DISCARD

DATE DUE

OCT 01 2001		
MAR 2 4 2002		

Demco, Inc. 38-293

CEIVED

551.55
Graywler Thomas

JUL 00 2001

The Tornado

the Tornado

Nature's Ultimate Windstorm

Thomas P. Grazulis

University of Oklahoma Press
Norman

Also by Thomas P. Grazulis

Significant Tornadoes, 1680–1993 (St. Johnsbury, Vt., 1993)

This book is published with the generous
assistance of Edith Gaylord Harper.

Library of Congress Cataloging-in-Publication Data

Grazulis, T. P.
    The tornado : nature's ultimate windstorm / Thomas
P. Grazulis.
        p.   cm.
    Includes bibliographical references and index.
    ISBN 0-8061-3258-2 (alk. paper)
    I. Tornadoes.   I. Title.

QC955 .G74 2001
551.55'3—dc21

                                        00-032609

The paper in this book meets the guidelines for perma-
nence and durability of the Committee on Production
Guidelines for Book Longevity of the Council on Library
Resources, Inc. ∞

1 2 3 4 5 6 7 8 9 10

To the memory of two friends
who passed away during the writing of this book,
weather historian David Ludlum (1910–97)
and
"Mr. Tornado," Ted Fujita (1920–98)

Contents

FIGURES AND TABLES

FIGURES

TABLES

PREFACE

The origins of this book can be traced to late spring 1953. At about 4:25 P.M. on June 9, fishermen on the north end of the Quabbin Reservoir in western Massachusetts watched as an unusual boiling and tumbling cloud took the form of an enormous, revolving cylinder. Minutes later the end of the cylinder reached down like an enormous finger, and trees began to snap in the woods of Petersham. Within a few minutes the finger took the shape of a huge funnel. For the next eighty-four minutes, that funnel would cut a damage swath of unprecedented size and intensity in the northeastern United States. Five minutes after touchdown the tornado encountered an unprepared couple in their Barre home. The house was blown apart, and the couple was thrown 300 feet to their deaths. As their bodies passed through trees, branches caught and held fragments of their clothing. Ahead lay an unsuspecting city of two hundred thousand.

People died in the open, in cars, in lakes, and under homes in what would be called the Worcester tornado. It lifted and carried tons of debris eastward; tar paper, shingles, sheet metal, and plywood rained down onto two dozen towns in eastern Massachusetts. Newspapers reported new discoveries of wreckage every day. Photographs and a piece of waterlogged, frozen mattress were found floating in the Atlantic Ocean. Trousers with a wallet were blown from the second floor of a home in Shrewsbury and dropped in Westwood, 25 miles east-southeast. Clotheslines in towns south of Boston were hung with pink insulation that had dropped from the sky. A Social Security card was returned to its owner from Hyannis on Cape Cod, 90 miles southeast of Worcester.

There was as much public interest in tornadoes in June 1953 as at any time in the history of this country (except perhaps during the opening week of the 1996 movie *Twister*). On May 11, 1953, 114 people died in a tornado at Waco, Texas. Two days before the Worcester tornado, on June 7, a family of 10 was killed near Arcadia, Nebraska. On June 8, 115 died at Flint, Michigan. In central Massachusetts, hundreds of miles from the traditional "tornado alley" of the United States, 94 people lay dead. Never before or since, at least not in recorded history, have such violent tornadoes occurred on three consecutive days. More than 500 people died in tornadoes during 1953, almost four times the average death toll of the previous five years. News reports speculated that aboveground atomic bomb tests in Nevada were drastically changing the weather. Senators insisted that it must be the nuclear tests; scientists insisted that the nuclear tests had nothing to do with it. The images and debates of the day were enhanced by the fear of nuclear attack and the "duck and cover" routines that pervaded the 1950s post–World War II mentality.

All of this was absorbed with both fascination and confusion by an eleven-year-old boy who lived just south of the track of the Worcester tornado. For the next week he and thousands of others would read and hear stories of vanishing homes and lives torn apart. Most impressive of all, the boy would witness armed militia guarding a large part of his hometown against, of all things, looting. His search for additional information about tornadoes was frustrating and short-lived. He eventually found only a small gray book on tornadoes.

The Worcester tornado of June 9, 1953, made a lasting impression on many other people. Forty miles east, at Chelsea, Massachusetts, a five-year-old boy watched in awe as the sky to the southwest turned a strange yellow-green. It was the edge of the Worcester thunderstorm; it produced an image in his memory that he vividly recalls today. He returned to the house only after his mother reminded him that tornadoes particularly like little boys. The five-year-old boy, Howard B. Bluestein, is now professor of meteorology at the University of Oklahoma. He is a premier storm chaser, and it was he who first brought portable Doppler radar to within half a mile of a violent tornado for a wind-speed measurement. A twenty-year-old student at the Massachusetts Institute of Technology (MIT), in Cambridge, 40 miles east of Worcester, was bicycling to a shopping area. He noticed huge clouds and shredded leaves falling from great heights into the street. It was immediately apparent that the cloud to the southwest must contain an exceptional windstorm. A year later he moved to Westwood, one of the towns that had been festooned with clothes and insulation from the Worcester tornado. In the woods near his home was a 5-pound piece of roofing, looking as if it had been there about a year. Edwin Kessler, the MIT student, would become director of the National Severe Storms Laboratory in Norman, Oklahoma, for its first twenty-five years. He would oversee the birth of scientific storm chasing, the development of a national Doppler radar system, and countless other advances.

Also in 1953, while the Weather Bureau wrestled with the newly established science of tornado forecasting, the University of Oklahoma Press was printing the first general book on tornadoes written in the twentieth century. This 194-page, gray hardbound volume, *Tornadoes of the United States*, by the Kansas climatologist Snowden Flora, coincided perfectly with this renewed interest in tornadoes. It became one of the best-selling books in the press's history. Not since John Park Finley's *Tornadoes* (1887) and Henry Allen Hazen's *The Tornado* (1890) had there been a text devoted to general information on the subject.

Flora rewrote a portion of the original book to include the great killer tornadoes of 1953. He died in 1957, however, and did not witness the golden age of tornado research that was just beginning at that time. Studies of the well-photographed tornadoes at Dallas, Texas, and Fargo, North Dakota, in 1957 ushered in a new era of sophistication. Flora would know nothing of portable Doppler radar, multiple vortices, mesocyclones, wall clouds, rear flank downdrafts, tornado chasers, the Fujita Scale, photogrammetry of tornado movies, and people's reactions to tornadoes as recorded today with home videocameras. He was, however, a major influence on an entire generation of people interested in the weather.

Unable to locate anything except Flora's book, the eleven-year-old in Worcester temporarily gave up his search for information. He would not go on to make the major technical and conceptual contributions that Kessler and Bluestein have made. However, after studying meteorology at Florida State University, he eventually began a search for information about every significant tornado that has ever struck the United States. The study would take twenty-five years and fill an eight-pound, 1,450-page book entitled

Significant Tornadoes. That eleven-year-old from Worcester is now the author of this book, a fifty-seven-year-old in Vermont, resting his eyes after the many years of searching through some thirty thousand reels of newspaper microfilm, under grants from the Nuclear Regulatory Commission (NRC) and the National Science Foundation (NSF). The gathering of information from thousands of far-flung sources was an effort to make the work of other scientists more efficient and productive. That project completed, the task of writing this book, built upon the foundation of Snowden Flora's work, began in 1991. The book is being completed here on a small farm, in late summer 1999, with a much-traveled copy of Flora's book never very far away.

My personal interest in tornadoes arises first from the fact that it is a natural weather phenomenon. I am also fascinated by the extraordinary human drama that accompanies so many tornado touchdowns and the refusal of this phenomenon to yield even its most basic secrets. An endless stream of unanswered and poorly defined questions surrounds the tornado.

For me, the questions began in 1953. What effect, if any, did the atomic bomb tests have? How often does Worcester or any other place in the United States get hit by a tornado? How fast are the winds? Do tornadoes really seek out and hit trailer parks? Can they actually defeather a chicken? How many tornadoes hit the United States each year? Do other countries have tornadoes? How big can tornadoes get? In 1953 I did not yet have the sophistication to ask the key questions, such as, what is the source of the tornado's incredible rotation?

Each of these questions leads to a host of related questions. What is meant by wind speed? Vertical wind or horizontal wind? The speed of a one-minute wind gust or a one-second gust? Does that gust affect 1 square inch or 100 square yards? What is meant by "big"? Big in height, width, path length, or area covered? These unanswered questions create research problems in all parts of the tornado life cycle.

My goal has been to write a book for the general public that touches on the full scope of tornado studies and answers most of the commonly asked questions. I have tried to set the record straight about tornado "risk," the Fujita Scale, the number of tornadoes that touch down annually, and certain myths that will not go away. I have tried to shed light on misconceptions and contradictory ideas about tornadoes.

I introduce several chapters with stories of previous tornado experiences. These narratives impart the incredible drama that so often accompanies any interaction between people and tornadoes. Some of these stories have a clear message: tornadoes can be horrible things that randomly destroy the lives of unsuspecting people. Most of the book gives a different message, however: tornadoes are an incredible marvel of nature and among the most fascinating scientific puzzles on this planet, one that may take the better part of the next century to unravel. By necessity, much of this book is about previous research and occurrences. If one wants to have any sense of what is in store for the future, historical perspective has always been one of the best teachers.

In the course of my research, I jotted down thousands of anecdotes concerning tornado occurrences, appearances, and oddities. Many of them are included in this book, but only the most important are specifically referenced; to cite all of them would have produced more clutter than insight. A large number of anecdotes are referenced in other books. For instance, in chapter 12, virtually all the details concerning tornadoes before 1870 are fully referenced in David Ludlum's *Early American Tornadoes.* That book, included in my references, contains a list of every newspaper, diary, and personal correspondence from which the anecdotes were taken.

My own research creates something of a dilemma in writing the parts of this book that involve tornado statistics. I and others have found many oversights and omissions in the official record. For instance, a recent and reliable study of the Worcester tornado (O'Toole 1993) revealed the death toll to be 94, not 90 as stated in official documents. Two tornadoes in 1955 killed 23 people in and around Mississippi schools and are not listed in official records. An officially listed New York tornado, one that killed 9 students in a school, was probably not a tornado at all. The most experienced severe storm specialists found it to be a kind of nonrotating wind known as a downburst.

All numbers used herein are my best estimate and may differ from those published by the National Weather Service (NWS). For instance, mixed into the official NWS "public consumption" tornado death statistics are a scattering of lightning and flood deaths. I hope that these differences do not cause confusion, but I cannot publish numbers that I know to be wrong. There are actually two sets of "official" NWS tornado data. One is based on a computerized, 80-digit database that is created annually. These numbers are rarely subject to change and are the source of statistics issued to the public. Professionals use this database only to obtain a broad perspective. There is also a more correct database, contained in the monthly publication *Storm Data.* These events are corrected and updated monthly. For instance, for public consumption, a new record of thirty-three tornadoes was set in Arkansas for the month of March 1997. However, the *Storm Data* text clearly states that there were only twenty Arkansas tornadoes in March 1997, affecting thirty-three counties. The numbers used in this book are from *Storm Data,* with additional refinements extracted from newspapers and research papers. I have tried to extract the best set of numbers. Maintaining error-free tornado data is not a priority for the NWS, a source of continuous frustration to me and many of my colleagues over the past three decades. While making climatological research a bit more tedious, this lack of top-quality data has no short-term impact on public safety. The data are adequate for all but highly refined risk analyses. The NWS must make budget decisions, and when it comes to choosing between data improvement and forecasting improvement, the money falls on the forecasting side. Then someone makes the point that you cannot improve forecasting without high-quality verification data, and the debate continues. Data problems will surface in several chapters of this book.

I have had the good fortune to have lived in the right place, at the right time—the United States, during a golden age of tornado research. I have gained insight through countless guided tours, walks, lunches, conferences, storm chases, research partnerships, and cherished friendships with many of the true pioneers in tornado research. I have met or listened to virtually every notable scholar in the field before their passing, save for one, Snowden Flora. My hope is that these influences are properly reflected in this book and that they will allow the reader to discover an even greater fascination in the endless pageant of the weather and its most spectacular and puzzling feature, the tornado.

This book is mostly my interpretation of other people's ideas. But my interpretation may not be entirely faithful to my colleagues' beliefs. One of the ongoing problems has been that in the years it took to write this book, many ideas have changed, especially on the subject of tornado formation. Not every colleague finds the new ideas worthy of inclusion.

I am deeply indebted to many atmospheric scientists, especially Don Burgess and Charles Doswell, who have taken valuable time to clarify concepts about tornado forecasting and dynamics for me. Any errors, or misconceptions, are my own. If I have stumbled into genuine insight, credit belongs to them.

Considerable thanks go to Howard B. Bluestein and Edwin Kessler, who were very helpful in choosing the content for this book and in focusing my attention on details that needed improvement. I also owe immense gratitude to the following people and many others, without whom I could never have carved out a career in severe storms: David Ludlum, for the inspiration he provided by paving the way into the distant past of American weather; Robert Abbey, Ted Fujita, Jim McDonald, and Joe Schaefer, all of whom posed very tough questions about tornado climatology in 1979 and then helped me to search for answers in the ensuing twenty years; Matt Biddle, Roy Britt, Jon Davies, Tim Marshall, Gene Rhoden, Robert Prentice, Dave Hoadley, Jim Leonard, Erik Rasmussen, and Mark Herndon, for their insights into storms and storm chasing; Doris Grazulis, wife, adviser, webmaster, and the glue that holds the Tornado Project together; Nora Sabadell of the National Science Foundation (NSF) for letting me roam freely through the past few centuries of tornadoes; and Lanny Cascaden, a lifelong student of the history of science, the English language, and the work of Snowden Flora. These people, through their contributions, have made this book much more readable.

The Tornado

CHAPTER 1

Tornadoes Past and Present

On May 25, 1932, on a northwestern Kansas farm just south of the Nebraska border, John Newport looked to the west and saw storm clouds building. He stopped cultivating potatoes, sent his family to the house, and put the horses in the barn. Life was not easy on the Great Plains of Rawlins County, Kansas. For the members of the Newport family, life was about to become even harder. A muffled roar in the distance grew sharper and louder. John saw the tornado, in the southwest, and thought it was moving to the east, as were most of the clouds. The funnel was, however, moving directly toward the farm (see fig. 1.1). He joined the family in the house. His wife, Merna, went to the bedroom where Paul, the youngest, was asleep.

Within the next few seconds, seven people would make life or death decisions about valued possessions, family members, and self-preservation. The rotating cloud had changed from transparent mist to solid brown mass at the edge of the plowed fields and continued to advance relentlessly on the small cluster of farm buildings. On the Newport farm the entrance to the cellar was just outside the house but now out of reach in the flying debris,

Fig. 1.1. This tornado just missed a house north of Cheyenne, Wyoming, on July 16, 1979. The appearance of this tornado is probably similar to the Rawlins County, Kansas, event in 1932. Debris in this funnel is from a mobile home park. Copyright Peter Willing.

which, as the daughter, Eleanor, would recall sixty-five years later, was "so thick you couldn't see six feet outside."

The thirty-year-old cottonwood trees that surrounded the house began to snap. John ran to the bedroom where his wife and son were huddled. As the leading edge of the vortex hit, the tornado lifted up one end of the lightly anchored prairie home. Eleanor remembered light coming in at the base of the walls. The outer walls of the home blew away and exposed the interior of the house to even stronger winds. In news stories following the event, none of the children mentioned whether there was, between the parents, a final glance at one another, or final words above the deafening roar. In an instant, a lifetime of work—walls, beams, furniture, tools, clothes, toys, books, and family treasures—were airborne. Some would fall only a few hundred feet away; smaller bits and pieces may have been carried 100 miles or more. Sheet metal and boards flew across the barnyard at perhaps 150 feet per second, impaling anything that was standing. The 12-inch-thick hand-hewn sills, on which the house had sat for forty years, would hit the ground a quarter mile away and plunge 8 feet into the prairie soil. An entire cottonwood tree was found 2 miles away.

A minute later, the four eldest children lifted their heads, dazed and injured, lying at various places in the farmyard and fields. The hail began falling at an increasing rate, and they found shelter under a board from the basement stairway. They heard the cries of Paul and found him with the lifeless body of their mother about 200 yards from the empty foundation, across the road in Nebraska. Their father was barely alive. His last words were instructions to get to the nearest neighbor for help, a half mile away. He fell into unconsciousness in the arms of his eldest daughter. The children, Mildred, Martha, Eleanor, Dean (John, Jr.), and Paul, ages fifteen to three, suddenly found themselves facing a very different life than they had experienced just minutes earlier. That unexpected altering of the course of one's life is often a tornado's legacy.

In my visit with Eleanor, sixty-five years after the storm, she told of arriving at the next farm, with the rest of the children, battered and bloodied and with broken arms and ribs. Their father died a few hours later in their neighbor's living room. The children began new lives in the depths of the Great Depression with their grandparents, aunts, uncles, and the good people of southwestern Nebraska. The Newport family, like thousands of families before them and thousands more since, were the victims of the most violent windstorm that nature produces on the surface of the earth, a tornado.

Since the first known death in Massachusetts more than three hundred years ago, at least 13,000 people have died in tornadoes in the United States. More than 150,000 others have been injured. This Rawlins County tornado took place at a time when hundreds more people died annually in tornadoes than do today. This was a time of growing cities, and yet there was still a large rural population. Radio was in its infancy and severe-storm forecasting was the distant dream of just a few meteorologists. In general, awareness of issues came through the print media, days or weeks after events had taken place.

Today we live in a world in which some might say there is an awareness overload with regard to tornadoes. Television stations compete to broadcast the most up-to-date warnings. Some hire storm chasers and build camera-equipped towers in an effort to beam live tornado pictures to their local audiences and even nationwide.

Government-issued weather watches and warnings, public education programs, rescue squads, amateur radio alert teams, and medical trauma units were almost unknown in the 1930s. Today it is rare to have a rural farm family caught by surprise in a tornado, and not just because there are fewer farmers. In modern times the Newport family might have awakened under a clear sky to radio reports of agricultural market prices and news that the county was in an outlook area that had a moderate or high risk for severe thunderstorms that day. By midday the family would have been alerted to a tornado or severe thunderstorm watch. The extended forecast might have told of the possibility of thunderstorms up to five days in advance. Weather radio or a police radio scanner would be tuned for reports of funnel cloud sightings or the placement of the county under a tornado warning. The same Internet connection that brings livestock prices can bring the latest Doppler radar images. The Newports might have had storm-spotter training. The children would have had annual safety instruction at school. The family might have seen to it that a designated area of the basement was set aside for tornado protection.

Advances in tornado forecasting and communication technology have created a vastly more aware and informed public. Today the formation of an intense tornado may be watched by several spotter teams and the alarm sounded in time to prevent a single death, even from the most intensely destructive tornadoes. Along with awareness and education have come changing perceptions about the tornado. A century ago it was thought of as an evil force that descended with the hellish odor of brimstone. Today most people see it for what it is, one of planet Earth's great natural spectacles rather than the work of the devil or the vengeful hand of the Lord.

For much of the general public, however, tornadoes still remain largely misunderstood. The general perception of tornadoes has been distorted by motion pictures such as *The Wizard of Oz* and *Twister*. Adding to the misconceptions are news reports written and presented by people with little or no knowledge of the subject. The actual risk from tornadoes is often exaggerated by the media, as they try desperately to compete for market share. In time tornadoes have come to be surrounded by myths and inaccuracies. Some of these misconceptions have been repeated so many times that they have been accepted as truths.

For many people, the difference between a tornado watch and a tornado warning is unclear. Radio disc jockeys often pass along weather information casually and irreverently. It is not uncommon to hear a local radio personality joke about opening windows and nonchalantly use the words *watch* and *warning* interchangeably. Some people incorrectly assume that there is no risk from tornadoes. Others assume, just as incorrectly, that the risk is quite high. The chapters that follow are an effort to set the record straight on issues ranging from death tolls to wind speeds, path lengths, trailer parks, opening windows, tornado numbers, and the actual risk from these airborne spectacles. First I will introduce some basic ideas.

THE TORNADO

Few other phenomena can form and vanish so quickly, leave behind such misery, and still be seen as beautiful. Tornadoes consist of little more than a mixture of insubstantial air and water vapor. Every year a few thousand people are witness to one of the most spectacular natural forces on this planet. Seemingly out of nothing, an enormous apparition takes shape in the sky. Within seconds it begins to evoke awe, curiosity, inspiration, insignificance, helplessness, even denial, and, for many, a closeness to the power of the Creator that they have never felt before. Unfortunately, this wonder of nature does not just inspire and challenge the senses, it randomly wreaks havoc on people's lives.

It is not difficult to understand why someone might be intrigued by an enormous funnel that seems to chew its way through a town. Something larger than the Empire State Building should not be able to move at all, much less gracefully. Some people dream about tornadoes. Others consider tornadoes to be the direct wrath of God. Many people see them as the perfect earthly link to the forces of the cosmos—gigantic in size, displaying immense power but not as unfathomable as a supernova or so rare as a planet-asteroid collision.

Tornadoes are very difficult to study. After a flood one can examine a river and its watershed. After a volcanic eruption one can study a crater and exhaust gases. After an earthquake one can survey faults. But after a tornado has "roped out" and the thunderstorm dissipated, we are left with nothing more than piles of debris and more questions.

The most intense tornadoes are born in the turbulence of a thunderstorm, arguably one of the most hostile environments on earth. The thunderstorm protects the tornado from researchers with 100-mph straight winds, baseball-sized hail, 30,000,000-volt lightning discharges, and blinding rain. After the tornado dissipates the problem of documentation arises. This is expensive and time-consuming work, often requiring detailed aerial and ground surveys. Most of the limited resources of the United States are put first into forecasting and then into rescue and cleanup. Very little money is devoted to tornado documentation.

Tornadoes do not just enter a home unexpectedly. They rip it apart and scatter the accumulated possessions of a lifetime to the four winds. They present a much different threat than do floods, lava flows, and earthquakes. Rivers, volcanoes, and faults are ever-present signatures of a risk that some people willingly accept. Automobiles, swimming pools, and railroad crossings are vastly greater threats to human life than are tornadoes. They take 40,000, 4,000, and 1,000 lives a year, respectively, compared to only about 80 for tornadoes. The difference is that these other risks are obvious, and we accept them as part of an improved lifestyle. For many people, that acceptance of risk does not extend to tornadoes. The potential loss of all one's possessions in the blink of an eye is hard to live with. It is this aspect of tornadoes, along with its visible display of power, that is the source of so much inappropriate worry.

Despite the frequency of newspaper stories about them and the availability of images on videotape, tornadoes are uncommon. Only about one in a thousand thunderstorms produces a tornado. Most tornadoes (more than 80 percent) are weak and inflict no more damage than would straight-line winds in a severe thunderstorm. Less than 1 percent of the American population will ever be in the path of even the weakest tornado during their lives. Even in the most tornado-prone areas of the country, a home can expect to be hit only about once in a thousand years. The frequency of actual destruction of any given house in the heart of tornado alley is only about once in 10,000 to 1,000,000 years, depending largely on one's definition of the word *destruction.*

While an unlikely part of most of our lives, tornadoes are a force that cannot be ignored. The most intense tornadoes can carry automobiles half a mile and level a well-built home. Some have crossed mountains, seemingly unimpeded. Tornadoes have carried people as far as a mile from their homes. They have lasted for more than an hour while scouring the earth with wind speeds of 250 mph. Tornadoes have occurred in every state, and each area of the country has its own unique "tornado season." In a few states they have occurred in every month and at all times of day and night. Tornadoes are not unique to the United States. They have killed up to one thousand people in a single swath across Bangladesh, for example.

A tornado is a comparatively organized structure. In its simplest form it is a single vortex in which air, often laden with dust and debris, is moving at very high speeds in an upward spiral. The rising air enters the vortex at its base and exits in the upper part of the funnel. Most of the debris is centrifuged out very quickly, in the bottom few hundred feet. Some of the lighter debris, however, can become caught in the upward spiral and carried for several miles above the earth's surface. The vortex itself can extend 5 miles or more upward from the surface, high into the parent thunderstorm. We may see only the bottom 10 percent of it protruding from the base of the thunderstorm as a "tornado" (fig. 1.2).

In a single-vortex tornado, the surrounding air rushes inward toward a central low pressure, then upward within the outer wall of the tornado. The

Fig. 1.2. Professor Howard B. Bluestein of the University of Oklahoma photographed this tornado near Spearman, Texas, on May 30, 1990. It formed near the back edge of a supercell thunderstorm. Copyright Howard B. Bluestein.

speed of the upward moving air may be about the same as the horizontal speed or rotation. The funnel could have air rotating at 100 mph and rising at 100 mph. The combined wind speed at any given point in this spiral may vary from less than 70 mph to (very rarely) as much as 300 mph. In some tornadoes the upward component may greatly exceed the horizontal rotation, lifting buildings and causing extreme levels of destruction.

To be called a tornado, the phenomenon must be a naturally occurring atmospheric vortex whose circulation extends from the ground at least to the base of a convective cloud. Dust devils form under a clear sky and are never called tornadoes. Oil-fire, forest-fire, and prairie-fire vortices are also not classified as tornadoes, even though some may connect with an overhead cloud produced by the fire. Fire-induced vortices are not considered tornadoes, even if they look like one, travel away from the fire, and kill people, as one did in California in 1926 (see chap. 12).

The tornado funnel can take a variety of forms, depending on the immediate conditions of air pressure, temperature, moisture, dust, the rate at which air flows into the vortex, and whether the air in the core of the tornado is moving upward or downward.

Tornadoes have been colorfully described in many ways: a giant serpent with its head feeding on the ground; the finger of God (fig. 1.3); a huge elephant's trunk searching for food; a monstrous snake, writhing, biting, and kissing the ground; a giant barrel hanging in the air; a great column surrounded by silvery ribbons; or as ropes, balloons, beehives, or hourglasses. Some tornadoes emit only a faint, high-pitched whine. Others have been described as sounding like a waterfall, a freight train, the buzzing of a million bees, and even the bellowing of a million mad bulls. The degree of interaction with the ground may have something to do with the sound that is generated. A tornado is a very long, whirling tube of air, an enormous acoustical instrument, with a hollow core and debris-filled cone or cylinder. No one has fully explored the sound-generating properties of such an object.

The typical (median) tornado is only about 50 yards wide and has a path length of about 1 mile (Schaefer, Kelly, and Abbey 1986). However, each year a few grow to a half mile wide and stay on the ground for an hour or more, carving out a 40-mile or longer path of destruction. About one thousand tornadoes a year are counted, but twice as many may actually touch down. (See chap. 11.)

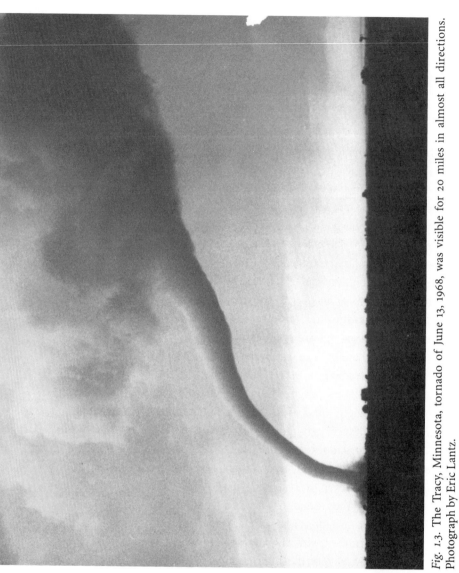

Fig. 1.3. The Tracy, Minnesota, tornado of June 13, 1968, was visible for 20 miles in almost all directions. Photograph by Eric Lantz.

On rare occasions, perhaps only a few times each century, someone with good observational skills has an opportunity like that of Will Keller, of Greensburg, Kansas (Flora 1953). On June 16, 1928, Mr. Keller looked directly up into the hollow core of a mature tornado (the date is often cited incorrectly as June 22, the date of his newspaper interview). His was a very unusual experience, for most tornadoes do not lift and travel so conveniently above ground level. Most tornadoes dissipate into a diffuse mass or narrow to a thin rope.

Will, a man whose "reputation for truthfulness and sobriety was of the best," was in his field looking over the ruins of the wheat crop that had just been destroyed by hail. He and his family ran to their storm cellar when he saw three tornadoes hanging from an umbrella-shaped cloud. The larger one, looking from a distance like a sawed-off cylinder, was heading directly for his farm. Will described what happened:

> Steadily the cloud came on, the end gradually rising above the ground. At last the great shaggy end of the funnel hung directly overhead. Everything was still as death. There was a strong, gassy odor, and it seemed as though I could not breathe. There was a screaming, hissing sound coming directly from the end of the funnel. I looked up and to my astonishment I saw right into the heart of the tornado. There was a circular opening in the center of the funnel, about 50 or 100 feet in diameter and extending straight upwards for a distance of at least half a mile, as best I could judge under the circumstances. The walls of this opening were of rotating clouds and the whole was made brilliantly visible by constant flashes of lightning which zigzagged from side to side. Had it not been for the lightning, I could not have seen the opening, or any distance up into it.
>
> Around the lower rim of the great vortex small tornadoes were constantly forming and breaking away. These looked like tails as they writhed their way around the end of the funnel. It was these that made the hissing noise. I noticed that the direction of rotation of the great whirl was anticlockwise, but the small twisters rotated both ways, . . . some one way and some another.
>
> The opening was entirely hollow, except for something which I could not exactly make out, but suppose it was a detached wind cloud. This thing was in the center and was moving up and down. The tornado was not traveling

at a great speed. I had plenty of time to get a good view of the whole thing, inside and out.

About half an hour later, another tornado from the same parent cloud was said to have moved very slowly and plowed furrows 4 to 6 feet deep, a mile long. One farmer noted that they were "deep enough to bury a horse."

When seen for the first time, the damage caused by a tornado is incomprehensible to many people. It certainly was to me. When the tornado's vertical wind in excess of 100 mph counteracts the force of gravity, resulting damage from the horizontal component of the winds can be amazing. Tornadoes can lift objects with both of these wind components. Horizontal winds passing over flat surfaces can create aerodynamic lift, the kind that gets airplanes off the ground. The vertical wind speed and the horizontal direction may change rapidly, creating a complex mixture of forces that create damage unlike any other natural phenomenon. We will look at some of these tornadic feats in the next chapter. We will see that tornadoes do not defy the laws of physics; they combine these laws in ways that we have very little experience with.

CHAPTER 2

In the Wake
of a Tornado

The encounter between a town and a well-developed tornado can create a surreal world of mangled trailers, cars wrapped around trees, and devastated neighborhoods that look like battlefields. One house can be leveled to the ground while a neighboring one is almost untouched. On closer inspection the effects can range from the merely unexpected to events so unusual that people find spiritual significance in them. There has been an almost mystical belief that tornadoes are capable of any imaginable damage. Some newspaper reporters have perhaps been overly eager to feed the public's interest in tornado oddities. Sometimes it is difficult to tell where reality ends and a reporter's enthusiasm begins.

On the evening of November 10, 1915, the citizens of Great Bend, Kansas, experienced the most oddity-filled tornado in recorded history. The newspapers in and around Barton County (available at the Kansas State Historical Library in Topeka) added new stories daily for several weeks. Perhaps the funnel had a unique multiple-vortex structure. Perhaps the rising air within this tornado was especially strong. Perhaps nothing was unique about the tornado at all. There must, of course, be one tornado that has more strange occurrences than any other; this was to be it. It was an unusual time of the year for a violent tornado this far west. The funnel touched down 16 miles southwest of Great Bend and was visible only during flashes of lightning. The strange occurrences began southwest of Pawnee Rock where a farm was leveled to the ground and two people were killed. From a short distance away, one could not tell that a farmstead had ever existed there. Five horses were the only uninjured survivors. They were supposedly carried from the barn a distance of a quarter mile. All were unhurt, all were found together, and all were supposedly still hitched to the same rail.

At the edge of Great Bend, the Charles Hammond house was unroofed. The family heard a passing roar and went outside to survey the neighbor's damage. Only then did they realize that their own roof was missing. At Grant Jones's store, the south wall was blown down and scattered, but shelves and canned goods that stood against the wall were not moved an inch. The Riverside Steam Laundry, built of stone and cement block, was left with only a fragment of upright wall, yet two nearby wooden shacks seemed almost untouched. A nearby iron water hydrant was supposedly found full of splinters.

Even the means of survival were unusual. During the destruction of the railroad yard, one worker survived by climbing into the firebox of a steam locomotive that had still not fully cooled down. At the Moses Brothers and Clayton Ranch on the east edge of town, 1,000 (out of a flock of 3,500) sheep were killed, the most ever by a single U.S. tornado. A canceled check from Great Bend was found in a cornfield, one mile outside of Palmyra, Nebraska, 210 miles to the northeast. This would stand for seventy-five years as the record for the longest-known distance that debris was carried. A rain of debris, receipts, checks, photographs, ledger sheets, money, clothing, shingles, and fragments of books, fell on almost every farm north and west of Glasco, 80 miles northeast.

A necktie rack with ten ties still attached was reportedly carried 40 miles. Mail was lifted from the railroad depot and scattered for miles to the northeast. A four-page letter "from a swain to his fair damsel in which he promised all" was carried 70 miles. It was returned to Great Bend, but other letters were sent on to their addressees from wherever they were found—

one of the earliest forms of airmail. A flour sack from the Walnut Creek Mill was found 110 miles to the northeast, perhaps the longest distance ever recorded for an object weighing more than one pound. Up to forty-five thousand migrating ducks were reported killed at Cheyenne Bottoms migratory bird refuge. Dead ducks fell from the sky 40 miles northeast of the marsh. Farmers living 2 miles from town were unaware of the tragedy and were dumbfounded when they visited town the next day and beheld the tragic spectacle. More than twenty thousand visitors viewed the wreckage the following Sunday.

Fictional events were added almost daily to the growing list of stories. An iron jug was said to have been blown inside out. A rooster was supposedly blown into a jug, with only its head sticking out of the neck of the container. Some of these reported oddities were probably at least close to the truth. The iron hydrant that was described as being full of splinters conjures up the image of small bits of wood driven directly into solid metal. A likelier version is that wood splinters were caught in small cracks in the iron and in spaces around the pipe fittings.

ODDITIES IN GENERAL

There are in fact peculiar happenings in tornadoes, as in everyday life. The number of strange things that can take place in and around a tornado is astronomically large. The chances of any one of them occurring is microscopically small. Since there are so many possibilities, the chances of at least one happening are quite good. Predicting just which oddity will happen is, of course, impossible.

Tens of thousands of tornadoes have encountered barns. It should not be surprising that at least one barn has had its door blown open and the wagon blown out, turned around, blown back in, and the barn door shut behind. A week after the Jackson County, Alabama, tornado of March 21, 1932, a live chicken was found in a dresser drawer. It is not hard to envision a dresser flying through the air along with one hundred chickens passing like bullets. A drawer could easily have opened and shut just as it passed a chicken and then been gently set down out of the way of the cleanup crew. What is at work here is probability, the high probability that at least one of millions of low-probability events can and will occur. When one of these

Fig. 2.1. A phonograph record was blown into a crack in a utility pole at Ada, Oklahoma, on April 20, 1973. Courtesy of NOAA.

low-probability events happens in everyday life, it is not uncommon for people to attach spiritual significance to it.

If enough trunks are blown out of enough attics, one is likely to land in the attic of an unroofed home a few blocks away. If enough cars are thrown into enough trees, then at some point the high winds will split a large tree just as an automobile is being hurled by, closing onto the car as if it were in a vise. Both of these events were reported in Flora's 1953 book as having happened on June 22, 1919, at Fergus Falls, Minnesota.

If enough phonograph records are scattered along with enough of their owners, someone is bound to land next to a recording of the song "Stormy Weather." That supposedly happened on June 10, 1958, at Eldorado, Kansas, but I could find no first- or secondhand reference for it. In a few cases photographic evidence does exist. If enough records are blown from enough homes, at enough telephone poles, a phonograph record will eventually lodge in a crack (fig. 2.1).

OF FISH AND FOWL

As reported on page 7 of the *Times of London* on March 10, 1859, it was February 9 of that year when John Lewis, a sawyer in the town of Mountain Ash, England, was startled. "Something [was] falling all over me," he related, "down my neck, on my head, and on my back. They were little fish. I saw the whole ground covered with them. I took off my hat, the brim of which was full of them. They were jumping all about. They covered the ground in a long strip of about 80 yards by 12, as we measured afterwards." He and his co-worker gathered a bucket full of them. A few were kept alive and put on exhibit at a London zoo. What was unusual about this story was not just the rain of fish but that it was well documented. Because most stories like this cannot be traced to their sources and cannot be verified with the names of real people, many of them seem to be hearsay. This one was apparently true, as both a scientist and a minister verified the story. How often fish fall from the sky is unknown. The accounts are amusing, and there are at least one hundred of them, dating back to biblical times.

Only rarely is one of these stories told in a respected publication. One of the most convincing was noted in the April 22, 1949, issue of the journal *Science*. As that story goes, the director of the bank at Marksville, Louisiana, rose from bed on the morning of October 23, 1947, to find that his and a neighbor's yard were covered with fish. A bank employee and two merchants were struck by fish as they walked to work at 7:45 A.M. There were fish in the street and fish on the roofs. Two biologists for the state Fish and Wildlife Department were in town at the time and collected samples. The largest fish was a 9-inch-long largemouth black bass. There was no thunderstorm in the area at the time. The swath of fish was about 1,000 feet long and 80 feet wide, in a north-south alignment.

Falling fish, frogs, snails, and salamanders are almost certainly related to unreported tornadoes or waterspouts. The fish- or frog-laden water is blown horizontally and becomes entrained in the spiraling upward airflow. To state that the fish were "sucked" from a pond would imply that the water rose from the pond as a continuous column, as liquids rise in a straw. That is not the mechanism at work here. Neither fish nor frogs are very heavy. Rain may have lured them to the surface of the pond. A rain of fish is probably sufficient evidence to confirm the existence of a tornado.

Fig. 2.2. This partially plucked chicken was found after a tornado at Anoka, Minnesota, on June 18, 1939. Courtesy of the Minnesota Historical Society and the *Minneapolis Star*.

While I do not doubt the stories, my natural skepticism awaits a well-documented account that directly links the fall of high-altitude frozen fish with a known tornado. I have personally talked with someone whose car was pelted with fish from the Red River in Oklahoma while he was watching a tornado cross that river. That, however, is not the same as frozen fish falling from the sky at a considerable distance from a body of water.

A few oddities are readily explainable, among them the ubiquitous plucked chicken (fig. 2.2). In the descriptions of damage caused by rural tornadoes there will likely be mention of a fowl "stripped clean of every feather." It has been suggested that the feathers explode off the bird in the tornado's low pressure. That explanation does not hold up, because the bird would be blown away long before experiencing the lowest pressure at the center of the tornado. In addition, the lowest pressure in a tornado is probably not low enough to explode a feather—if indeed a feather could explode. It is curious how the exploding-feather theory became accepted by so many people when the remains of an exploded feather were never found. But when it comes to tornadoes, facts, evidence, and accurate descriptions have never bothered amateur tornado theoreticians or much of the news media.

In 1842 Elias Loomis performed a bizarre experiment that obviously made sense to him at the time. He hoped to learn what wind speed was needed to defeather a chicken. An account written a few years later states:

> In order to determine the velocity needed to strip feathers, the six-pounder [cannon] was loaded with five ounces of powder, and for a ball, a chicken was killed. The gun was pointed upwards and fired. The feathers rose twenty or thirty feet and were scattered by the wind. On examination, they were found to be pulled out clean, the skin seldom adhering to them. The body was torn into small fragments, only a part of which could be found. The velocity was 341 miles per hour. (Hazen 1890)

Loomis speculated that if a live bird were fired at 100 mph, the results would be more successful, but to my knowledge he never attempted it. He did, however, place dead chickens under a vacuum jar to see if the feathers would explode. They did not. A widely accepted alternative theory in the nineteenth century was that opposing electric charges during the tornado's passage stripped feathers from chickens and tore the clothes from people. It was supposed that the highly charged tornado induced an opposite charge in objects as it approached, causing them to be sent flying. Although static electricity is undoubtedly present in a debris-filled funnel, this makes no scientific sense whatever. There is no mechanism that would produce powerful opposing charges on the bird and on the feather at the same time.

The likeliest explanation (Vonnegut 1975) for the defeathering of a chicken is the protective response called "flight molt." Chickens are not stripped clean but lose a large percentage of their feathers under stress. Flight molt would give the predator a mouthful of feathers instead of fresh fowl. In a tornado, the panicked chicken's feathers simply become loose and are blown off. Stories of chickens found dead, sitting at attention and stripped clean of feathers, may be on a par with reports of the blowing of a cow's horn, a two-gallon jug being blown into a quart bottle without cracking, or that poor rooster in a jug. Despite their ridiculous nature, it is fun to come across old newspaper accounts, such as the

Fergus, Ontario, News Record of July 26, 1906, which noted that tornadoes can "turn a well inside out, a cellar upside down, blow the staves out of a barrel leaving only the hole, change the day of the week, blow the cracks out of a fence; and knock the wind out of a politician."

LONG-DISTANCE DEBRIS AND LONG-DISTANCE PEOPLE

The carrying of checks or receipts for 30 miles or more occurs almost every year, but even objects weighing a pound or more have been carried up to 100 miles. Commonly, tornado debris is flat and thin, with large surface areas for aerodynamic lifting and yet relatively lightweight. Letters, postcards, receipts, photographs, grain sacks, signs, and even panes of glass have been found in excess of 50 miles from the point of origin. This debris would have to be initially sheltered from or somehow withstand the winds at the outer edge of a tornado. Most debris is rapidly centrifuged out and away from the tornado. The outer walls of a house might protect a desk that contains checks or receipts. The walls of the building would eventually give way, just as the upward-spiraling winds near the center of the vortex encounter the desk. The receipts are then caught in the upward spiral, held aloft by the thunderstorm updraft, and carried far downwind.

The carrying ability of the tornado and its parent thunderstorm was demonstrated long ago and studied in detail in more recent years by the University of Oklahoma Tornado Debris Project (Snow et al. 1995). On August 9, 1878, a tornado carried receipts from a home in Wallingford, Connecticut, 65 miles to Peacedale, Rhode Island. After a newspaper published the home owner's name and noted that $50 in cash was lost, the man received donations of $55 (Ludlum 1970). The Great Tri-State Tornado of 1925, the deadliest in history, reportedly carried a pair of trousers 39 miles with $95 remaining in a pocket (Flora 1953).

According to Amy Wyatt (pers. com.) of the University of Oklahoma Tornado Debris Project, the longest-known distance that any debris has been carried is 223 miles. This was a personal check that traveled from Stockton, Kansas, to Winnetoon, Nebraska, on April 11, 1991. Stories of people and farm animals being carried long distances have been hard to verify and tend to be more frequently exaggerated than the movement of pieces of paper. On June 11, 1915, three mules were reportedly carried 2 miles by the tornado at Mullinville, Kansas. "Witnesses" reported hoofprints lead-ing only outward from the spot where the mules were supposedly dropped.

It is not uncommon for people to be carried 100 to 400 yards to their deaths in major tornadoes. My own research (Grazulis 1993), in more than thirty thousand issues of various newspapers, has uncovered only a single carefully measured and documented case of a person being carried more than a mile. That single case, substantiated by the county sheriff and reported in local newspapers, took place on May 1, 1930, at Kickapoo, Kansas. Lawrence Kern and his wife and three children were sitting down for supper, unaware that a tornado was approaching from the southwest. The funnel, which had "left a 25-mile-long trail of dead livestock" was spotted a few hundred feet from the house. All ran to the door, for the storm cellar was 30 feet from the house. When Kern's thirteen-year-old son, John, reached the shelter door, he turned to find that he was alone; his house and family were gone. Lawrence, barely alive, was found just over 1 mile from the empty foundation, his head buried in the ground to the shoulders. His wife, Augusta, was 200 yards away from the homesite, lying near her other children, Wilhemina and Joseph. The children recovered, but both parents died in the hospital. More than fifty thousand people toured the devastated farm area the following weekend; about two thousand viewed the bodies at a Leavenworth funeral home.

Some newspapers erroneously reported that Kern was carried over the Missouri River and several miles beyond. The floor of the home may have acted as a sail. In years past many homes were set directly on stones rather than bolted to concrete foundations as they are today. The floors of these homes could be lifted intact more easily than can today's floors, so we may not see this event repeated.

Of those persons carried less than a mile, the most interesting of the documented cases took place in Edmunds County, South Dakota, on July 1, 1955. According to local newspapers, nine-year-old, 80-pound Sharon Weron was returning home from a friend's house on horseback, while her mother and three other children returned in a car. Sharon took a shortcut and was 150 feet from the house when the tornado appeared in full view of every-one. The horse put its back to the wind and took off over a hill and across a valley. It was just before the second hill that the funnel caught them, as the mother followed desperately in the car. She saw them airborne but was forced by intense hail to stop and wait. Sharon said that her landing was "just like a plane . . . on [her] tummy." How long the horse was airborne is not known, but it was seen in the air by Sharon's mother. The girl's injuries were not caused by the tornado but from hail while she lay in a ditch, 1,000 feet from where she became airborne. By coincidence L. Frank Baum, author of *The Wizard of Oz,* had lived just a few miles away, in Aberdeen.

There have been unsubstantiated press reports of people taking much longer rides. On May 26, 1908, a tornado destroyed thirteen farms and hundreds of cattle near Alva, Oklahoma. Four people were killed in one home in Alfalfa County, and a mother and baby (presumably) died north-west of Ingersol. That baby was not found after two weeks of searching. One rumor in the national press was that the missing baby was carried for 17 miles, but I could not locate its source in local newspapers.

The supposed 10-mile flight of a baby took place during the March 21, 1932, tornado outbreak in Alabama. A week after the outbreak, national newspapers, including the respected *Atlanta Constitution,* carried the story of twenty-two-month-old Jewel Butler. She was supposedly found in a field on the day of the outbreak and taken by the farm owners into their home. As the story goes, Jewel was regularly taken to town in the hope that she would be recognized. She eventually was. The story added that her two sisters had been killed and her parents hospitalized when their home was obliterated, 10 miles from where she was found. The name of the town where these events were to have taken place was not given in the national press. The author located the Butler farm in Chilton County, Alabama, where thirty-eight people died that afternoon. No Alabama newspaper, not even the local county newspaper, made any mention of a 10-mile flight. In general, the more distant the newspaper from the tornado, the farther the body was reported as having been carried. In all likelihood, the flight of Jewel Butler never occurred.

COINCIDENCES

There are so-called coincidences that accompany every tornado. A barn was destroyed while the owners were out buying paint for it; a man received his tornado insurance policy in the mail, then ran for cover as the house was destroyed. But since people are frequently improving their property, through purchase or work, whether or not a tornado is in the area the number of these "coincidences" is practically limitless, and of no significance except to the individual home owner.

If enough butter churns were blown from the porches of enough farmhouses, then one was bound to eventually drop on the head of a cow in a distant field. With that in mind, one should not be surprised if a Bible was left undisturbed and opened to Ezekiel 1:4 ("and, behold, a whirlwind came out of the north") or Hosea 8:7 ("For they have sown the wind, and they shall reap the whirlwind"). Paul Smith's home was destroyed at Gainesville, Georgia, in 1932. He recalled finding his Bible open to the twenty-seventh chapter of Acts. The passage at the top of the page began, "But not long after there arose a tempestuous wind. . . ."

Among the most frequently cited coincidences (Flora 1953) is the passage of a tornado through the township of Codell, Kansas, on the same day for three straight years. There were significant tornadoes in or near Codell on May 20 in 1916, 1917, and 1918. Only in 1918 did the storm pass through downtown Codell. There were no fatalities in town, but nine deaths occurred on nearby farms in 1918. No May 20 tornado has hit Codell, or Rooks County, before or since.

Not all tornado paths are exactly parallel to one another, from southwest to northeast. Many move from west to east, south to north, and northwest to southeast. Therefore, over the years there will be intersection points, and some of those intersection points will have had structures on them at the time of the storms. About once every few years a building, or its successor, is hit by a tornado for the second time. In Logan County, Nebraska, only two homes have been leveled by a tornado in the past one hundred years; they were on the same homesite both times, on October 29, 1956, and June 18, 1975, near the town of Arnold. Leon Morgan of Eastwood, Missouri, was injured as his house was destroyed by a tornado on December 2, 1982. He moved a mobile home onto the lot. On Christmas Eve, just twenty-two days later, another tornado struck the trailer and killed him. Kathleen Gaines was just five days old when her home at Gainesville, Georgia, was torn apart by a tornado in 1903. Her father, Leon, arrived home to find Kathleen and her mother lying in a pool of water. In 1936 Leon was cranking the car at 8:30 A.M., about to take his thirty-two-year-old daughter, Kathleen, to her teaching job, when he saw a tornado approach. He raced to the house as it collapsed onto the family, killing Kathleen and her mother.

The Gainesville tornadoes of 1903 and 1936 themselves constitute an interesting coincidence. Never before or since has such a small city (population 17,000) been so devastated twice. In 1936 there were stories of superhuman strength as a man tore down a 6-inch-thick door to free people from bursting ammonia pipes in an ice-cream factory. Nearby, more than forty young girls and women were cremated in the fiery collapse and destruction of the Cooper Pants factory, which was hit by the tornado just as they started work. One of the women at the pants factory was Mrs. Boyd Shaw. As the women in her group rushed in terror to the stairway, Mrs. Shaw caught her dress on her sewing machine. As she struggled to free herself, the tornado ripped the roof from the factory, causing it to collapse. She was then picked up, ripped free from her dress, carried through the air, and dropped a block away with only minor injuries. None of her co-workers made it beyond the top of the stairway.

The above stories were taken from local newspapers printed shortly after the time of the tornado, as well as from five- to fifty-year anniversary issues. The Gainesville stories were from the fortieth anniversary issue of the *Journal*. These commemorative sections contain particularly interesting accounts, as old-timers recall the event to eager reporters. One has to wonder whether the passage of time has enhanced some of the details. After the fiftieth anniversary of the event, new stories become less numerous, as fewer and fewer survivors are available and the best stories have been told and reprinted several times.

For some people, these anecdotes have raised an endless list of questions about the nature and structure of tornadoes. Inquisitive people in the eighteenth century, such as Benjamin Franklin (see chap. 12), began to look beyond the stories and to come up with crude hypotheses about why tornadoes form and whether tornadoes actually rotate. It was not until late in the nineteenth century that genuine scientific progress was made, however. Success came first in the field of tornado forecasting, then in understanding the tornado life cycle and why tornadoes form. We will look at these areas in a slightly different order. Forecasting will be discussed third, after considerable terminology has been introduced. This gives us the best opportunity to understand forecasting, which is more important in our daily lives.

CHAPTER 3

TORNADO LIFE CYCLE

According to the *Hull Index* and the *Sioux County Herald* of May 10, 1895, even old-timers in Sioux County, Iowa, were awestruck by the appearance of the sky in the early afternoon of May 3, 1895. "A sudden darkness began to hover over the entire scope of the country, and the hearts of all began to grow quail and faint." In the schools that were about to be destroyed, "the dark was so intense that work was stopped and lamps lighted."

"The heavens were of a greenish-blue color," M. B. Coombs observed from his farm. "Two clouds came together and a finger reached to the earth, no larger than a wagon wheel." He barely had time to reach the house. His wife and younger children were already in the basement, and within seconds the building was torn in half. His older children were at the Coombs School, a mile to the north. The teacher, Miss Anna Marsden, could only huddle and pray with her students as the funnel approached. Perhaps she thought of her brother, George, teaching at another school 4 miles to the northeast. Both were new teachers, recently arrived from Wisconsin. A few minutes earlier Mr. C. R. Steel had looked at the sky, ridden to the school, and brought his son home. There were no storm cellars at any of the five schools (all in session) that would be blown apart in the next fifteen minutes. To those left at the Coombs School, it appeared that the tornado might miss the building. But as the edge of the funnel passed nearby, the school was "lifted on end, collapsed like an egg shell, and blown into a thousand fragments." Anna Marsden and two Coombs children were killed.

At the Haggie School, we do not know whether Anna's brother and the dozen children saw the tornado at all. The funnel was now a half mile wide and filled with mud. The school was "annihilated," killing George Marsden and two of the children. At the next school, Miss Dystrata was frightened by the appearance of the sky and sent all the students running for their homes, some a mile or more away. Two of the Koster children almost made it home and were apparently near their house. The Koster farm "had every piece of furniture or clothing swept from the face of the earth." The mother may have seen the daughters running to the house, for she too was killed in the front yard, along with the infant in her arms.

In District 6 of Welcome Township, Miss Faustina Boyton saw the storm coming and "took refuge with her students in a willow hedge" (probably in a low-lying area) as the school was destroyed. No one was injured. A few miles to the northeast, still another school was "lifted into the air and carried across the fields." But early in its flight "the floor fell out and the children escaped without serious injury." Miss DeBoor and the students were all bruised and covered with mud. Fence posts and trees were covered to a depth of several inches with mud, as were the sides of buildings. The layer "had to be removed with a hammer after a few days of drying."

During the past several centuries, countless descriptions have been written that, taken together, cover all of the tornado's visible life cycle. But these accounts are of little scientific value, for each describes only part of the storm. We have been told hundreds of times that funnels begin aloft, grow downward, start small, then grow rapidly in size. Occasionally other bits of useful information have been added, for example, the idea that powerful winds extend beyond the visible funnel. But the exaggerations and florid prose often cast doubt on the accuracy of the entire story. Meteorologists find phrases like "clouds driven to madness," "funnels that vomited lightning," or "two clouds coming together" interesting but not very useful.

In his widely quoted 1887 book, *Tornadoes,* Finley reinforced the long-held idea that tornadoes begin after "two clouds come together." For the next half century, newspapers used those words in their tornado descriptions. Storm chasers have looked for this phenomenon for decades without seeing it. They have seen rotation under a thunderstorm and airflows converging toward the updraft. "Two clouds coming together" is a poor way to describe this combination of rotation and convergence. Lacking the right words, the awestruck observers were probably comfortable with the "two clouds" idea and repeated the phrase year after year. A proper organization and vocabulary began to take shape in the late 1940s. The struggle to classify and name what we see in the sky continues today.

In 1946 The Thunderstorm Project became the first multiagency field experiment on severe storms and marked the start of large-scale, federally funded, peacetime weather research. From that study of Florida and Ohio thunderstorms came the concept of the three stages of a thunderstorm's life cycle: towering cumulus stage, mature stage, and dissipating stage (Byers and Braham 1949).

In 1949 Edward Brooks of St. Louis University proposed that certain large thunderstorms contain a small area of rotating low pressure that spawns destructive tornadoes. He called this area the "tornado cyclone" (Brooks 1949). The idea came from pressure and wind direction data at Weather Bureau offices (primarily St. Louis) that had been near a tornado. After this, individual storms, in the right place at the right time, would be the stimulus for advancing our understanding.

Below is my personal list of the ten most significant severe weather events that led up to the formal definition of the visible life cycle of a tornado. The most important discoveries did not come from the deadliest tornadoes. One of the events involved a storm that did not spawn a tornado and did not even occur in the United States; another did not even involve a thunderstorm.

STORM #1. On April 9, 1953, the McCormick family of Bismarck, Illinois, and others in the area grabbed their children and ran for cover as their homes and farms were blown to bits. There were no tornado warnings, no interrupted television programs with live, multicolored Doppler radar views of the approaching storm. That technology would not be available for

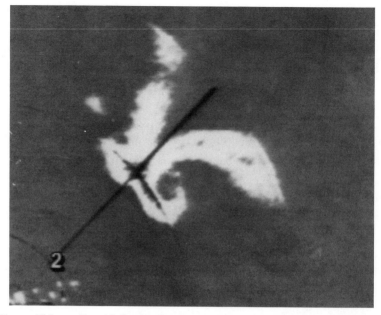

Fig. 3.1. This 5-mile-wide hook echo appeared on a radar screen at Champaign, Illinois, on April 9, 1953. It was the first tornado-related hook to be identified in real time. The hook is the reflection of precipitation being wrapped around a mesocyclone. Courtesy of Ted Fujita.

another thirty-five years. In Champaign, Illinois, however, south and south-west of the tornado, an early step in the development of that technology was being taken. By coincidence, an electrical engineer, Daniel Staggs, was testing a newly rebuilt World War II–style weather radar at the State Water Survey office. During the test, he put it into full operation. A shape could be seen on the screen that looked like a huge hook (fig. 3.1).

The image was obviously associated with the thunderstorm in progress to the north. Although tracking the storm was not part of his duties that day, Staggs wisely kept the radar unit in operation, recording on film the entire life of this hook-shaped structure. Later analysis would show that this hook was closely associated with the tornado itself (Stout and Huff 1953; Fujita 1958). The hook was not the tornado but a band of rain and hail sweeping around Brooks's "tornado cyclone." The era of tornado research with radar was born. A few years later Ted Fujita, of the University of Chicago, renamed this area the "mesocyclone." He felt that the term "tornado cyclone" was inappropriate, since a tornado did not always form in this rotating area. Despite a great deal of initial enthusiasm, a study by Stuart Bigler in the early 1950s showed that in radar photos of thirty-three tornado or funnel-cloud events, only three showed hook echoes on these primitive, World War II era radar displays. Most storms were too distant, and radar resolution too poor, for a hook to be recognized easily.

STORM #2. Randomly scattered tornado photographs are of little scientific use. But by 1955 the veterans of World War II had fathered the baby boom generation, and there were more cameras than ever, ready to take pictures of their children. As of June 27, 1955, we would no longer be limited by single photographs or the uncertainties of eyewitnesses. That day gave us thirteen rather slow-moving tornadoes near Scottsbluff, Nebraska. Walter Hoecker (1959) studied at least forty-five photographs and four motion pictures of these funnels, the first reliable photographic record of funnel development.

STORM #3. The Dallas, Texas, tornado of April 2, 1957, posed for hundreds of photographs and more than 2,000 feet of motion picture film. This historic event was again studied by Hoecker (1960; Hoecker et al. 1960) in landmark papers on the life cycle and wind speeds associated with a destructive tornado.

STORM #4. Just two months after the Dallas tornado, on June 20, 1957, ten people died at Fargo, North Dakota, including six children in one family. More people might have died, but the city had advance warning from motorists heading eastbound on U.S. 10. The approach of the tornado was announced on television and radio, and the funnel was greeted by a large number of amateur photographers. After learning of these pictures, Horace Byers asked Fujita to survey the storm. Dewey Bergquist, a well-known meteorologist on WDAY-TV, announced on the air that Fujita needed photographs. More than one hundred fifty were collected from his viewing audience, along with five motion pictures. Fujita and Bergquist located the exact spot from which each picture was taken.

The detailed study at Fargo (Fujita 1960) was a landmark in storm analysis that in some ways is unequaled even today. Fujita's drawings (fig. 3.2)

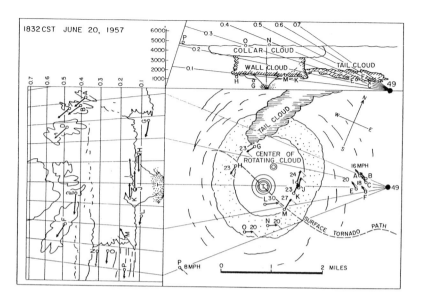

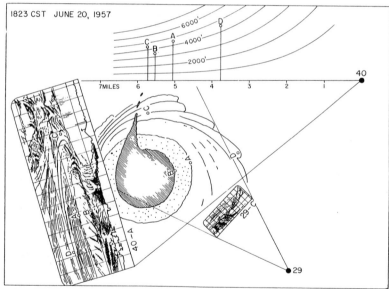

Fig. 3.2. Fujita's drawings of the Fargo storm of June 20, 1957, included perspective drawings and new terminology. Courtesy of Ted Fujita.

and his new vocabulary—"wall cloud," "collar cloud," "tail cloud"—gave us a better means of comparing and discussing storms. He had outlined the external architecture of a "supercell" but did not coin the term. The concept of the supercell, and the term, originated in England.

STORM #5. On July 9, 1959, Frank Ludlam had five radar units in place, along with a small army of more than two thousand volunteer observers around his East Hill installation. Seven convective storms crossed England that day. One of them, the Wokingham storm, developed over France, crossed the English Channel, and laid down a 130-mile-long hail swath across southeastern England. The storm passed directly over the East Hill station, and 442 "ground truth" observation points lay within the storm area. The town of Wokingham was pelted with nearly baseball-sized hail. Ludlam and his student Keith Browning analyzed the storm in extraordinary detail (Browning and Ludlam 1962). They coordinated the radar images with exact times from the observer network, allowing them to deduce the life history of the storm, including its internal airflow structure. They were especially surprised that the storm entered an almost unchanging steady state condition for an hour. It was unheard of for something as chaotic and changeable as a thunderstorm to do this.

It was here that the supercell concept was born. A key observation was that the storm appeared to have a large hole in it, as seen on radar. Browning called it an "echo-free vault," an open, domelike structure within the thunderstorm where precipitation was held aloft. Today it is called the "bounded weak echo region," or BWER. Above this hole or vault, hail grew to abnormally large sizes, creating a strongly reflective upper boundary as seen on radar. The Wokingham thunderstorm was the first identified "supercell," having been casually given the name by Browning (1962). After graduation, Browning moved to the U.S. Air Force Laboratory at Cambridge, Massachusetts, where another radar pioneer, Ralph Donaldson, also worked.

STORM #6. In the early 1960s thunderstorm research was well under way in Oklahoma. Neil Ward, a researcher for the National Severe Storms Project (NSSP), was convinced that he could find a potentially tornadic storm, drive to it, and perhaps even photograph the tornado. That now historic supercell passed 50 miles west of Oklahoma City on May 4, 1961.

Ward made plans to track a storm with radar guidance, and May 4 was the day. His link with the radar station near Oklahoma City was through an Oklahoma Highway Patrol radio car. As luck would have it, the updraft vault showed up on radar as a hole in the storm, and Ward raced in that direction. Near Geary, Oklahoma, he shot the first motion and still pictures of a tornado taken on a storm chase (see chap. 10). In addition, the life of the storm was filmed and studied on radar by Browning and Donaldson (1963). Comparison of the Geary and Wokingham storms showed striking similarities. It was obvious that this was one of those special kinds of storms.

STORM #7.   On May 26, 1963, two tornadic thunderstorms passed either near or over the radar at Oklahoma City. Donaldson himself was at the radar station near Tinker Air Force Base and saw the tornado form almost directly overhead and touch down to the east. He also saw, in person and on radar, how rain curtains from one storm were drawn into the other. The thunderstorms' mature stage lasted hours longer than most thunderstorms and moved gradually to the right of the prevailing winds, instead of with the prevailing winds. The storms developed unique radar structures, such as a vault, a hook echo, and precipitation-free areas at the rear. These 1963 storms led to the recognition of a new stage in the development of thunderstorms: the severe/right-moving, or SR, stage. It was considered to be a unique kind of storm phenomenon, not a normal part of thunderstorm evolution.

STORM #8.   The unprecedented outbreak on Palm Sunday, April 11, 1965, changed the course of how the government informs people about storms (see chap. 5). It also provided Fujita with the opportunity to study tornado families in more detail than ever before (Fujita, Bradbury, and van Thullenar 1970). After an aerial survey of the Palm Sunday damage, Fujita concluded that the main vortices of some tornadoes may indeed contain very powerful miniature vortices, essentially tornadoes inside a tornado.

STORM #9.   A defined life cycle of waterspouts (Golden 1974) preceded similar work on the life cycle of tornadoes (Golden and Purcell 1978) by four years. The waterspout research started with a very lucky sightseeing flight from Key West to Miami in September 1967. On board was Joseph Golden, a Florida State University meteorology student who was a summer employee of the National Hurricane Center. The flight passed a huge waterspout near Matecumbe Key, about 50 miles south of Miami. This encounter led to the idea that waterspouts could be studied from the air. The eager graduate student was told that little could be learned, for only one or two waterspouts could be studied each year. Persistence overcame skepticism, and the Florida Keys Waterspout Project began in 1969 as a doctoral dissertation. The reported annual number of waterspouts turned out to be low by a factor of one hundred. The project had a shoestring budget and survived with help from off-duty pilots, donated smoke flares from the U.S. Navy, and an occasional ride on a hurricane-hunter plane. In 1969 alone, 140 waterspouts (fig. 3.3) were studied at every stage of development, perhaps the most detailed study of any natural vortex ever done in so short a time.

STORM #10. It was not until May 24, 1973, that scientific chase teams from the National Severe Storms Laboratory (NSSL) and the University of Oklahoma (OU) finally documented a tornado well enough to define the steps in its visible life cycle. NSSL and OU chase teams raced to an area of suspected activity just 30 miles west of Norman. The entire life cycle of a major tornado was recorded on film from distances of 3 to 8 miles. They literally surrounded the tornado at Union City from beginning to end. The storm chase at Union City was one of the first organized chases and one of the most successful. It combined accurate forecasting, direct observation by scientists, high-quality motion picture photography, and experimental Doppler radar. Joseph Golden was one of the lead chasers.

LIFE CYCLE STAGES

The stages in the life cycle of a tornado are based on observations at Union City in 1973. Golden and Daniel Purcell (1978) list four stages, combining the dust whirl and organizing stages, and Robert Davies-Jones (1985) lists five. I follow Davies-Jones and use the drawings by David Hoadley (fig. 3.4) here. The time needed to pass through each stage can

Fig. 3.3. A giant waterspout photographed on September 10, 1969, in the Florida Keys. Note the smoke flares streaming away from the vortex. They are under the influence of air flowing out of the storm that spawned the waterspout. Copyright Joseph Golden.

vary widely, and not every tornado goes through all stages. The Union City time spans should not necessarily be considered typical for all tornadoes. The visible life cycle lasted 26 minutes, which is longer than most tornadoes but less than half as long as some. The funnel moved east-southeast at 20 mph, which is slower than the 30 to 40 mph typical for most destructive tornadoes. Moreover, the tornado did not travel in the most common direction, which is to the northeast. Nonetheless, Union City is the benchmark for the tornado life cycle.

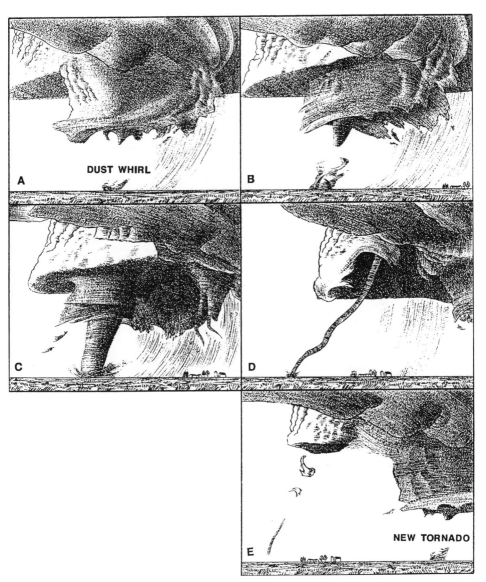

Fig. 3.4. The five stages of tornado formation—dust whirl, organizing, mature, shrinking, decaying or rope—were drawn by David Hoadley for Tim Marshall's *Storm Talk.*

STAGE 1: DUST WHIRL

To an observer in the field, the first sign of a tornado is usually dust swirling upward from the ground and a short pendant funnel cloud hanging from the base of the parent cloud. In this first stage, the funnel cloud aloft and the dust swirl below may not appear to be connected. If both are present, however, the circulation must be continuous from the cloud to ground, and a true tornado has indeed formed. If only a pendant funnel is visible, with no dust swirl, the event is called a funnel cloud aloft and is not counted as a tornado. The tornado may develop under a lowered cloud base, called a "wall cloud." This wall cloud structure can preexist any tornado formation for 1 to 30 minutes or even longer. Thunderstorms can, however, produce a tornado without developing a wall cloud. It is not uncommon to have several wall clouds form before any tornado appears.

STAGE 2: ORGANIZING

It is during the organizing stage that the vortex becomes visible. The condensation funnel usually forms aloft, at cloud base, because the temperature is cooler and humidity higher there. The visible funnel appears to extend downward as more humid air is drawn into the tornado, where it encounters lower pressure and cools as it expands. The expansion causes the air to cool below its dew point temperature. As the vortex spins faster, the pressure inside the funnel drops farther and some of the moisture in that inrushing air condenses into cloud droplets. Eventually a full condensation funnel appears. The funnel seems to form from above and descend to the ground, but it is possible that the funnel actually forms from the ground up. The tornado may now increase in size and intensity, or vanish into thin air. At Union City, the combined dust whirl and organizing stages lasted about 10 minutes. Some tornadoes mature and become destructive much faster than that.

STAGE 3: MATURE

The tornado, now at its greatest size, is vertical or only slightly tilted. If conditions in and around the thunderstorm are not ideal, the tornado can skip from stage 2 to stage 5, completely omitting the mature and shrinking stages. The mature stage lasted 8 minutes at Union City as the funnel rapidly widened and intensified. The maximum visible size was about 150 yards, with a damage track of about 500 yards wide.

The supercell updraft, the inflow, and the various downdrafts can all work in harmony to maintain the mesocyclone and the mature stage of the tornado in an almost steady state and produce intense, potentially deadly, long-track tornadoes. In that state single tornadoes can be maintained for an hour or more with path lengths of 50 miles or more.

STAGE 4: SHRINKING

The diameter of the tornado now shrinks, and the funnel begins to tilt. The lower end of the tornado usually lags behind the upper part. As the funnel width decreases, it may rotate even more rapidly, as ice skaters do when they draw their outstretched arms inward. The rotating air conserves angular momentum by spinning faster. This rapid spin can make the funnel even more dangerous, although the path is narrower. The wall cloud shrinks and disappears. This stage lasted about 6 minutes at Union City. The damage path narrowed from 500 yards to 150 yards, and twenty homes were destroyed, along with various churches and commercial buildings.

STAGE 5: DECAYING, OR ROPE

The rope stage can last 10 minutes or more, and it can be very erratic. The cooler air of the rear flank downdraft flows down and around the tornado. This apparently cuts off the inflow to the funnel. With upward-spiraling air in contact with downward-moving air, the tornado stretches into a "rope," occasionally a mile or more long (fig. 3.5). Sometimes the rope may extend out from under the base of the thunderstorm and dissipate under a clear sky. The decaying stage lasted 2 minutes at Union City.

The rope tornado can still be destructive. The circulation has contracted even further, and a small but intense circulation can stay on the ground even after the upper part of the tornado has completely disappeared. At Union City, a family tried to outrun the tornado in a car, but the tornado

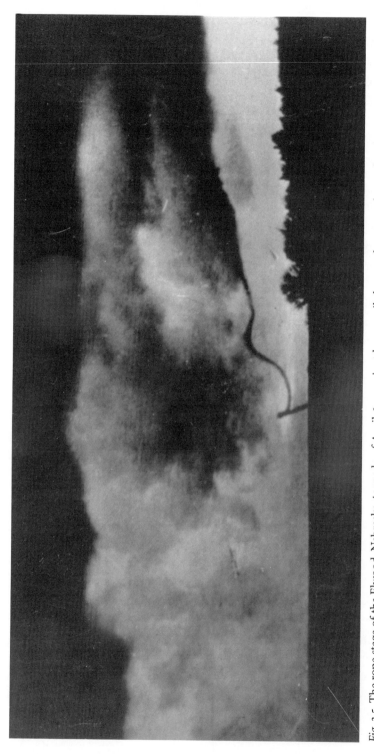

Fig. 3.5. The rope stage of the Elwood, Nebraska, tornado of April 6, 1919, is at least a mile long and seems to have a bend in it. This is only an illusion, because the lower part of the funnel is seen along its length. Photo from Snowden D. Flora, *Tornadoes of the United States* (Norman: University of Oklahoma Press, 1953), courtesy W. A. Wood.

caught up with them, overturned the car, and destroyed a house. Some tornadoes do not actually "rope out" but instead grow wider and weaker as they dissipate. This may occur as the updraft weakens.

A tornado can make rather quick movements to one side or another if it is buffeted by strong downdrafts. These movements may be especially unpredictable during the rope stage. The most famous of all tornadoes, the studio-created funnel in *The Wizard of Oz,* is seen swinging from side to side in the scene in which Dorothy is looking for her relatives. That tornado is doing far too much swinging; the gyrations are too frequent. Downdraft winds that are strong enough to produce that motion would probably disrupt the circulation, destroying the vortex. However, people have lost their lives by misjudging rapid changes in funnel direction.

The five stages of the tornado's life cycle can overlap, or even repeat, making it impossible to identify the exact point of transition from one to another. Some tornadoes never display a condensation funnel. The air flowing into the tornado may be too warm and dry for condensation to create visible cloud droplets. It is likely that some tornadoes never reach a fully visible stage and thus are not reported. Just how many of these undocumented tornadoes occur annually is unknown (see chap. 11).

THE APPEARANCE OF THE TORNADO

A tornado can last from less than 10 seconds to more than 2 hours. In that time the funnel may vary in forward speed, direction, erratic movement, path width, path length, internal structure, wind speed, color, sound, dust and debris content, and altitude of the parent cloud base, and probably in ways we have not yet imagined. Processes that involve temperatures, pressures, and humidities inside the funnel make them all look a little different.

Very few tornadoes look like true funnels; the tornado shown in figure 3.6 is more the exception than the rule. Because temperatures are warmer nearer the ground, there can be less condensation near the ground than aloft, giving the tornado a tapered appearance, although its true form is that of a column. Also, convergence of air into the vortex mostly occurs near the ground, which tends to pinch the base into a funnel shape.

Fig. 3.6. The tornado at Lake Park, Iowa, on May 30, 1942, took the shape of a true funnel. Tornado descriptions frequently use the word *funnel,* but few tornadoes actually look like one. A tail cloud is obvious to the right of the funnel. Courtesy of the S. D. Flora Collection of the Western History Collections, University of Oklahoma Library.

Fig. 3.7. The damage at Xenia, Ohio, on April 3, 1974, was done by a multiple-vortex tornado. Some houses in the middle of the path received only roof and wall damage while surrounding houses were nearly obliterated. Courtesy of the American Red Cross.

Little is known about the airflows and conditions inside a tornado. Rapid changes in the dust and moisture content of the funnel sometimes give us a brief glimpse of the intricate workings inside a tornado. These changes can best be seen in tornadoes captured on videotape.

MULTIPLE VORTICES

For as long as tornadoes have been described, eyewitnesses have reported tornado "tails," "silvery ribbons," and forms resembling "egg beaters." At least one large tornado every year engulfs an entire neighborhood, destroying one home and leaving an adjacent house seemingly untouched (see fig. 3.7). Aerial surveys not only have photographed unusual damage patterns but also have recorded spiral ground markings like those in figure 3.8. Eventually these markings, the "egg beaters," and the irregular damage

Fig. 3.8. These spiral ground markings were photographed near Kokomo, Indiana, by Ted Fujita after the Palm Sunday outbreak of April 11, 1965. From Fujita et al. 1970.

patterns were linked by a single concept, the multiple vortex tornado. They are visible in a few photographs from the 1940s, but in general they do not show up well in still photographs. So many tornado photographs and videos are taken today that at least a few every year show them distinctly, as in figure 3.9. Multiple-vortex tornadoes are not a new phenomenon, only a newly recognized one. They have been around as long as tornadoes have been around, as the story below illustrates.

A headline in the *Chicago Tribune* of May 9, 1876, read "Cyclone Ravages City," and the accompanying story contained this vivid description of the tornado as it moved away over Lake Michigan.

Fig. 3.9. Only a few times a year are the multiple vortices of a tornado seen clearly as they were at Jarrell, Texas, on May 27, 1997. Photograph by Scott Beckwith.

[When it was about a mile from shore] it was composed of eight or ten columns grouped together, all whirling around a central point. The columns, or spirals, twisted and writhed like snakes. The group was about 500 feet in diameter, the various parts leaning at the top towards the centre, and bulging slightly at the middle. Now and then a column would draw away from its fellows and then sweep back. The down rush of air in the vacuum drew the cloud down. Directly under the mass the lake was flat and still. Around it the waters were lashed and torn. The waves dashed upon the spirals as if driven to madness by the attack. As the pillars curled around, binding themselves together, the cloud vomited lightning, as though sick of the performance. Another such scene may never come in this generation, and it is to be regretted that the cylinder could not have been caught and pickled for scientific investigation.

These observations are astute, given that the date of the tornado was May 7, 1876, nearly a century before the multiple-vortex phenomenon was explained. Remarkably, downward-moving air is involved in the modern-day explanation.

The pieces of the multiple-vortex puzzle were put together by Ted Fujita and Neil Ward. They worked independently, by attacking the problem from different directions. Both had puzzled over unusual damage patterns and spiral ground markings. Both focused on the unique tornadic events of May 24, 1962, at Newton, Kansas, when dozens of small funnels seemed to encircle the town.

Ward (1972) perfected a physical model that produced multiple vortices similar to those he had seen in dust devils. Experiments began in his garage during 1956, about fifteen years before any other comparable models were created. He produced an intertwining, double helix and up to three multiple-vortex tornadoes. The Ward model was perfected at Purdue University in the mid-1970s by Chris Church, John Snow, and Ernest Agee (see Church et al. 1979; Church and Snow 1993). The Purdue team was able to produce double-helical vortices and model tornadoes with six or more subvortices, all under controlled conditions.

At about the same time, at the University of Chicago, Fujita was studying aerial survey photographs of damage in the Palm Sunday outbreak of April 11, 1965. He drew his conclusions from photographs such as figure 3.8. Fujita theorized that to produce these markings, some tornadoes must contain three to five secondary vortices within the walls of the main funnel. He initially called them "suction spots" and later changed the name to "suction vortices."

Fujita (1970) studied the relationship between spiral ground markings and tornado-related deaths in the Lubbock, Texas, tornado of May 11, 1970 (see chap. 12). Most of the deaths were in the paths of those intense suction spots, which may add an extra 100 mph to the maximum winds inside a tornado. (See chap. 6.) It was now clear that tornadoes do not "skip" when they create odd damage patterns. The intense vortices inside the funnel make the damage worse in some areas. By contrast, the area between the paths of the multiple vortices appear relatively untouched, as in figures 3.7 and 3.10.

Figure 3.11 simplifies the gradual change of a single-vortex tornado into a multiple-vortex form. The figure is a series of two-dimensional, vertical cross sections of what is a very complex three-dimensional structure. These drawings from Davies-Jones (1985) do not show the relative speed of the airflows. Figure 3.11a shows the cross section of a single-vortex tornado with the air flowing inward and upward. The air swirls about the axis of the vortex

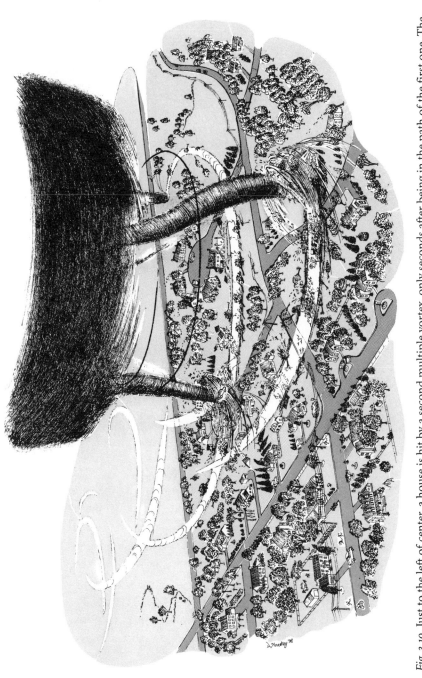

Fig. 3.10. Just to the left of center, a house is hit by a second multiple vortex, only seconds after being in the path of the first one. The entire neighborhood was severely damaged in this situation. However, David Hoadley has not drawn that damage so that the effect of multiple vortices could be emphasized.

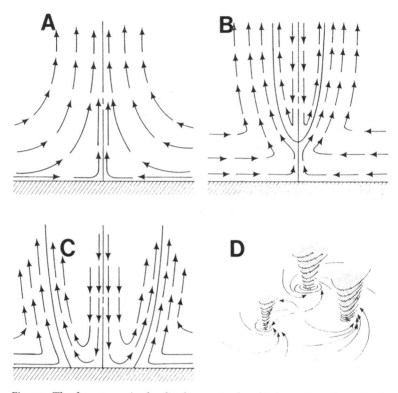

Fig. 3.11. The four stages in the development of multiple vortices. From Davies-Jones 1985.

at increasing speed while the pressure in the center of the vortex continues to drop. Figure 3.11b shows that this pressure drop causes the vortex to fill in from above; air begins to descend in the core of the funnel. This is the process known as "vortex breakdown." In figure 3.11c the descending air reaches the surface and flows outward toward the walls of the tornado. There it meets inward-flowing air. In figure 3.11d that interaction produces three subvortices. They form and disappear readily. No single suction vortex may actually make one full revolution around the core of the tornado.

Atmospheric scientists are fairly confident that intense tornadoes are related to supercells, that tornadoes have a fairly predictable life cycle, and that they understand at least the theoretical aspects of multiple vortices.

LOOKING TO THE PAST AND TO THE FUTURE

Describing, classifying, and explaining what is seen is the easy part. Just identifying the supercell and deciding that tornadoes had five visible stages took a century of observations, several revolutions in photography, and the invention and refinement of radar. What seems so obvious now was not obvious at all until the hard work and keen insight of earlier meteorologists opened our eyes. And hard work it was. The task of creating and gathering data from a network of two thousand volunteer observers in England is a monumental effort in itself. But Ludlam then took their observations and mentally created a three-dimensional picture of the storm. Another, different challenge was Fujita's effort to track down, visit, and map the exact location from which every Fargo tornado photograph and movie was taken. He also constructed a three-dimensional view of the storm in his mind and created perspective drawings. Unique skills come in many forms, but the ability to do multidimensional visualization is critical in making breakthroughs in understanding severe storms.

The hard part lies ahead. We must now try to explain the tornado formation processes that are hidden inside the thunderstorm and are at work in the transparent air outside the thunderstorm. That first hint of a funnel cloud may be the product of dozens of earlier, mostly unknown, steps. A little of what we know about these processes, the ones that actually cause the tornadic vortex to form, is the subject of the next chapter.

CHAPTER 4

TORNADO
FORMATION

The mystery of how and why tornadoes form, or tornadogenesis, may be decades away from a satisfactory explanation. Progress is very slow. From the time a hook echo was detected on conventional radar in 1953, it was fifteen years until a mesocyclone was detected on Doppler radar and then another twenty-seven years until a portable Doppler radar was able to get close enough to a tornado to reveal the complex airflow in and around an actual funnel. Here is a brief summary of these two events.

On August 9, 1968, 100-mph winds seemed to come out of nowhere at Marblehead, Massachusetts. Harbormaster John Wolfgram was unaware of rotating clouds overhead or that this storm was to become a part of meteorological history. His only concern was that dozens of boats were being destroyed in this small section of the Massachusetts coast. It was of no consequence to the boat owners that 20 miles west, at Sudbury, Ralph Donaldson was heading a research team that was beaming a radar signal into the storm, 3 miles over Wolfgram's head.

Donaldson was steering the radar beam horizontally, across the thunderstorm. The returning signal from a small area in the storm indicated motion toward the radar unit. Two miles to the right, motion was away from the unit. This meant that the storm was rotating. For the first time the rotation of a mesocyclone was detected by radar using the frequency shift in radiowaves known as the Doppler effect (Donaldson 1970). The initial signs of rotation occurred one full hour before the storm hit Marblehead and ushered in an era in which we can study the rotary motions inside a potentially tornadic thunderstorm, even when the storm is up to 100 miles from the radar.

Twenty-seven years later, on June 2, 1995, Carlos Calvert and his wife huddled in their basement while most of their Dimmitt, Texas, house was being ripped to splinters and scattered. A few seconds earlier the tornado had peeled slabs of pavement from Highway 86 and tossed them more than 500 feet. While families below ground prayed that they would survive this ordeal, above ground more than one hundred scientists and storm chasers had the tornado surrounded by a meteorological armada. Radio communications crackled with phrases such as "FC [Field Coordinator] this is Probe 2, touchdown is imminent west of Highway 385." "Probe 2, what are your coordinates?" "FC, this is Probe 1, the tornado is on the ground passing 1 mile south of us, here are our digits." More than fifteen fully instrumented chase vehicles and two mobile radar platforms were gathering data from preassigned positions. One was a Doppler on wheels (DOW), mounted on a flatbed truck. This mobile radar station was comparable to what we might expect to find at a permanent weather station. But now it was less than 2 miles from a major tornado, and part of history's greatest scientific storm-chasing endeavor.

At Dimmitt, for the first time, an intense tornado was fully resolved on the radar screen with feeder bands, an open core, and rotating winds of at least 155 mph (Straka, Wurman, and Rasmussen 1996). The DOW was fielded by Josh Wurman of the University of Oklahoma as part of VORTEX (Verification of the Origins of Rotation in Tornadoes EXperiment), a full-scale assault on the problem of understanding tornado formation (Rasmussen et al. 1994). The Dimmitt tornado had become the most completely documented tornado in history. Another one hundred or so events like these, during the course of the next several decades, and the problem will at least be better understood.

The tornado formation puzzle has taken so long to resolve in part because large and long-lasting tornadoes are rare events. We cannot actually build one, or find one when it is convenient. In *Twister*, tornadoes seem to be easy to locate; in real life, it may take years of storm chasing to bring the right piece of equipment to the right storm.

The secrets of tornado formation are, however, slowly yielding to genius and determination on three fronts. Storm-chasing scientists, armed with weather and communications gear, have surrounded tornadic thunderstorms to gather airflow information. Unfortunately, this happens only about once or twice a year. Storms are also explored by the probing eyes of Doppler radar, which can "see" into the supercell and map circulation patterns that would otherwise remain hidden.

The third assault on the tornado puzzle cannot have a real-life tornado story as an introduction. It takes place in an environment in which no actual severe storms ever rage—inside supercomputers (Wicker and Wilhelmson 1993). Given the equations of airflow, basic principles of physics, and a set of initial conditions, computer programs can produce a digital supercell and tornado-like vortices.

Oversimplified explanations say that tornadoes form during a twisting clash of air masses. If it were that simple, there would be hundreds of tornadoes every day. The clash of cool and warm air occurs daily in the United States and in other countries where, unlike here, tornadoes are virtually unknown. "Battling air masses" may be a nice sound bite for the six o'clock news, but it is absolutely useless to anyone with the responsibility of issuing a forecast and warning a community that might be in imminent danger. Something as dynamic as a giant funnel cloud rotating at 200 mph does not happen just because air masses "clash." There are specific sources of that incredible rotation, and a specific sequence of events in which rotation and updraft combine to produce a tornado. We will not understand tornadoes until those sources are identified.

The tornado recipe has many airflow ingredients, most of them invisible. They are either transparent or hidden by clouds and rain. The zone where the most important ingredients may hide is especially hard to study. VORTEX mesonet chase vehicles reach only up to 10 feet. Above that we have virtually no temperature and humidity measurements. Distant NEXRAD radar stations usually can probe only well above the cloud base. This leaves the space from 10 feet to 5,000 feet somewhat of a mystery zone, one in which critically important processes occur. The bottom mile of the atmosphere is 99 percent out of reach, except for very expensive tools like the DOW. The lowest altitude measurable by the DOW is about 300 feet, so a critical area from 10 to 300 feet above ground level is devoid of any measurements. My own experiments with physical tornado models indicate that airflow in the bottom 5 percent of the tornado chamber may be critical to the tornado formation process (Grazulis 2000).

At all levels of the atmosphere, from the surface to 10 miles up, we must know precisely what airflows are moving in what directions, and with what temperatures, pressures, and moisture levels. From studies of how they move, rotate, and interact, we are gradually developing an understanding of how and why tornadoes form. The gathering and synthesis of data and ideas operate within a set of general, largely unwritten, commonsense rules called "the scientific method."

TORNADO FORMATION, THE SCIENTIFIC METHOD, AND LIGHTNING

A prime goal of the scientific method is to come up with a theory. As yet there is no generally accepted theory of tornado formation. When people gather and talk, it is not uncommon to hear someone say that he or she has a "theory." This could be a theory about a highly publicized murder, alien abductions, or the quality of professional sports. In the proper sense of the word, these ideas are not theories. They are hypotheses, untested speculations. Only after a hypothesis is tested, revised, tested again, then submitted to expert review for intense scrutiny and accepted by experts does a hypothesis become theory. The scientific method is a rigorous process, one that many people have no patience for. Jumping off the deep end of the idea pool is much easier. Public speculations about cold nuclear fusion, life-prolonging herbs, and global warming can propel someone to instant celebrity and sell a lot of books, but they are not theories.

Occasionally an untested speculation about tornado formation finds its way into the news media and is proclaimed a "theory." The idea that there is an electrical attraction between mobile homes and tornadoes, or that opposing movements of interstate highway traffic can trigger tornadoes, is outlandish speculation, not theory. An untested idea that sounds good has particular appeal in an area of study as important, yet painfully slow, as severe-storm meteorology. For tornadoes, a single trip through the scientific method cycle can take ten years, depending on the grandeur of the experiment. Somewhere between speculation and the testing phase is the fund-raising phase. Field experiments and supercomputers can be very expensive.

In my lifetime the world has seen several examples of the scientific method at work in the earth sciences. Drifting continents, black holes, and dinosaur extinctions by asteroids were once considered either wild speculations or flights of pure fantasy. Years of speculation, testing, and revision have brought all three at least to the threshold of viable theory and, in the view of some people, "truth." It is hard to determine just when hypothesis becomes theory. A few basic principles can be considered "laws," for example, the law of gravity. But complex processes generally advance only to theory. The scientific method works well because scientists do not think alike and ideas are rarely revealed in a flash of brilliant reasoning. Experimental results can be interpreted differently by everyone who sees them. Each of these different ideas can spawn a new avenue of speculation and research.

The theory that tornadoes are produced by electricity was widely promoted by stars of the nineteenth-century scientific lecture circuit such as the chemist Robert Hare and "Professor" John H. Tice, the "weather prophet of St. Louis." Tice (1883) made outlandish forecasts and preached that all aspects of the weather were electrical in nature. He used the occasion of the Delphos, Kansas, tornado of May 30, 1879, to explain that Delphos was a railroad town and that "railroad and telegraph lines obey the laws of induction and give rise to the necessary electrical charges to produce storms." The leading tornado authority of the time, U.S. Army Lt. John Park Finley, despised the electrical theory of tornadoes and may have thoroughly enjoyed pointing out that Delphos actually had no railroad and no telegraph (Finley 1887). The town had only promoted itself as having them. This is an example of the pseudoscientific debates that plagued tornado studies for nearly a century and that continue today.

In the nineteenth century there were many demonstrations using electricity, magnetism, and rotation. It was "reasoned" without any hard evidence that electricity produced tornadoes. Lightning is electricity, electricity can produce rotation, lightning accompanies tornadoes, therefore electricity causes tornadoes. It was as simple as that. Electricity, new and exciting at the time, provided a means to explain many complex questions in meteorology. Droughts and floods on the plains were attributed to the westward spread of railroads and the "magnetic induction" of the steel rails. Then, as in the pseudosciences of today, observation was followed by speculation and conclusion.

In later years serious scientists suggested that heating by atmospheric electricity was needed to supplement mechanical forces to create extreme tornadic winds (Vonnegut 1960). This idea now seems unlikely, however, as we no longer need to explain winds of 600 mph. In addition, storm chasers rarely see frequent lightning near a funnel. Many tornadic storms have very little lightning; others have intense lightning. No solid evidence for a relationship exists, just speculations that are very hard to test in the field. We do know that lightning is related to updrafts and how the updrafts distribute precipitation in a storm. We also know that tornadoes are related to strong updrafts. There seems to be no direct link, however, between lightning and tornadoes. This is not to say that lightning will not be useful in tornado studies. The changing frequency and type of lightning, as viewed from satellites, might tell us a great deal about the development of a particular thunderstorm. Rather than a cause of tornadoes, lightning may turn out to be a tornado forecasting tool in the future.

THE SUPERCELL AND THE SOURCES OF ROTATION

The most productive era of tornado research began when meteorologists began trying to understand the storms that give rise to violent tornadoes. Not until the late 1950s and early 1960s, when supercells were identified as the generators of the deadliest tornadoes, did the pieces of the tornado formation puzzle finally start falling into place. Part of that puzzle is understanding just where the rotation comes from and how it gets so concentrated. And the puzzle pieces must fit; the numerical value of the tornado's rotation cannot be more than the sum of all the rotational parts.

More than a century ago, William Ferrel (1889) suggested that tornadoes rotate and that they form when the updraft of the thunderstorm encounters a rotating or "gyratory wind field." He was correct, but it took about seventy years to identify even the first source of rotation. Ferrel probably looked for a "gyratory wind field" with a vertical axis. Little did he know that it probably has a horizonal axis, parallel to the ground.

ROTATING TUBES AND ROTATION OF THE SUPERCELL UPDRAFT

The idea that the rotation of the supercell updraft comes from environmental wind shear has advanced to the level of accepted theory. Ideas about the rotation of the actual tornado have not advanced that far. The word *environmental* refers to winds around the thunderstorm, not within the storm. Wind shear in general is the changing of either the wind speed or the wind direction at different altitudes.

On the left in figure 4.1 is an illustration showing how wind shear gives rise to horizontal rotation near the surface, producing vortex tubes. In this situation, the wind is gradually changing direction with altitude. Near the surface the wind might blow from the southeast; at one-half mile above ground level it might be blowing from the south; at one mile up it might be blowing from the southwest. If winds were sheared this way, they would cause the horizontal tube to rotate clockwise. The heating of the ground by the sun would then produce updrafts that cause the rotating tube to tilt into a vertical position, as in the right portion of figure 4.1. It is the spin, or "vorticity," of the tube that is lifted into a vertical position and is probably the source of rotation for the updraft, the midlevel mesocyclone(s), and perhaps some of the rotation of the tornado.

There is a good reason that we do not try to measure the rotation of these large tubes. Although the vortex tube model is frequently used in newspaper and magazine articles, the tubes do not actually exist. Nowhere is there a one-mile-diameter rotating tube of air lying on its side. Solid-body analogies, using cylinders and tubes, do not always apply to moving fluids like air. It does not matter if you picture one big tube or hundreds of little ones. The vortex tube is a conceptual model that allows us to more easily work with the tricky subjects of wind shear and vorticity. The idea that the vertical axis of rotation in a supercell begins in a horizontal position

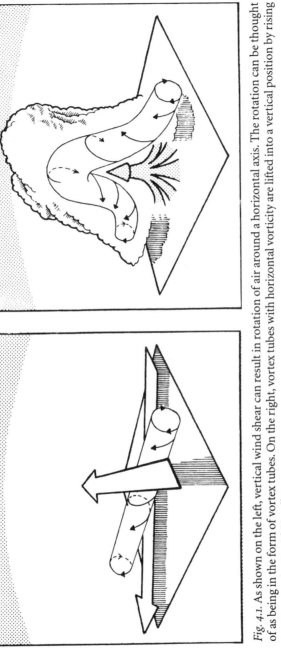

Fig. 4.1. As shown on the left, vertical wind shear can result in rotation of air around a horizontal axis. The rotation can be thought of as being in the form of vortex tubes. On the right, vortex tubes with horizontal vorticity are lifted into a vertical position by rising air. Drawing by David Hoadley.

was suggested by Keith Browning and Charles Landry (1963) and then refined by Stanley Barnes (1968, 1970).

THE PUZZLING QUANTITY CALLED VORTICITY

It is quite easy to imagine air having temperature, humidity, speed, and direction. We feel these quantities every day. We also can feel "shear" and a tendency to rotate if someone bumps our shoulders while passing in a crowd. Air parcels can also experience this stress. If there is any difference in the speed or the direction of the moving air on either side of an air parcel, the parcel becomes stressed and starts to rotate. "Vorticity" is the name we give to this rotational stress, and it has a numerical value in rotations per second. The rotational stress increases an air parcel's vorticity and the vorticity of an entire airstream. For example, as air is streaming into a thunderstorm updraft, it may be stressed by different air movements above and below it. This makes the updraft rotate. We measure vorticity by measuring the wind shear; they are basically the same thing. The vorticity of the airflow in a strong tornado is about one rotation per second. This is 10,000 to 100,000 times greater than the vorticity of the air outside the funnel.

The rotation from wind shear around the thunderstorm is called "environmental vorticity." It explains only the rotation of the updraft and the midlevel mesocyclone, 2 to 3 miles above ground level. It does not explain how the tornado forms all the way to the ground. Wind shear and vorticity are ingredients in tornado formation, not theories. Supercells are an ingredient, not a theory, of tornado formation. A complete theory must explain why many supercells form without ever producing a tornado. It must describe the sources of rotation, along with how and why the rotation gets properly positioned and concentrated. We know the ingredients quite well, even though they are mostly invisible. It may be many years or even many decades, however, before we have the recipe.

SUPERCELL FORMATION, STRUCTURE, AND TYPES

A supercell thunderstorm is a constantly evolving heat engine that spawns and keeps alive the devastating tornadoes that appear at the top of the killer tornado lists. It is more than just a severe thunderstorm. A supercell tends

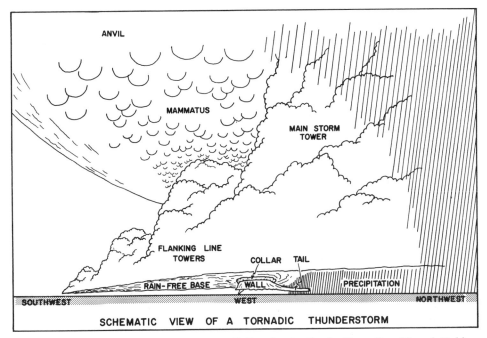

ANVIL

MAMMATUS

MAIN STORM
TOWER

FLANKING LINE
TOWERS

COLLAR TAIL

RAIN-FREE BASE WALL PRECIPITATION

SOUTHWEST WEST NORTHWEST

SCHEMATIC VIEW OF A TORNADIC THUNDERSTORM

Fig. 4.2. The main features of a classic supercell. Drawing by Charles Doswell and Joseph Golden.

to have a unique structure, with many recognizable features (fig. 4.2). It is
an isolated thunderstorm dominated by its overall rotation and the presence of a unique area of rotation called a mesocyclone. That "meso," as it
is often called, would be positioned as a vertical column between the wall
cloud and the overshooting top.

The supercell has a long-lived, intense, rotating updraft that sustains the
storm in its mature stage for up to six hours or more. The supercell's
updraft feeds moist air, loaded with latent heat energy stored in the water
molecules, high into the atmosphere. The updraft eventually becomes
surrounded by multiple downdrafts.

Typically, in late afternoon, the first storm clouds grow larger and higher
into a structure called a "multicellular" thunderstorm. This massive cloud
contains many individual, short-lived (45 minutes or less) billowing storm
towers, each with its own updraft. One of these thunderstorm cells, often
the one on the right, or southeast, side of the cluster, may become larger
and isolated and begin moving farther to the right. As large volumes of air

rise, compensating downdrafts develop and suppress the growth of neighboring clouds, leaving the future supercell relatively free from the interference of other thunderstorm cells. This one cloud may dominate the area and billow up in spectacular fashion for thousands of feet above the other clouds. When a strong rotating updraft develops, the storm is considered by most meteorologists to have become a supercell. It may take two hours or just a few minutes for a disorganized multicellular storm to become a tornadic supercell.

Wind shear helps to tilt the updraft slightly forward, and rain falls downstream in the front portion the storm. This rain generates large amounts of sinking cool air, especially as it evaporates. This cool air flow is the front flank downdraft (FFD). The air hits the ground and spreads out. The leading edge is called a "gust front." Many of us have felt this cold gust of air in advance of an approaching thunderstorm.

The updraft is now at the rear (often the southwestern part) of the growing thunderstorm, which is left relatively rain-free. The updraft is fed by air entering the storm from the southeast or south. Much of the precipitation within the updraft is held aloft by the rapidly rising air. This is a nearly precipitation-free, but not cloud-free, weak echo region (WER) on radar.

At 40,000 to 60,000 feet, the updraft slows down, which causes the rising air to spread out. Upper-air winds move this mass of air and water vapor downstream, giving it shape and direction, helping to create an enormous "anvil" extending out for hundreds of miles. Here, the temperature has dropped to as low as -80°F, and the anvil is composed of ice crystals. The updraft may be powerful enough to push moist air above the altitude where it would normally stop. A domelike structure above the anvil, called the "overshooting top," then becomes prominent and may enter the stratosphere.

Some of the precipitation being held aloft may freeze into hail. Updrafts may reach 150 mph and can hold grapefruit-sized hail aloft. Any shift, weakening, or fluctuations in this updraft can be followed by a barrage of falling ice, a hailstorm. The supercell has grown in size, intensity, and complexity, rising to nearly twice the height of Mount Everest.

In this stage, a structure known as a midlevel mesocyclone may form about 4 miles above the ground. The mesocyclone and the rotating updraft are in the same area of the storm. The mesocyclone is an area of low pressure, initially inside the thunderstorm updraft. Air enters it through the bottom and leaves at the top. This rotating area begins to spin faster, contracts to a smaller diameter, and stretches both upward and downward. It may start with a diameter of 7 miles and eventually shrink to a diameter of 2 or 3 miles while growing to a height of 8 miles. The midlevel mesocyclone rotation is detectable by Doppler radar up to 80 miles away and is a sure sign that severe weather is in progress or very soon to follow.

TORNADO FORMATION IN A SUPERCELL

Just before tornado formation, several events seem to occur almost simultaneously within the supercell. The mesocyclone shifts from the center of the updraft toward the rear of the storm. Within the mesocyclone, now partially separated from the updraft, the intensification of a more concentrated vortex, the tornadic vortex signature (TVS), may begin. Also in the rear of the storm, within the mesocyclone, a clearly defined downward cascade of cool air begins descending to the ground. This is the rear flank downdraft (RFD), which is drawn as the dominant part of figure 4.3.

The RFD plunges to the surface in the back of a supercell thunderstorm, spreads out, and creates a gust front. This RFD gust front is swept cyclonically around the existing FFD gust front and distorts it. Beneath the mesocyclone, the boundaries between the updraft and the two main downdrafts create cold, warm, stationary, and occluded fronts that resemble a miniature weather map (see fig. 4.3). The tornado is at the interface, or occlusion point, of these airflows. Once formed, the tornado may live for just a few seconds, or it may cut a devastating path for an hour or more.

One possibility is that the RFD forms when midlevel air (2–3 miles, 10,000–15,000 feet above ground level) from the west encounters the strong thunderstorm updraft, which blocks its flow. Some of the midlevel airflow turns downward, becoming the RFD, and some of the air enters the storm. The dryness of the RFD air may cause evaporation of the cloud and cooling of the descending air. This cooling process adds to the speed of the downward flow. Other hypotheses suggest that the RFD is formed entirely by processes inside the supercell.

As the RFD hits the ground, its gust front surges outward. It can be a dangerous wind of 70 mph or more and can blow a storm-chase vehicle

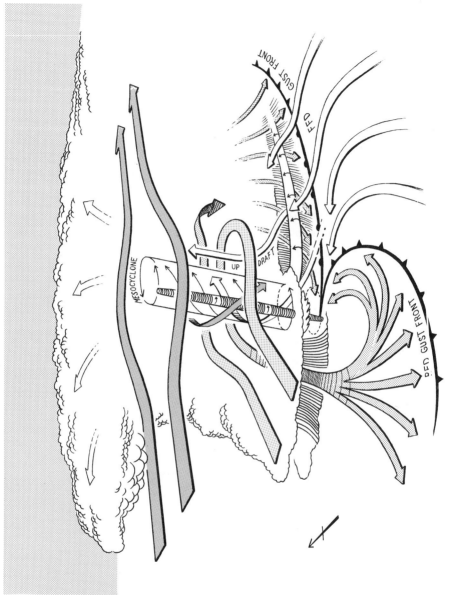

Fig. 4.3. Airflow near the back of a supercell. Drawing by David Hoadley.

from the road or derail boxcars on a freight train. At ground level, some of the RFD is drawn toward the updraft. The RFD undercuts the updraft and encounters the cool FFD air on the front side of the updraft. This complete cutoff, the occlusion, may be a key step in tornado formation. Like the role of the TVS and midlevel mesocyclone rotation, that of the RFD is not yet understood.

After being cut off by the RFD, the updraft may shift and produce a new mesocyclone or mesocyclone core in a nearby part of the storm. This is often to the east or northeast of the old mesocyclone core. The whole process starts over again, and a second tornado may touch down.

A well-placed observer may find ample evidence of the RFD, including the roar of its approach and a rush of air. On the back and right side of the mesocyclone's wall cloud, the dry air of the RFD evaporates some of the cloud base, creating what is called a "clear slot," a brightening of the sky just west of the mesocyclone. This is another indication to storm spotters and chasers that a tornado is in progress or may be about to form.

THE SEARCH FOR PIECES OF THE PUZZLE

Pieces of the tornado formation puzzle have come from many different avenues of research, and not every piece fits the way we initially think that it might. The 1970s proved to be a confusing time in this regard.

For many years the idea that environmental wind shear is the main source of the tornado's rotation was incorrectly accepted as theory. The Union City tornado of May 24, 1973, gave the idea a strong boost. That tornado was the first such event close enough to the NSSL experimental Doppler radar in Norman to allow scrutiny of mesocyclones inside the storm.

Several months after the tornado, close examination of radar records identified a more concentrated area of rotation, within the midlevel meso-cyclone, about 3 miles above ground level. This was the TVS. Excitement built around the idea that the TVS could be the embryonic tornado. It was shown by Burgess (1976) to be present 33 minutes before the first tornado damage. The actual TVS would be too small to detect in most cases and could not be the sole basis of a warning system. However, the idea took hold that the midlevel mesocyclone was the spawning ground for tornadoes. It seemed logical (again by reason, rather than experiment) that the TVS built downward, along with the midlevel mesocyclone, through processes called "vortex stretching" and the "dynamic pipe effect." During the 1980s, almost every up-to-date magazine article repeated this idea.

In the later 1980s serious doubts about this idea began to surface, largely based on findings by Joseph Klemp (1987). The final nail in the coffin for the "midlevel to surface" idea as the sole mechanism for tornado formation was VORTEX. Some of the most spectacular and intense tornadoes studied in VORTEX were not spawned under a midlevel mesocyclone. In some cases, such as at Dimmitt in 1995, the tornado formed at about the same time as its low-level mesocyclone, and the system built upward.

Tornado formation turned out to be much more complex than just the downward extension of a TVS from 3 miles up in a midlevel mesocyclone. Even today, more than twenty years after the TVS was identified, we do not really know where the midlevel meso fits into the puzzle. If nothing else, its presence is very useful in identifying a thunderstorm as potentially severe. Even though the midlevel mesocyclone may not be the triggering mechanism for tornadoes, many tornado warnings are issued when a well-formed midlevel mesocyclone is detected by Doppler radar. This is called a "radar-indicated" warning. Midlevel mesos form in dangerous storms, storms that have a much higher frequency of tornado production than thunderstorms without a mesocyclone.

Research on the TVS and the dynamic pipe effect is still under way (e.g., Trapp and Davies-Jones 1996). This work can be seen as valuable branches off the main stem of research. The main stem has it roots in a 1979 paper by Les Lemon and Charles Doswell.

Part of the process of building a theory is to make observations and try to break a problem down into manageable pieces. The mesocyclone, its relationship to the tornado, and its relationship to the supercell are such pieces. By 1974 the supercell was becoming the focus of tornado research and forecasting. For the next five years, NSSL/OU storm chasers and radar meteorologists studied the life and death of dozens of storms. By the end of the decade, Lemon and Doswell (1979) analyzed, synthesized, summarized, and interpreted thirty such observations. What they suggested about the life cycle of the supercell and the mesocyclone has stood the test of scrutiny year after year. While it is still under refinement, it will probably be a major part of any final theory of tornado formation.

Based on thirty case histories, Lemon and Doswell reported that the mesocyclone eventually divides into updraft and downdraft and that tornadoes are not born at the center of the updraft, as they are in physical models. Instead a tornado seems to form under the mesocyclone, at the interface of these two opposing airflows. Theirs was the first effort to pull all life cycle pieces together into a series of events leading from a cluster of cumulus clouds to the touchdown of a mesocyclone/supercell tornado. In the Lemon and Doswell model, the RFD descends in the rear portion of the supercell and the RFD gust front undercuts the updraft and flows toward the FFD. The tornado formation process occurs at the intersection of these three airflows, under the mesocyclone, as noted earlier.

The Lemon and Doswell paper was not intended as a theory of tornado formation, however; it is a theory of tornadic supercell structure and the relationship of that structure to the tornado. It does not explain why tornadoes form. It was a historic piece of work, and a great starting point for the next round of ideas. It focused research on contrasting airflows and their convergence under the mesocyclone.

COMPUTER SIMULATIONS

Throughout the 1970s computer memory and processing speed increased every year. Programmers made good use of these improvements in perfecting Doppler radar, as well as in creating computer simulations of clouds. Computer simulations of storms begin with a set of initial weather conditions, the equations of airflow, and the basic principles of physics, such as the release of latent heat stored in the water molecules. Digital simulations generate storms from real weather conditions. They do not merely animate what people have observed in nature. Robert Schlesinger (1975), a pioneer in numerical cloud modeling at the University of Wisconsin, made a major breakthrough in computer simulations. His was the first three-dimensional computer simulation of a convective cloud that included wind shear. Severe storm research would never be the same. Some of the most important ideas would come from storms that formed only in microprocessors.

After Schlesinger, extraordinary computer models were created by Joseph Klemp of the National Center for Atmospheric Research (NCAR) in Boulder,

Colorado, and Robert Wilhelmson (1978) of the University of Illinois. Their digital supercells had a rotating updraft, storm splitting, an RFD, an FFD, a mesocyclone with both upward and downward moving air, a clear slot, and a flanking line.

In the late 1980s the entire life of a digital supercell was created inside a supercomputer. The effort took eleven months with a computer capable of 10 billion operations per second (10 gigaflops). If the speed was 1,000 billion operations per second (a terraflop), the 7-minute video could be created in just an hour (Corcoran 1991). Researchers could then alter the parameters and run it again in a reasonable time. Greater levels of computer speed may reveal, at last, the true nature of tornado formation. Just as some people long for the next chase season, others long for the next advance in chip technology and processing design of supercomputers.

It was these numerical models that revealed clues about important airflows within one mile of the ground. Among them was the idea that rain-cooled air at low levels, behind the FFD and near the updraft, may be important in producing an intense tornado. That additional horizontal rotation may be a very important source of vorticity for a tornado. It occurs when the pressure gradient is forcing cool air under the warm air along the FFD gust front. Meteorologists call this a "baroclinic" condition (fig. 4.4).

When the cool air flows under the warm air, a horizontal vortex tube is the result. This baroclinic zone vorticity along the FFD is eventually drawn into the updraft (see fig.4.3). This additional vorticity may indeed be enough to create a low-level mesocyclone and possibly even a tornado. Without this additional vorticity, say some computer simulation experts, the low-level mesocyclone may not form.

By the early 1990s increased processing power and smaller grid spacing allowed Lou Wicker and Robert Wilhelmson (1993) to simulate the coarse features of a large, weak, tornado-like vortex extending from the bottom of the digital thunderstorm. They were able to introduce another ingredient into the model, surface friction. With each increase in computer speed and memory, other aspects can be introduced, and the grid size of the model can be made finer and finer, to reveal smaller and smaller details.

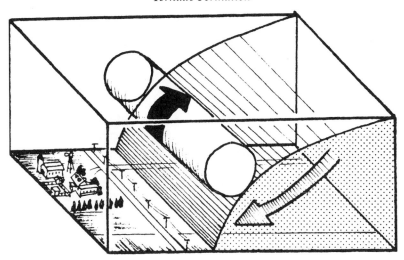

Fig. 4.4. Air can flow out of the forward flank downdraft and undercut the warm updraft. Along this baroclinic zone, air develops a rotational tendency, shown here as a rotating vortex tube. The vorticity is drawn into the thunderstorm, turned upward, and concentrated through stretching. It may enhance the formation of a tornado or a low-level mesocyclone.

FIELD OBSERVATIONS AND PRECIPITATION

In the 1980s storm-chasing scientists like Howard Bluestein, Charles Doswell, and Alan Moller were finding more pieces of the tornado formation puzzle with their field observations. During the off-season, discussion would lead to speculation and plans for the next chase season. Some of these speculations involved tornadoes and rain. It had been long established that rain-cooled downdrafts produced the FFD gust front and that tornadoes seem to form near the FFD gust front, the RFD gust front, and the updraft occlusion. They had observed that some supercells had little or no rain and others had almost every feature obscured by heavy rain.

A classification system for supercells was developed in the 1980s, based on the amount of rain in the storm. The rain-tornado relationship emerged with this system. Burgess and Donaldson (1979) identified a unique type of supercell that had little rainfall and rarely produced tornadoes. Bluestein and Parks (1983) named it the low precipitation, or LP, supercell. Not being obscured by rain and surrounding clouds, LP supercells often showed spectacular rotation. We could speculate that without rain-cooled air flowing near the surface, there is no side-by-side, cold/warm airflow. With no additional baroclinic zones, tornadoes are not so easily produced.

The heavy precipitation, or HP, supercell idea was developed by Moller, Doswell, and Ron Przybylinski (1990). This is probably the most common type of supercell. It can produce flash floods and is more likely than an LP supercell to have tornadoes. With all this energy from condensed moisture, and plenty of rain-cooled downdrafts, one might expect tornadoes to be common in HP supercells. That is not the case, however. Brooks, Doswell, and Davies-Jones (1993) suggested that the stronger outflow from the large area of rain-cooled air sweeps away the low-level vorticity and prevents the formation of a low-level meso and the tornado.

Between the HP and LP types are the Lemon and Doswell "classic" supercells. These storms have classic radar features, such as hook echoes. They can be prolific tornado producers and seem to spawn the great majority of violent tornadoes. We can speculate that precipitation amounts, types, and positions are just right in classic supercells. This classification system is described by Doswell and Burgess (1993).

No generally accepted unified theory of tornado formation is yet in place. However, Doswell summarized many observations on his World Wide Web home page, after VORTEX was completed. He noted that tornadoes seemed to form in association with miscellaneous "fine lines" as seen on radar and "cloud lines" as seen on satellite photographs. These "lines" are all manner of air mass boundaries, each one unique to that day and that situation. If these boundaries are a necessary part of tornado formation, then each situation would be unique. This prospect is both frightening and exciting. Frightening because it would make forecasting much more difficult than meteorologists had imagined; whether a given storm will become tornadic may depend on processes we cannot currently observe very well, if at all. The excitement comes from the challenging research that is needed to identify and classify new ingredients in the tornado formation puzzle. There is so much we do not know.

Doswell has also suggested that a possible role for the midlevel mesocyclone is to "condition" the lower levels of atmosphere by wrapping rain curtains around the mesocyclone in such a way as to improve the possibility that a low-level mesocyclone will form. In addition, he suggested that the low-level mesocyclone and the tornado might have a longer life if they were aligned vertically with the midlevel mesocyclone.

Erik Rasmussen, VORTEX field coordinator and director, speculated that the RFD is a crucial factor in tornado formation. He suggested that RFD interaction with the updraft and the FFD was the catalyst that actually produced the tornado. He hypothesized (pers. com.) that the RFD may acquire an anticyclonic spin as it descends. The RFD hits the ground anticyclonically and makes a 180° change in apparent direction, as it turns into the updraft. The RFD is then stretched into the tornado by the updraft as it rises into the low-level mesocyclone. This event might mark the birth of the tornado from the ground upward, rather than from the cloud downward.

The RFD may give the tornado life, or it may enhance the strength of an existing tornado. But it is also the RFD that helps in the destruction of the funnel. The demise of the tornado may also be due to RFD inflow that gradually becomes too cold to be efficiently lifted into the storm.

A SPECTRUM OF TORNADO TYPES

Ray Wolf and Edward Szoke (1996) suggested that there may be a complete spectrum of tornadoes, with the isolated classic mesocyclone/supercell tornado on one end and the landspout on the other. The former takes hours to form, if measured from the first appearance of a convective cloud. Such a tornado can last for more than an hour and become very violent. Near the middle of the spectrum would be tornadoes from "minisupercells" and tornadoes that spawn from squall line thunderstorms. Some disorganized squall lines may imitate supercells for a brief period and develop a mesocyclone, but the entire storm would not rotate. Toward the weaker end would be the so-called spout tornadoes, the landspout and waterspout.

LANDSPOUTS AND WATERSPOUTS

Some tornadoes occur well away from supercells and mesocyclones and are created by a simpler set of ingredients. They can form on the fringes of supercells and or under growing cumulus clouds that do not appear to be very threatening. These are the landspouts. The waterspout (see fig. 3.3) has been recognized for centuries; the landspout was identified as a unique type of tornado and given its name by Bluestein (1985). Their seeming simplicity is apparent in diagrams in a paper by Roger Wakimoto and James Wilson (1989). The stages in their formation are pictured in figure 4.5. On the left and in the center there are eddies swirling along the boundary between two air masses. The swirls probably begin as waves in the boundary zone as the two air masses slide along one another. On the right a cumulus cloud and its updraft have moved over a low-level swirl. The swirl has been stretched upward by the updraft and a landspout has formed, from the ground up.

The wind shear that helps to produce a landspout is analogous to the shear on a pencil that is held vertically between the palms of your hands. When the palms are slid in opposite directions, the pencil rotates. If only the mere presence of this horizontal wind shear and an updraft was needed, landspouts (fig. 4.6) might form by the thousands each year. Local wind shears and updrafts are numerous all over the world. The range of critical values of wind shear and updraft is narrow enough, however, to limit the number in the United States to several hundred annually. Landspouts often occur in groups, perhaps three to ten within a 5,000-square-mile area of convective activity. VORTEX did not document any landspouts, but they have been computer modeled (Lee and Wilhelmson 1997). One of the few areas in which landspout formation is occasionally predictable is near the Front Range of Colorado. This area is called the Denver Convergence Vorticity Zone (DCVZ), or the Denver Cyclone. When the surface air flows across the Colorado plains from the south or southeast, this Denver Cyclone can develop downstream of an east-west–oriented ridge known as the Palmer Lake Divide. An air mass can move northward over the prairie and meet air flowing eastward off the Rocky Mountains. This encounter can produce convective clouds and numerous landspouts.

GUSTNADOES

Off the spectrum are smaller, shorter-lived, and weaker vortices called gustnadoes. Most meteorologists do not include the gustnado as a true tornado.

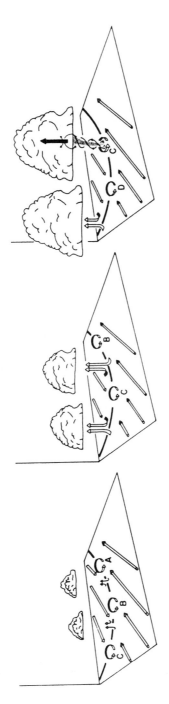

Fig. 4.5. The three stages in the life cycle of a landspout. From Wakimoto and Wilson 1989.

Fig. 4.6. A landspout near the Denver, Colorado, airport on May 30, 1976. Copyright *Denver Post*.

Gustnadoes form as cool outflow surges forward at the edges of a super-cell or in front of a squall line. The leading edge of the gust front can develop an irregular edge, with bulges and lobes. The gustnadoes seem to develop at the cusp, the middle of the concave portion between bulges. They may be strong enough to damage a car, flip a mobile home, and do roof damage to a frame home. The swirls can be drawn upward and stretched into weak vortices that resemble a tornado. In my opinion gustnadoes should not qual-ify as tornadoes unless they are clearly attached to an overhead convective cloud. It is probable that every year unworthy (unattached overhead) gust-nadoes are reported as tornadoes and slip into the database (see chap. 11). It is possible that when a gustnado flips an unanchored mobile home, the owner or a neighbor will report the event in such a convincing manner that it is counted as a tornado. If the vortex does reach cloud base, then the event is a tornado, something akin to a landspout. A name for this comes to mind, a "gustspout," but I hope that term will not enter the vocabulary.

There is, to date, no generally accepted classification system for these various types of tornadoes. Doswell and Burgess suggested to me that the dynamics of formation is the most important criterion for classifying tornadoes. Unfortunately, no data for such a system are currently part of any official tornado documentation.

There needs to be a classification system with terminology that better reflects real processes. "Spout" variations can be traced back to the archaic term "waterspout," which came into use when water was presumed to be spouting out of the ocean. The "spout" terminology is an unfortunate one, implying that they are different kinds of phenomena rather than variations of one phenomenon. All landspouts and waterspouts are true tornadoes. A waterspout is a tornado over water. The ocean can set up unique condi-tions that can produce hundreds of waterspouts in a single month. The presence of sea breezes, land breezes, and warm ocean currents with convective clouds and showers can create all manner of shear zones. But this does not make them, meteorologically, any less of a tornado. The NWS has chosen not to include tornadoes over water in the official database, unless they touch land. This is true for supercell tornadoes over the ocean or any shear-zone tornado that occurs entirely over water.

ANTICYCLONIC TORNADOES

Anticyclonic tornadoes rotate clockwise, which is the opposite direction of what is normal in the Northern Hemisphere. We know from motion pictures and video that they occur (Fujita 1977). Anticyclonic tornadoes have been seen by storm chasers on the south and southeast side of a supercell. When the RFD reaches the updraft, a part of the RFD can be shunted to its right. The part of the flow that moves to the right does so with an anticyclonic, or clockwise, swirl. An anticyclonic curvature near an updraft may lead to the formation of small anticyclonic tornadoes. It is also possible that the airflows that give rise to landspouts could, on rare occasions, interact in the opposite sense as described above and produce an anticyclonic tornado. Only about 1 percent of documented U.S. tornadoes rotate anticyclonically.

TORNADO FAMILIES

Tornadoes spawned by the same parent supercell/mesocyclone are said to be part of a tornado "family." The concept of tornado families developed gradually during the twentieth century, with major refinements added by Brooks (1949), with his tornado cyclone ideas, by Hoecker (1959) at Scottsbluff, by Fujita (1960) at Fargo, and by Fujita again in his Palm Sunday outbreak studies.

At the end of the life cycle of the first member of a tornado family, the hook echo and the RFD continues to wrap around the area of the supercell, and much of this old mesocyclone is destroyed in descending precipitation and cool air. While the updraft associated with the first tornado is being cut off, air is still flowing into the thunderstorm. There is now a repositioning of the main updraft, and a new updraft forms to the right, usually the southeast. A new mesocyclone or mesocyclone core takes form, and the tornado life cycle begins once again. The cycle for each new mesocyclone and a new tornado family member takes about 45 minutes. The new member of that tornado family may touch down before the first tornado has dissipated, as in figure 4.7.

SUMMARY

Tornadoes form when the right amount of rotation is present under the right amount of updraft. But the devil, as they say, is in the details. We have

Fig. 4.7. Two members of the same tornado family are seen near Wamego, Kansas, on May 15, 1943. The funnel on the right is roping out; the tornado on the left is recently formed. Photo from Snowden D. Flora, *Tornadoes of the United States* (Norman: University of Oklahoma Press, 1953), courtesy Kathryn Mitchell.

identified many of the ingredients, but we do not yet have the recipe with which nature combines them. Nor do we know the source of all ingredients. Until the exact roles of environmental vorticity, baroclinic vorticity, multiple storm interactions, the RFD, midlevel and low-level mesocyclones, rain curtains around a meso, and airflow boundaries from old thunderstorms are known, tornado formation will remain a mystery. Some supercell tornadoes are associated only with low-level mesocyclones. Others may have a low-level and a midlevel mesocyclone that are aligned vertically. Some may have built downward from midlevels; others may build upward from near ground level. Still others may be triggered by rain-induced outflow from other storms. Many may be RFD-dependent.

The RFD alone presents an enormous challenge. What part of a tornado's rotation, if any, is directly supplied by the RFD? Does the RFD both trigger tornado formation and provide protection for the fragile early stages of the tornado? Do rain curtains help the RFD to protect the embryonic vortex from disruptive airflows? How important is the RFD temperature or the angle at which it approaches the updraft? What causes the RFD to form in the first place? At least we have a list of questions. Such a list is an essential part of the scientific method.

In previous years research has focused on trying to find a mechanism that would allow the TVS rotation and midlevel mesocyclone to develop downward through 3 miles of updraft. Today the search is primarily for airflows at lower levels that converge, interact, lift, rotate, stretch, and finally produce a tornado. Sometime in the future ideas from storm-chasing scientists and supercomputer simulators will converge into a genuine theory of how and why tornadoes form. Then begins the challenge to find a way to incorporate them into operational forecasting procedures.

CHAPTER 5

TORNADO FORECASTING AND WARNINGS

The official watch/warning system of the National Weather Service dates back to the early 1950s, but the people of the American heartland have watched threatening skies and warned their neighbors of approaching tornadoes for more than a century. The following is an account of the watching of the skies and the personal warnings that were sounded by the people of northeastern Nebraska on September 13, 1928.

WATCHES AND WARNINGS IN NEBRASKA, 1928 VERSION

It had been a busy Tuesday in Thurston County, Nebraska, for young Dale Larson. It was obvious to all farmers and their children that the day would be stormy. The harvest was under way, and prewinter projects were still competing with daily chores on the Larson farm 3 miles east of Pender.

A mile from the Larson farm sat the James School. Miss Dorothy Smith was only slightly uneasy about the threat of bad weather. The storm cave was only a few feet from the school, and September was not tornado season.

Seven miles to the north-northeast was the Lamere School, where twenty-two-year-old Phyliss Stewart was conducting class for her pupils. She also was not especially concerned about the weather. Another 10 miles to the northeast, nineteen-year-old Helen Rooney, teacher at the O'Connor School, was nervous in the stormy weather, as she always was. Her school was situated on an exposed hilltop, and she frequently dispersed the children to their homes on neighboring farms on those occasions when weather turned severe.

Thunderstorms grew in the southwest and passed over the county on that balmy fall afternoon. After a heavy rain, the storm seemed to be over. The students at the James School were about to be dismissed. At the O'Connor School, heeding the advice of a neighboring farmer, Miss Rooney had already dismissed her students early, but she stayed to work on lessons for the next day.

At 3:50 P.M., seventeen-year-old Dale Larson and his father looked out from their hilltop farm and saw the rain drifting off to the northeast. They also glanced to the southwest and noticed a black low-hanging cloud near the ground. They knew in an instant what it could be and what had to be done. The James School was on the northeast side of a hill, and the approaching tornado would not be seen by either the students or the teacher. The massive funnel was moving steadily and directly toward the little building. Without hesitation, Dale leaped into the family Ford and began racing toward the school, heading directly into the path of the oncoming twister. Losing a tire as he spun out of the driveway, the race to the school seemed endless, although it lasted only two minutes. He arrived seconds before the school began to disintegrate. Until the moment that Dale burst into the classroom, Dorothy Smith and her twenty-nine students were unaware that they were in any danger. Dale hurled himself into the building and shouted "Get into the cave! Cyclone!" In just a few seconds, the thirty-one people, ages six to twenty-four, packed themselves into the tiny storm cave.

As the children were passing through the cloakroom, Dale almost instinctively grabbed a skipping rope. He tied it to the storm cave door and, with the help of two older boys, was able to keep the door closed while a deafening noise rose and fell outside. Ten minutes after the noise subsided they emerged into sunshine and found nothing left but fragments of a

Fig. 5.1. Dale Larson and the survivors at the site of the former James School. The storm cave (cellar) is to the left of center. Courtesy of the Heritage Museum of Thurston County, Nebraska.

foundation, the posts from the swing, and the pump at the well, set in concrete. Pieces of the Larson family car, Miss Smith's car, and the teacher's hand bell were found more than 2 miles away. No one at the James School was even scratched (fig 5.1.). Fragments of schoolbooks were found in Iowa, 50 miles away. Whether they were from this or other schools in the tornado's path is not known.

Seven miles to the north-northeast, a curious-looking sky drew Eugene Keyser away from his chores. Concerned, he headed for the Lamere School to get his nine-year-old son. As he began walking, he saw the tornado approaching and watched in amazement as the adjoining farm was obliterated. Continuing to the school, but now running, he arrived a minute before the tornado. From the school the view to the southwest was blocked by a grove of trees, and the teacher was unaware and unprepared. Unlike the James School, there was no storm cave. Keyser, Miss Stewart, and twenty-three children joined hands and huddled in the center of the one-room school. One of the many newspaper stories written about this extraordinary event had the teacher playing the piano, hoping to ease the children's fear by singing, as the building was swept entirely away as if it were a paper box.

Animals from the adjoining farm were seen overhead. Two of the children were killed, including a ten-year-old girl found crushed by the piano, 50 feet from the empty foundation. All others were injured, including Miss Stewart, who was found more than 300 feet away. Mr. Keyser reportedly helped direct the rescue work, then collapsed and was taken to the hospital delirious and semiconscious. Students recovering in the hospital argued whether it was the white or the gray horse that passed overhead. A photograph of Gail Dean, the eldest of the four Dean children injured at the school, was carried 110 miles to a golf course in Sheldon, Iowa. It was returned to her parents, whose home was leveled by the tornado.

We can only imagine the horror of Miss Rooney's last moments at the O'Connor School. Her lifeless body was found against a tree, 100 feet from the empty foundation, the knob of the school door still clutched tightly in one hand.

Over the next few weeks fifty thousand people visited the area and $27,000 in tolls were collected at the Sioux City, Iowa, bridge. Most of it went into a relief fund. Laws requiring schools to have storm cellars would soon be written. The seven other families whose children were saved bought the Larson family a new Ford later in fall 1928. In 1978, fifty years after the tornado, the students presented Dale Larson, a Pender businessman, with a commemorative plaque at their reunion.

Tornado forecasting did not exist on September 13, 1928, and the only warning systems people had were the informal ones that have always been present in small farming communities. There were no severe weather outlooks, tornado watches, amateur radio or spotter networks, community sirens, commercial television or radio alerts, or awareness programs in northeastern Nebraska in 1928. There were only people who watched the skies and were ready to risk their own lives to help a neighbor. The heroism displayed by Dale Larson and Eugene Keyser is similar to that shown by countless people during the past century across the Great Plains.

If identical weather conditions were to occur today, Thurston County probably would have been alerted to the possibility of thunderstorms several days in advance of the tornado. Anyone keeping track of the weather would certainly have been warned of the imminent danger of severe thunderstorms for several hours beforehand. Thurston County would have been warned of the tornado's approach because spotter groups in Cuming County, southwest of Pender, might have seen the tornado almost immediately. Even before that, the mesocyclone rotation inside the thunderstorm would have been seen on NWS Doppler radar. A warning would be broadcast on National Oceanographic and Atmospheric Administration (NOAA) Weather Radio while the storm was still 30 miles away, and thousands of eyes would be focused on the southwest horizon.

A BRIEF HISTORY OF TORNADO FORECASTING

Tornado and severe storm forecasting is as difficult a task as any in meteorology. It has a long and fascinating history that includes visionary thinking, political pressures, bureaucratic squabbles, uncertainty about the reaction of the general public, courageous decision making, and some genuine luck.

In 1847, two years after the telegraph went into public use, the Smithsonian Institution established a volunteer national weather-observing system. The system initially had 150 stations, which grew in number to more than 500 at the start of the Civil War in 1860. The director of the Smithsonian eventually issued a special request asking for thunderstorm and tornado observations. These and other weather observations would become the basis for the very first tornado forecasting.

In 1874 the U.S. Army Signal Corps took responsibility for the weather-observer network and for making rough national forecasts called "outlooks." The history of tornado forecasting, as we know it today, can be traced to the data-gathering efforts of a farmer's son from Ypsilanti, Michigan, who joined the U.S. Army in 1877. John Park Finley enlisted and was assigned, after Signal Corps schooling, to the Philadelphia office (Galway 1985). There he began a systematic study of tornadoes, marking the dawn of modern tornado climatology and forecasting.

In 1882 Sergeant Finley suggested that a tornado reporting system be devised, and he was allowed to pursue the idea from a base in Kansas City, Missouri. He traveled through at least seven states enlisting volunteer "tornado reporters." They would help him to verify the forecasts and gather data about weather conditions prior to actual tornadoes. These data would be added to other tornado-related weather information dating back to the Smithsonian era. By June 1884 the network had grown to 957 reporters. By 1887 there were 2,403 volunteer reporters, but by then, as we shall see, they were of little value.

In 1884 Finley and his tornado studies project were transferred to the Weather Research Unit in Washington, D.C. He had tirelessly researched all known tornadoes and available weather data surrounding those tornado dates. On March 10, 1884, he began experimental predictions. The country east of the Rockies was broken down into eighteen permanent districts. Each district was divided into four sections, each about the size of a modern "watch." At least once a day Finley would make a prediction, based on his checklist of tornado weather conditions that we now call "parameters." He would forecast whether tornadoes would occur in each section. Since Finley's prediction of no tornadoes in a section was counted as a success-ful one, his success score was very high, about 97 percent. Tornadoes are rare events, and if Finley had predicted no tornadoes in all districts, all of the time, he actually would have been 98 percent correct. The point of fore-casting is, of course, not to get the best "score." The point is to get people to be alert to changing weather conditions, to get them to look at the sky and give them a chance to save their own lives.

Finley made 2,803 forecasts in three months during 1884. If we count only his forecasts of tornadoes that actually occurred, he was correct 28 percent of the time (Murphy 1996). Given that only about a tenth of docu-mentable tornadoes were reported at that time, a 28 percent score is an admirable result. This suggests that forecasting a sizable percentage of significant tornadoes is not a particularly difficult task. Forecasting all significant tornadoes is, however, incredibly difficult. Yet forecasting all tornadoes is, unfortunately, what many expect forecasters to do. And if they do not, there are hungry reporters eager to manufacture a story out of what they will call a "busted" forecast.

Finley had developed an empirical system, decades ahead of his time, for forecasting severe weather. As with any empirical system, no under-standing of just why the tornadoes occur was necessary. The system merely identified conditions under which they had occurred in the past. Forecasts of tornadoes were then made when those conditions reappeared (Schaefer 1986). Unfortunately, Finley was never able to refine his techniques. Fate and politics would intervene.

Among Finley's checklist of patterns and parameters were key ingredients of today's checklists. These included the presence of a deepening low-pressure area, large temperature differences across the low-pressure area, increasing humidity on the southeast side of the low, and a northward curve of the temperature lines in the southeast part of the low. Today that northward curve is called a "thermal ridge." The temperature differences are separated by a cold front, which is a weather feature that was not formally identified and mapped until about 1920. If these conditions were present, Finley would forecast severe weather and tornadoes in the sections that were several hundred miles to the southeast of the center of the low. The system worked quite well for a number of outbreaks, but instead of being refined and put to wider use, it was cast aside in 1887.

That year, General Adolphus Greely became chief Signal Corps officer after the death of the science-oriented General Hazen. Greely ended tornado research and prediction. He believed that the harm done by prediction was "greater than that which results from the tornado itself." A ban on the use of the word *tornado* in any public forecast was reinstituted, having been lifted temporarily by General Hazen. The ban was based on the idea that people would panic at the first warnings, then grow complacent and ignore subsequent warnings. The ban would be in place for the next sixty-five years.

There was a long-standing feud as to whether the data gathering and forecasting of weather should be in civilian or military hands (Galway 1992). It became clear that civilian control would win out and that Finley's experimental tornado forecast days were definitely over. Weather data and forecasting duties were given to the Department of Agriculture in 1891.

But by 1897 official tornado documentation had ceased entirely. This "dark age" of tornado records lasted until 1916. Finley spent much of this time successfully, without force, pacifying a hostile tribe in the Philippines. He also created a dictionary of their language. Finley eventually returned to meteorology but not as a tornado forecaster. He died in 1943, a visionary to the end, having foreseen the now-important role of private-sector meteorology. He was one of the first private forecasters and consulting meteorologists to the insurance industry and the agricultural community.

Documentation of the most obvious and damaging tornadoes began again in 1916, but forecasting remained a remote dream. If Finley's methods were experimented with, it was done in private. There was, however, a gradual accumulation of insights. In 1920 Vincent Jakl noted some startling data from kite-flying experiments in Nebraska. For several years large instrumented kites were being flown to altitudes of more than 2 miles at Drexel, Nebraska. On the morning of March 20, 1920, Jakl noted the unusual situation in which the surface was getting a warm south wind while 2 miles above ground the air was colder and blowing from the west. This situation might not have been considered remarkable, except that the afternoon produced nineteen killer tornadoes farther to the east. Jakl (1920) related the two correctly, and tornado forecasting had taken its first major published step in thirty-five years. Outbreaks would be forever linked to airflows in the upper atmosphere.

As balloon and kite observations increased, it became obvious that cold, dry air aloft was an important component in severe thunderstorm and tornado formation. It was added to every parameter checklist. Upper-air data for the outbreaks of March 15 and March 30, 1938, were studied by J. R. Lloyd (1942). The outbreaks produced thirteen killer tornadoes. He would use these data to devise forecasting techniques based on the position of what he called "upper-air cold fronts." This concept would not be very useful, but it brought a greater focus on the all-important upper-air conditions.

It was in the 1930s that techniques for instrumented balloon sounding of the upper atmosphere (for temperature, pressure, and humidity) were refined and put into regular use. These "radiosondes" were developed in France, Russia, and Germany in the 1920s and were refined in the United States in the 1930s. The tracking of the device as it drifted downstream, thus measuring the changing wind speed and direction as the balloon rose, was first done in the United States in 1930. By 1938 there were six upper-air radio wind-sounding balloons (rawinsondes) each day. The system expanded widely in the 1940s, as the importance of upper-air observation became more obvious. Even after becoming digital in 1981, the basic system is little changed since World War II. There are only two launchings a day, at 7:00 A.M. and 7:00 P.M. EST, from widely spaced stations, 150 to 300 miles apart. Severe storm forecasts for the afternoon may have to use upper-air measurements that were taken ten hours earlier at a station 150 miles away.

During World War II the ban on using the word *tornado* in forecasts was partially lifted. Only disaster relief agencies such as the Red Cross were given tornado outlooks, however. Concern for the threat of tornadoes at large ammunition depots and factories encouraged Albert Showalter and Joe Fulks (1943) to refine empirical forecasting systems. Their publication on tornado forecasting was labeled "restricted" but not "classified."

There were sixty killer tornadoes in 1942. The worst included fifty-two deaths near an ammunition factory at Pryor, Oklahoma. The public and press began demanding forecasts, despite the wartime censorship imposed on weather information. Understanding how imperfect tornado forecasting still was, the Weather Bureau hierarchy resisted pressure to issue public tornado forecasts. There was still a mentality that assumed the public would panic and then act with indifference to future forecasts if earlier forecast tornadoes did not occur as predicted. As it has turned out, they were quite wrong in assuming that the public would panic but at least partly correct in the assumption that future forecasts would be treated with indifference by at least some of the population.

In 1943 experimental tornado warning systems were set up for Wichita, Kansas, Kansas City, Missouri, and St. Louis, Missouri. Tornado spotter and warning networks were set up around airfields, training camps, and other military installations. More than two hundred spotter and warning networks were in place by the end of the war in 1945. Weather Bureau officials still felt that tornado alerts were more trouble than they were worth, however. It was in 1948 that luck would intervene and tornado forecasting would become a reality.

On March 20, 1948, a tornado hit Tinker Air Force Base near Oklahoma City, destroying more than $10 million in aircraft and other property. The meteorologists in charge of the Tinker weather station were Colonel Edward Fawbush and Major Robert Miller. For years they had been gathering data on weather systems that accompanied Oklahoma tornadoes, hoping eventually to create a reliable forecasting system.

After meeting with a military board of inquiry on March 21, Fawbush and Miller were given the go-ahead to develop a forecasting strategy as quickly as possible. Just four days later the basic weather ingredients of the system were all present in central Oklahoma again. If they announced a tornado alert for the base and the tornado failed to materialize, as was quite likely, they faced ridicule and perhaps rejection of the whole idea of empirical forecasting. Deciding to risk the embarrassment, they met with base officials. All movable property on the base was made secure by noon, even though no thunderstorm was in sight. Thunderstorms began to form in southwestern Oklahoma by about 3:00 P.M. and a tornado touched down on the base at 6:00 P.M. Damage was extensive, but less than that in the previous tornado. The forecast was among the most successful tornado forecasts in history. It was also one of the luckiest, for the tornado could just as easily have touched down 50 miles from the base under nearly identical conditions. The odds of a tornado passing within a mile of a particular location in a watch area are about 1 in 1,000, if any tornado forms at all. Luck, as I like to define it, is opportunity meeting preparation. That is exactly what happened at Tinker Air Force Base in March 1948. The odds against two tornadoes striking in the same week on the same air base where the world's two premier tornado forecasters happened to be stationed are almost beyond calculation.

The Fawbush-Miller technique had nothing to do with an understanding of how tornadoes form. It used the empirical concept that a certain combination of weather conditions results in tornadic thunderstorms. Fawbush and Miller's checklist of parameters seems very simple and obvious. In spring 1948 it was not simple or obvious at all; it was risky, and the consequences of broadcasting a forecast based on them were as unpredictable as the tornado itself. Some of the original Fawbush-Miller conditions (1951) are listed below and strongly suggest a refined Finley system.

1. A layer of moist air moving north in a wedge or tongue from the Gulf of Mexico that is from 3,000 to 9,000 feet thick, extending from the surface to that altitude. Other thicknesses might produce severe thunderstorms, but tornadoes would be less likely. The moisture distribution in the surface layer should have a clear maximum in a narrow band called the "moisture ridge."
2. Temperature, pressure, and moisture conditions that produce "conditional instability."
3. Humid air overlain by a layer of dry air centered at about 10,000 feet. The influx of dry air aloft is usually from the west or south-

west. This dry air changes the "lapse rate," or rate at which air changes temperature with height.

4. A narrow band of high winds, now called the jet stream, present at about 20,000 feet AGL. The projected center line or axis of the upper level winds must intersect the axis of the moisture ridge. In a typical situation, the strongest thunderstorms might be expected to develop 50 to 150 miles south of the core of this jet stream and west of the axis of the moisture ridge.

5. A humid layer subjected to lifting. We know today that this lifting is caused by fronts, dry lines, and outflow boundaries.

Today forecasters still use this type of checklist as a tool for issuing watches. The rules today are more numerous, far more complex, and less empirical. While much of tornado formation remains a mystery, the parameters involve considerable understanding of the dynamics of tornadic supercell formation. By 1951, a year before the Weather Bureau activated its severe storms forecast unit, Fawbush and Miller (1953) showed these and other parameters on a successful forecast map (see fig. 5.2.)

In figure 5.2, what would have been a modern day "watch" was drawn to the west of the moisture ridge or moisture axis, which is the core of the moist air moving northward at 5,000 feet. As noted in step 4 above, it appears at about 150 miles south of the main jet stream axis. The dry air aloft is shown as a relative humidity (RH) of 40 percent at the 700 millibar pressure level (about 10,000 feet). The west edge of the moist air, the 55°F surface dew point is also shown. "LFC 650 mb" is a mapping of the level of free convection, or LFC. The LFC is the altitude at which, if they can attain it, the convective clouds begin rapid and massive vertical growth. Fawbush and Miller obviously thought that plotting the area with an LFC at about 12,000 feet above sea level (the 650 millibar pressure level) revealed the east-west extent of an outbreak. Recognizing this type of severe storm situation is not a great challenge to forecasters today. There are many other patterns, much less obvious than this one, that can produce violent tornadoes.

In the early 1950s Fawbush and Miller continued their experimental tornado forecasts, which were sent only to air force weather officers. The existence of the forecasts were "leaked" to the public and the media, which applauded the air force and criticized the Weather Bureau for its inaction

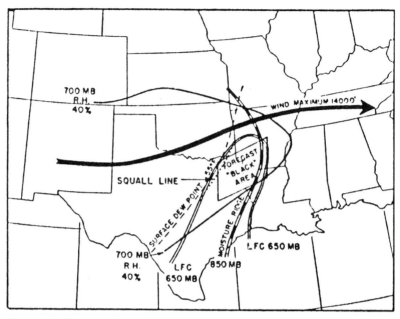

Fig. 5.2. The "forecast black area" (now called a tornado watch area) for March 17, 1951, as shown in Fawbush and Miller 1953. Courtesy of the American Meteorological Society.

in distributing tornado forecasts. Most of their forecasts successfully predicted tornadoes, although there were also many tornadoes in areas where no forecasts were made. It was clear that the method had great potential but was not perfect.

Most Weather Bureau officials and senior forecasters urged that tornado forecasting policy remain unchanged, mostly because the technique did not pinpoint tornado locations. Despite this, Francis Reichelderfer, chief of the Weather Bureau, started a crash program to investigate and test the Fawbush-Miller technique. The air force methods continued to be praised in the media, which served to further embarrass the Weather Bureau.

At about this time, J. R. Lloyd, who had become meteorologist-in-charge at the Weather Bureau office in Kansas City, took matters into his own hands. Lloyd had experimented with tornado forecasting techniques for a decade and was known as a man who set his own priorities. He began rewording the air force forecasts and leaking them to the press (Galway 1992).

The year 1950 also saw the beginning of the first major field experiments in tornado forecasting. The "pressure-jump line" theory (Flora 1953) led to limited data gathering around Washington, D.C., and eventually to a 134-station microbarograph experiment across Oklahoma and Kansas in the mid- to late 1950s. The goal was to see if barometric pressure change could be used in tornado forecasting. The pressure-jump line network greatly expanded our knowledge of pressure fields in and around severe storms. It also showed that the pressure-jump system was to be of little value as a forecasting technique. We understand today that the cold fronts and squall lines that produce the pressure-jump lines are on a larger scale than tornadic supercells.

In January 1952 Lloyd set up his own special unit in Kansas City to test the air force methods and his own upper-air cold front ideas. This action by Lloyd and continued criticism by the media forced Chief Reichelderfer to give the go-ahead for a special forecasting unit in Washington, D.C. On March 17, 1952, the U.S. Weather Bureau at last issued a public tornado forecast. This was four years after Fawbush and Miller's first success and sixty-eight years after Finley's first forecast.

The success of the "forecasts" (renamed "watches" in 1966) for March 21, 1952, prompted the Weather Bureau to continue forecasting and to create the Severe Weather Unit (SWU) in May. With the establishment of this group there were many incremental refinements in the science of forecasting, albeit few major innovations, with little recognition from the general public. Forecasters improved their technique by inventing new conceptual tools, such as the Lifted Index.

The discovery of the hook echo in 1953 gave forecasters a new, if imperfect, tool for warning communities of an impending tornado. We would learn, however, that a hook echo sometimes forms without an accompanying tornado and that a tornado can form without a hook echo. The association was close enough so that it became a well-known, if somewhat overpublicized, short-range nowcasting and warning tool.

The ultimate goal of forecasting is to save lives and property. But in 1953, the first full year of Weather Bureau tornado forecasting, nature produced some of the most intense tornadoes ever to hit cities during the twentieth century. Tornadoes killed 19, 114, 115, 94, and 38 people, respectively, in such widely scattered locations as Georgia, Texas, Michigan, Massachusetts, and

Mississippi. The need to improve forecasting became very evident, and debate raged as to whether a crash program should be started to install weather radar that would cover the entire country. The Weather Bureau SWU was under heavy criticism for the timing, positioning, and size of forecast areas. Many people, both inside and outside the Weather Bureau, thought tornado forecasting was doomed to failure. In June 1953 the name of the SWU changed to the Severe Local Storms (SELS) unit. In late summer 1953 SELS moved from Washington, D.C., to Kansas City, Missouri.

Gradual improvements in forecasting techniques continued year after year. On May 25, 1955, a tornado killed 77 people in Udall, Kansas, and 5 children south of town. As of this writing, no town in America would again suffer 50 or more deaths. Before 1953 at least thirty-two American cities or towns had experienced 50 or more deaths in a single tornado event. Although there is no way to measure the number of lives saved by tornado forecasting, statistics like this suggest that the awareness and forecasting programs have been very effective. The first tornado preparedness film, *Tornado,* was made and distributed in 1956. Built around the fictional Oklahoma community of Elmville, it drew large audiences and was credited with saving many lives. It was shown by virtually every television station in the country and was the general public's first look at the actual drawing of a watch on a map. It contained some bad advice, however. The film told viewers to open windows and to hide in the southwest corner of their basements. But many lives were undoubtedly saved simply by increasing awareness and by highlighting the need for an understanding of the warning system and for developing community preparedness plans. After 114 people died in the 1953 tornado at Waco, Texas, that state took the lead and set up the Texas Tornado Radar Warning Network. Its goal was to cover the entire state with twenty advanced 200-mile-range weather radar units. Its first success was on April 5, 1956 (Bigler 1956). Operators of the radar unit at Texas A&M University in College Station identified a hook echo near Bryan, Texas, and issued a warning. There were no deaths or injuries even though the tornado did $250,000 worth of damage across the south side of town.

Significant progress on the supercell concept began in the early 1960s (see chap. 3), and the links between supercells and tornado formation were made in the 1970s (see chap. 4). The supercell concept has allowed forecasters to time and position watches more accurately, especially for the long-track supercell tornadoes that cause most fatalities. Today much of tornado forecasting depends on predicting the environment that is favorable for supercell thunderstorm formation.

On Palm Sunday, April 11, 1965, an outbreak of extreme severity, with nineteen violent tornadoes, killed 256 people in six midwestern states. The tornado forecast areas were quite accurate. All killer tornadoes were in watch areas, but there were serious inadequacies in the communication of information to the public. In postevent surveys, the level of public awareness about safety and about the meaning of forecasts and warnings was found to be very low.

That outbreak gave birth to the SKYWARN spotter program, a NOAA weather radio system, greater focus on public awareness, and a new award-winning, color version of *Tornado*. Allen Pearson, a member of the Palm Sunday survey team, was committed to public education and media relations. He became director of the SELS unit and eventually the first director of the larger forecast complex called the National Severe Storms Forecast Center (NSSFC). In 1997 the NSSFC moved from Kansas City to Norman and was renamed the Storm Prediction Center (SPC).

In 1966 the name of the severe storm and tornado "forecast" was finally changed to "watch." The terms "watch" and "warning" had been used in hurricane forecasts since the mid-1950s, and several Weather Bureau officials had suggested the name change as early as 1956. In retrospect it might have been wiser to choose two words that did not begin with the same letter, thus avoiding some of the confusion that exists today.

The first weather satellite, Television and Infrared Observation Satellite (TIROS), was launched in 1960, but it was not until the Applications and Technology Satellite (ATS) launch in 1967 that the United States had a camera on a geostationary platform. Only then could the cloud images be used in tornado outbreak studies. Fujita's satellite analysis of the Ohio Valley tornadoes of April 23, 1968, focused on linking the position of the jet stream, made visible by its accompanying cirrus clouds, to the developing outbreak. The movement of the jet stream could now be watched, and satellite imagery was added to a growing stockpile of tornado forecasting tools.

In the 1970s, study of the Union City tornado defined the stages of the tornado life cycle. It also set the stage for eventual development of a network of Doppler radar installations. Development of Doppler radar into an operational forecasting tool, with computer programs called algorithms, has helped forecasters interpret the patterns, but that would take about fifteen years.

By 1988 Doppler radar had been refined enough to be approved as an operating system, the WSR-88D (Weather Surveillance Radar-1988, Doppler version). The actual deployment of this next-generation doppler radar system (NEXRAD) began in the early 1990s. Throughout the 1970s, 1980s, and 1990s refinements in the understanding of supercells continued to improve our ability to judge the importance of parameters.

Each year would see great successes in forecasting. But because most of these involved no loss of life, they went unnoticed by most people except the forecast community. The few failures, however, became the fodder for newspaper and television headlines. Forecasting the Kansas/Oklahoma outbreak of April 26, 1991, was particularly successful. However, the tornadoes of that day revealed an ever-vulnerable segment of the population that may never be reached by watches and warnings (see chaps. 9, 15). Forecasting of the Plainfield, Illinois, tornado of August 28, 1990, was not as successful and therefore was even more widely publicized.

MODERN TORNADO FORECASTING

Doswell, Weiss, and Johns (1993) present a good introduction to the subject of modern severe storm and tornado forecasting. They break down forecasting into two parts: the anticipation of the potential for tornadoes and the recognition of thunderstorms that might produce tornadoes after the storms have formed. The first step can be broken down further.

There are three basic steps in trying to judge where and when tornadic supercells will form. In "pattern recognition," a forecaster watches large-scale weather patterns. These include the position of upper-level low-pressure areas, the northward movement of moist air from the Gulf of Mexico, and the flow of dry air from the southwest, along with the advance of cold fronts and jet streams. Several dozen times a year a weather pattern that is obviously favorable for severe storms takes shape over some part of the United States.

In "parameter evaluation," meteorologists combine basic information about temperature, wind, and humidity and come up with numbers that are a blend of conditions rather than just raw information. These combinations, or "parameters," are a classic case of the whole being greater than the sum of the parts. One such parameter is called convective available potential energy (CAPE). CAPE combines temperature and humidity at different elevations, as measured through about 50,000 feet of atmosphere, to estimate not just how much potential energy is locked in the water vapor molecules as latent heat but how much of that energy is available to build thunderstorms.

The lifted index, or LI parameter (Galway 1956), measures the same things that CAPE does but in a different way. To calculate the lifted index, we measure the average humidity and estimate the high temperature for the day in the bottom part of the atmosphere. We then theoretically lift and cool that average air parcel to a height of about 18,000 feet. The temperature of that mathematically "lifted" parcel is then subtracted from the actual measured temperature at that height by weather balloons. That temperature difference is a measure of how potentially "unstable" the air is. This is one measure of how strong the storms might grow that day. The more negative the number, the more unstable the layering of the air. Exactly why this is so is far beyond the scope of this book.

Another parameter, "helicity," uses the wind direction as measured at various altitudes. Helicity is not the wind direction or the speed of the wind; it is a combination of the two as they change in the bottom 2 miles of the atmosphere. It is a measure of the wind shear and a way to estimate the likelihood of supercells. There seems to be no end to the number of clever ways that values for wind, temperature, pressure, and humidity can be combined to give us some additional clue about what will happen with the weather in the next several hours.

Forecasters create maps of many parameters, often superimposed on one another (fig. 5.3). To the untrained eye, the layers of numbers, lines, and arrows may seem bewildering. To the trained eye, these patterns reveal where storms are likely to grow and what kind of severe weather we will probably have to face on the way home from work. In addition to those shown in figure 5.3, a dozen other parameters might also be studied simultaneously. Forecasters work at interactive computer screens on which parameters can be added or taken away with a keystroke or two.

All this does not forecast where tornadoes will touch down. Parameters help a forecaster judge the increased probability of tornadoes occurring

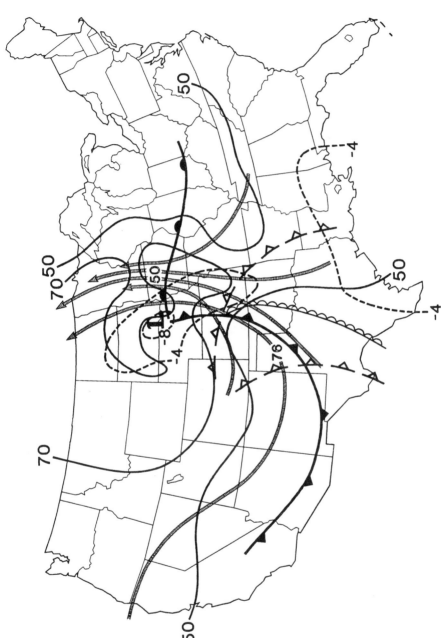

Fig. 5.3. This composite chart is a forecast of parameters as they would probably be positioned at 7:00 A.M. CDT on April 26, 1991. From Doswell et al. 1993.

somewhere in a specific area. Looking at figure 5.3, a trained eye would see lots of trouble ahead for Oklahoma and Kansas. The dashed lines with the numbers "-4" and "-8" are the LI. The thin solid lines, labeled "50" and "70," are the average humidity in the bottom 18,000 feet of the atmosphere. The thick black line, labeled "76," is the position of the jet stream with a 76-knot (84-mph) maximum indicated. The four bold lines streaming north over eastern Kansas show the airflow at about 5,000 feet above ground level (AGL), with a 50-knot (55-mph) maximum from the south. The position of the surface cold front, warm front, and dry line (unfilled semicircles) are also shown. The dashed line across Kansas is the position of the thermal ridge, where surface temperatures are highest. The intersection of the dry line, the thermal ridge, the strong northward airflow, and the "-4" LI line was a good indication that this was going to be a long and frightening day for parts of Kansas and Oklahoma. The "-8" LI was of lesser concern in that it was in colder air to the north.

Pattern recognition begins several days in advance of the tornado outbreak. Meteorologists receive a computer-generated forecast of airflow at about 18,000 feet over North America. The focus then moves to a smaller and smaller scale as the possible outbreak approaches. By the day of the outbreak, the task is to forecast severe weather in areas that would cover about one-third of a midwestern state. Finally, while the outbreak is in progress, "nowcasting" focuses on areas the size of a single county or even smaller. Nowcasting describes what is actually going on outside at the present time and predicts the movement of thunderstorms over the next several minutes to an hour. While nowcasting is done by the National Weather Service, a very large segment of the public is kept informed by meteorologists on local television stations, using NWS radar or their own Doppler radar units. The next step is to issue a "warning." Forecasting is the anticipation of storms, but warnings involve actual detection of those storms, especially important parts of the storm such as the mesocyclone. While they do overlap once the storm has formed, forecasting and warning are quite different, with different skills and different tools.

Climatology is also considered, as the forecaster questions whether there have ever been tornadoes under these weather conditions, in the threatened area, at this time of day or year. On any given day, one might hear that a 30 percent chance of thunderstorms is forecast for a particular town many hours before clouds have begun to form. Tornado information is not given in the same way that thunderstorm or general rainfall forecasts are presented. At present tornado forecast watches and the real-time warnings are either issued or not issued; there is no middle ground. In the future it may be possible to provide this product in probabilities (10%, 20%, etc.) that can express the confidence the forecaster has that a tornado will occur.

Tornado and severe storm information is given to the public in three stages. First, early on the day of the outbreak there is the severe weather forecast called an "outlook." Morning weather maps on television often show this area in red or orange. The risk for severe thunderstorms (and possibly tornadoes) is listed as "low," "moderate," or "high." The outlook is a forecast that may cover all or part of ten or more states and up to half a million square miles (fig. 5.4). The outlook statement may be followed by special weather statements if a tornado outbreak is expected to be very severe. As the outbreak approaches, forecasters make these gradually more specific in both area and time.

Second, the next forecast level, the tornado or severe thunderstorm "watch" is issued, covering about 20,000 square miles (fig. 5.5). A tornado watch indicates that conditions are favorable and the potential exists for severe thunderstorms that could contain tornadoes. The watches are issued two to seven hours in advance of the severe weather and are usually valid for up to six hours. People living in and near this watch are told to be alert for tornadoes and to take certain precautions.

In some cases only a small fraction, perhaps 5 percent, of the watch area will experience any kind of thunderstorm. In other cases the entire watch will be affected as a continuous line of thunderstorms sweeps across the forecast area. However, it is only in the very worst outbreaks that as much as 1 percent of the area of a watch will experience the actual winds of a tornado. In other words, even in the worst outbreaks 99 percent of the watch area will not be hit by a tornado. Each watch is given an expiration time. That time may be extended if storms redevelop or move more slowly than anticipated. The purpose of the watch is to allow the public and emergency managers to prepare for severe weather, to keep track of storm developments via television and radio, to deploy spotters, and to watch the skies.

The third stage is a real-time "warning," which means that a funnel cloud has actually been sighted or is strongly indicated by weather radar, in the

Fig. 5.4. The Day-1 Outlook for April 26, 1991. The larger area covers the moderate risk for severe weather. The inner area encloses the high risk for the day. The risks are not necessarily for tornadoes alone. For comparison, the paths of the tornadoes that actually touched down are also shown.

form of mesocyclone rotation within the storm. It is a take-cover message. Tornado warnings are issued for one or more counties and usually for less than one hour in duration. Warnings may be accompanied by the blaring of emergency management and police sirens. If the tornado has already formed, the first community near the touchdown point may have only a few seconds of warning. Sometimes that first town has 5 to 20 minutes of

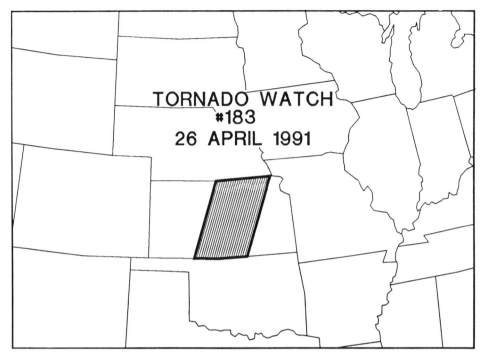

Fig. 5.5. NWS watch #183 was a tornado watch that enclosed an area along and 65 statute miles east and west of a line from 45 miles east-southeast of Medicine Lodge, Kansas, to 45 miles northeast of Concordia, Kansas.

lead time if strong mesocyclone rotation was seen on Doppler radar. Towns farther along the anticipated track may get a half-hour's warning. Whether sirens are used varies greatly from community to community. Some towns will hold back on blowing the sirens until a visible tornado has moved to the very edge of town, whereas others may sound their sirens each time a suspicious radar echo or funnel cloud is sighted. A tornado may cut the power to the sirens as it approaches. Tornadoes are not annual occurrences in every county, so sirens can fall into disrepair after years of minimal use. Many communities have consciously chosen not to buy sirens at all.

If only a severe thunderstorm is in progress, a "severe thunderstorm warning" may be issued. Every year, however, unpredictable tornadoes touch down in severe thunderstorm warning areas. It is not uncommon for tornadoes to be mentioned in a severe thunderstorm warning.

The ideal linear progression begins with an NWS outlook and proceeds to a watch, to a warning, and eventually to the sounding of sirens. But there are also local community warnings, initiated by local spotters, that do not directly involve the NWS.

CASE HISTORIES

THE TORNADO OUTBREAK OF APRIL 26, 1991

After a week with no tornadoes at all, forecasters had to deal with more than fifty in less than ten hours. On April 27, 1991, just after midnight, a tornado lifted from the ground just east of Victor, Iowa, and the worst tornado outbreak of the year was finally over. Across Kansas and Oklahoma, twenty-one people lay dead; damage totaled about $300 million. A violent tornado had just missed the heart of a major city and a billion-dollar flight line of B-1 bombers, some of which may have contained nuclear weapons. Forecasters at the NSSFC and at local NWS offices all over the Great Plains and Midwest could relax for the first time in several days. Tornado forecasting has often been likened to war, with hours of boredom punctuated by moments of sheer terror. The following sequence of events leading up to the tornado outbreak is a good illustration.

Under ideal conditions, the forecasting process can begin as many as ten days ahead, with a computer-generated 240-hour, upper-air forecast map. On Tuesday, April 16, 1991, ten days before the outbreak, this map showed the predicted positions of high-pressure ridges and low-pressure troughs at about 18,000 feet AGL.

At this point a forecaster cannot tell whether the severe weather will be in Texas, Nebraska, or Kentucky. The 240-hour forecast may indicate whether an upper-air trough, which is associated with cold fronts and jet streams that can trigger or enhance severe weather, will extend into the western United States. This ten-day forecast can alert a research team or advise a storm chaser whether to get ready for a Great Plains trip. But it will not tell a forecaster how much energy-laden moisture will be heading north from the Gulf of Mexico, or where that moisture will be concentrated. Ten days before the great outbreak of April 26, the 240-hour map showed a definite indication that within a few days of that date there would be just such a low-pressure trough extending down into the western United States.

On Sunday, April 21, 1991, five days before the outbreak, it was still diffi-cult to tell whether the severe weather would be in Texas, Nebraska, or Arkansas and whether tornadoes would even be a big part of the severe weather. Television stations might have been displaying maps of a projected severe weather area in their five-day forecast presentations. Only under rare and ideal conditions is it apparent that, five days in advance, a major tornado outbreak is imminent. This was one of those cases.

By Sunday the situation was looking increasingly grim for the end of the week. For two weeks a large low-pressure area had been anchored over the Gulf of Alaska, and a ridge of high pressure was situated over the central and eastern United States. A series of low-pressure areas were now migrat-ing from the Gulf of Alaska into the northwestern United States. It was apparent that by the end of the week one of these would extend southward and bring with it a strong cold front and very strong jet stream winds. Ahead of this system would be a great deal of warm, moist, unstable air. It was apparent to forecasters that the residents of some quiet and unsus-pecting American town might spend the weekend comforting their neigh-bors, searching the ruins of their houses, attempting to put their lives back together, and perhaps burying and mourning their dead. As fate would have it, that town proved to be Andover, Kansas.

On Thursday, April 25, 1991, at 3:00 A.M. CDT, 36 hours before the first tornado touchdown, it was evident that the tornado outbreak could be of major proportions. It was also apparent that an area from Oklahoma to Nebraska would be at the heart of the outbreak. This information appeared on the SELS "Day-2 Convective Outlook." This forecast of the area of pro-jected severe weather was created primarily from numerical weather predic-tion models, rather than satellite photographs or current weather maps.

When the NSSFC issued its Day-2 outlook for Friday, April 26, it advised everyone that "tornado activity was likely ahead of a cold front that was forecast to move eastward across the central and southern plains on Friday afternoon and evening." The potential severity of the outbreak was not yet publicized.

The upper-air low-pressure area had moved into the Pacific Northwest and had extended a low-pressure trough into Arizona. Jet stream winds

were in excess of 125 mph and were ready to introduce pressure and temperature changes that allowed explosive thunderstorm growth. It was clear that
April 26 was going to be the day; Kansas and Oklahoma were going to be
the place.

At 1:08 P.M. on Thursday, twenty-six hours before the first touchdown,
the update of the Day-2 outlook indicated "the potential for a significant
tornado outbreak in the central United States on Friday, April 26th."
Experienced storm chasers and weather observers, knowing how cautiously
the NWS chooses its words, realized this was serious and were waiting
anxiously for every available map, satellite photograph, and new weather
statement. Most people in central Kansas probably thought it was just
another severe weather situation, perhaps the five hundredth of their life-
times. Some meteorologists were attempting to relay the idea that this was
not "just another day with thunderstorms."

By 7:00 P.M. on Thursday, forecasters were able to draw weather maps
containing the projected position of key weather features and parameters
for the morning of the outbreak (see fig. 5.3). It was obvious that April 26
was going to be a rough day from southeastern Nebraska southward to
central Oklahoma.

On Friday, April 26, 1991, at 2:00 A.M., the Day-1 Outlook was issued.
The "high risk" designation is used by the NSSFC only for those situations when a major severe weather outbreak is anticipated. The words
"slight risk of severe thunderstorms" constitute a forecast of some kind of
severe thunderstorm activity. The words "moderate risk" are used only if
severe thunderstorm conditions are particularly good. The Day-1 Outlook
(see fig. 5.4) did indeed include rarely used terms such as "high risk" and
"damaging tornadoes." These words may seem unimportant to a casual
listener who must endure the exaggerations of the news media, but to those
who understand NWS terminology and procedures, they stood out in bold
relief.

Between 6:00 and 11:00 A.M. on April 26, weather systems were in place
(figs. 5.6, 5.7) and early morning thunderstorms formed in north central
Oklahoma and southeast Kansas. A supercell at Tonkawa, Oklahoma,
spawned a few weak tornadoes, but the storm weakened before noon. The
rain-cooled outflow from many morning thunderstorms that eventually
spread across southeastern Kansas may have enhanced the growth of the

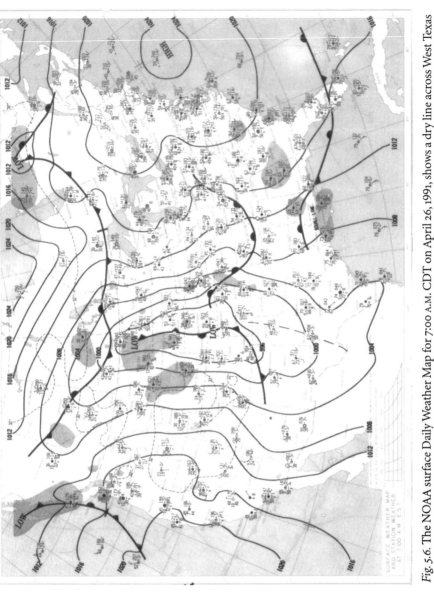

Fig. 5.6. The NOAA surface Daily Weather Map for 7:00 A.M. CDT on April 26, 1991, shows a dry line across West Texas with a dry 21°F dew point temperature at Amarillo and a humid 67°F dew point temperature at Oklahoma City. Warm humid air has spread over most of Kansas and Oklahoma. Compare this to the forecast parameter map in figure 5.3.

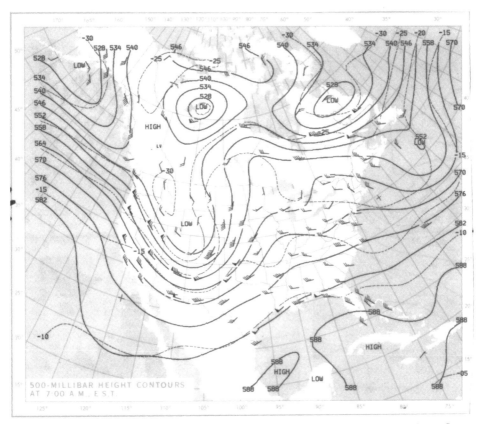

Fig. 5.7. This NOAA 500-millibar chart for 7:00 A.M. CDT on April 26, 1991, shows the airflow at about 18,000 feet. A big loop, a low pressure trough, is over the western United States. The fastest winds were in the jet stream at the southern edge of the trough, over New Mexico. Later in the day those maximum winds would be over Oklahoma and Kansas.

supercells. As the afternoon progressed, the surface low had moved to southeastern Nebraska and had helped to produce a dry line from western Kansas down to West Texas. That dry line was approaching the cool outflow boundary of the old thunderstorms.

In the outbreak area, winds at the surface were from the south-southeast. A mile above ground level, a low-level jet from the south, with 60-mph winds, was feeding humid air into Kansas. Two miles up, the wind veered to a more southwesterly direction. Three miles up, winds were from the west. That is a large directional change with height, or strong vertical wind shear. It is more than enough to give any heated air that is rising enough rotation to help turn a disorganized thunderstorm into a supercell. The LI was a very unstable -7 in the morning and a dangerous -12 after the sun rose and started heating the lower layers of atmosphere.

During the morning of the outbreak, only one instrumented balloon was launched into the volatile air mass that would sustain the outbreak. It was launched at 7:00 A.M. from Norman, 200 miles south of Wichita. That would be the most representative sounding, the best vertical profile of the atmosphere in the outbreak area for that day. The nearest station to the north, Topeka (140 miles from Wichita), was out of the warm air. Amarillo, Texas (300 miles to the southwest), and Dodge City, Kansas (155 miles to the west), were behind the outbreak. Figure 5.8 shows the Norman upper-air sounding. Two lines are plotted, the air temperature on the right and the dew point temperature on the left. On figure 5.8 an inversion is noted. It is a layer in the atmosphere where the temperature increases for a short distance. This small increase in temperature will stop cloud growth, at least for a while. When the inversion wears away, thunderstorms can develop rapidly and become more severe than if the inversion had not been there at all. The narrow spread of the sounding lines at the bottom means that the air and dew point temperatures are almost the same and the air is very humid. Above the inversion the air and dew point temperatures are far apart, meaning that the air is dry. When warm, humid air near the surface reaches this cold, dry air aloft, condensation and heat release will occur at an incredible rate. This "narrow at the base and wide at the top" profile, with an inversion in between, is what Fawbush and Miller (1951) called the "loaded gun" sounding.

Without a dense network of soundings, forecasters are forced to be creative in the use of available data. They have to use indirect clues, such as satellite photographs of cloud development, to understand what is going on above the ground and guess just where and when the outbreak will start.

On April 26, 1991, at 12:10 P.M., just three hours before the first touch-down, forecasters were taking charts produced by computers and recon-touring them by hand at smaller intervals, adding pressure change lines, boundary lines between slightly different air masses, and wind shift lines and dew point fronts, looking for any clues that might give a better idea of where this outbreak would start and how it would progress. At this time

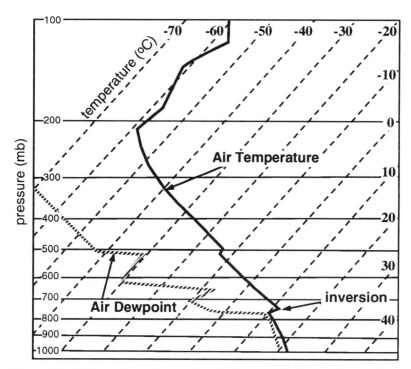

Fig. 5.8. The NWS rawinsonde sounding for Norman, Oklahoma, for April 26, 1991.

the first tornado watch (severe weather watch no. 183 for the year) was issued by SELS forecaster Bob Johns. It covered virtually all of central Kansas and was in effect for the next eight hours (see fig. 5.5). It was strongly worded, containing the phrases "Particularly Dangerous Situation" (PDS) and "the possibility of very damaging tornadoes." SELS would issue twenty-four watches on April 26. The fourteen watches on the evening shift were a new record. The watches were issued by SELS in Kansas City, but the actual warnings and public statements were the products of local NWS offices.

By 3:00 P.M. radar showed the first trace of the thunderstorm that would grow to supercell status and spawn the Wichita-Andover tornado family. At this time there was no indication as to which of the many dots on the radar screens would become the major players, the biggest supercells of the day. Shortly after 3:00 P.M. the first tornado touchdown of the day was caught on videotape by storm chasers near Washington, Kansas. One of the chasers was an off-duty NSSFC forecaster.

By 3:25 to 5:00 P.M. spotters had taken their positions on the edges of towns. Television stations in Kansas and Oklahoma were interrupting programs, running messages at the bottom of the screen, and inserting maps showing counties in the watch. Television meteorologists became the eyes and ears for millions of people who could not judge accurately what was happening outside.

At 5:10 P.M. the first member of the Wichita-Andover tornado family touched down 2 miles northeast of Anthony, Kansas, 40 miles south-southwest of Wichita. Longtime storm chaser Jim Leonard was there to capture it on video. The tornado would last only a few minutes. Jim was far from a telephone, and any report he could have phoned in might have been considered of questionable reliability. Despite the considerable expertise of some chasers in judging the intensity and movement of tornadoes, there was, and is, no established system or set of procedures for the reporting of tornadoes by storm chasers who live outside the area. That both the first tornado of the day and the first member of the Andover tornado family were caught on video by storm chasers is a tribute to modern short-range tornado forecasting. At the time of the outbreak, the problem was dissemination of new information, not inadequacies in forecasting.

By 5:15 P.M. Radio Amateur Civil Emergency Service (RACES) and Citizens Radio Emergency Services Team (CREST) volunteers arrived at the Wichita office of the NWS to staff the base station of the communications network. By about 5:20 P.M. the Anthony tornado had lifted and the second member of the tornado family formed under the supercell 5 miles west-southwest of Argonia. This funnel, although potentially destructive, would hit only open country before lifting 5 miles north of Conway Springs.

At 5:26 P.M. the NWS Wichita office issued the first tornado warning, based on reports of the Anthony tornado, sixteen minutes after its touchdown. The warning area included parts of Harper and Sumner counties, southwest of Wichita. The entire system was moving in the direction of that city. This was an ominous development for this NWS office, whose facilities did not yet include NEXRAD Doppler radar. The storm was about to move into the "ground clutter" area of the city, where the older radar received no storm echoes, only the echoes from buildings and hills. Wichita would have to rely solely on spotter reports for the tornado positions. This can be confusing, because reports of the same tornado can arrive from different areas at the same time, or from the same area at different times, giving the false impression that there is more than one tornado on the ground. These reports can take precious minutes to sort out.

At 5:46 P.M. a tornado warning was issued for all of Sedgwick County, including the city of Wichita, based on reports of the tornado at Conway Springs and the severity of the situation. The supercell continued to move to the northeast, but the tornado that would hit Wichita and Andover would not touch down for another 11 minutes.

At 5:57 P.M. the third member of the tornado family touched down just southeast of Clearwater, 15 miles southwest of Wichita. This one was destined to grow to violent intensity and hit the still largely unsuspecting town of Andover, 25 miles to the northeast, just over the Sedgwick-Butler County line. At 6:05 P.M. the tornado near Clearwater was reported to the Wichita office. For the next hour, the tornado moved to the northeast and grew more intense. A nearly continuous stream of statements and warnings were broadcast over virtually every media outlet in the area.

By 6:25 P.M. the tornado had crossed the Kansas Turnpike, passed through housing developments and trailer parks at the south edge of Wichita, and was advancing across McConnell Air Force Base. McConnell suffered $62 million in damage to base housing, the elementary school, recreation facilities, and the hospital, but no casualties. The tornado could now be easily seen from second-floor apartment balconies in Andover, just over the Butler County line, 12 miles away.

At 6:33 P.M. a tornado warning was extended to Butler County, specifically mentioning Andover, but the warning siren at Andover failed. The remote-controlled siren was said to be in good working order when tested in stress-free conditions. But the heavy radio traffic at the dispatcher's office had somehow interfered with the remote radio signal.

By 6:35 P.M. the tornado had left McConnell Air Force Base and was devastating residential areas at the eastern edge of Wichita. Homes were leveled. Four people were killed, all caught in the open as they ran for shelter. The group included two young children and their elderly aunt.

By 6:40 P.M. the tornado seemed to reach its maximum intensity just as it entered the town of Andover and its sprawling 244-unit Golden Spur Trailer Park. About 330 residents of the park were in the path of the tornado at this time. It had been more than half an hour since the first notification that a tornado was heading in the direction of Andover. Because of the failure of the community warning siren at Andover, a police car traveled the streets of the trailer park with its siren wailing. The mounted videocamera on the car captured one person running for cover and another casually strolling down the street with a dog. A half-mile-wide tornado was visible just a few miles away. Many residents refused to believe the warning until they saw the funnel for themselves. Some had heard sirens from Wichita. Some thought that the police siren was no more than an everyday ambulance emergency and ignored it. While the specific warning for Butler County was given 7 minutes before the tornado's arrival, some people had been watching the funnel for 10 minutes. According to the Center for Disease Control, about 146 (45 percent) of the residents had left the trailer park to escape the tornado. Another 45 percent had sought safety within the park. Many of these people stood at the edge of the community shelter until the last moments before the tornado hit. The underground shelter soon contained more than 100 people, and another 20 to 30 were in the basement of the police station. Andover was fortunate that the shelter existed. Many trailer parks have no such shelters. But about 10 percent of the residents, or about 35 people, did not find shelter in time. Thirteen died and the rest were injured. The trailer park was obliterated to such a degree that the landscape was unrecognizable to its residents when they emerged from the shelter. Now devoid of street signs and trees, maps were needed to locate debris-strewn, newly vacant lots.

An elderly couple died on the way to the shelter, along with a younger woman who managed the senior citizens' center and was helping the clients to seek shelter. Another woman died when she and her husband sought shelter in a storage shed. Reports said that she was torn from his arms. A man and his son died while shielding his wife in a ditch; they were driving into town on a visit when surprised by the tornado. Although a ditch is almost always a safe haven, the incredible barrage of sheet metal and other debris from 205 disintegrating trailers being shredded by 250-mph winds was unforgiving to anyone aboveground. Several others who died at the trailer park were either elderly or hard of hearing. One stubborn gentleman was killed soon after he flatly refused to go to the shelter. Another man was at the shelter but ran back to lock his home. His body was the last one found, after a twenty-hour search. The other victims may have been waiting for the siren.

By 6:52 P.M. the Wichita-Andover tornado was mercifully passing just east of Towanda and heading into the open terrain of the Flint Hills. But forecasters were anything but finished with their work. This was only the beginning of the outbreak. Howard Bluestein was 80 miles to the south, near Red Rock, Oklahoma, with his portable Doppler radar deployed in front of a monster tornado. The storm returned signals indicating a wind speed of at least 275 mph in the funnel. Along with him was Tulsa meteorologist Gary Shore, broadcasting directly back to KJRH-TV with live reports on the tornado's position. Also at this time, a $30 million hailstorm was in progress at Omaha.

At about 7:10 P.M. the Wichita-Andover tornado dissipated 6 miles north of El Dorado, after 73 minutes and 46 miles of destruction (fig. 5.9). At about 7:15 P.M. the fourth and final member of the tornado family touched down on El Dorado Lake, 5 miles east of the point where the Andover tornado lifted. It moved to the northeast, parallel to and just south of the Kansas Turnpike. At this time two cameramen from KSNW-TV in Wichita were heading southwest, returning from a story unrelated to the tornado. They crossed the median and began to photograph the funnel but soon headed to the northeast, with the tornado in hot pursuit. Reaching an underpass, they hid under the girders along with other motorists. The tornado circulation passed near or over the underpass while the camera continued to run. The video would be seen around the world and earn the pair an Emmy nomination. That video has helped to create what I believe is the suicidal myth that an underpass is a safe place to seek shelter from tornadoes. The practice invites accidents and highway backups that prevent people from getting out of a tornado's path. It also exposes people to flying debris. The myth was tested on May 3, 1999, near Oklahoma City, with tragic results (see chap. 12).

The underpass tornado lifted at 7:35 P.M. This supercell would spawn no more tornadoes. Forecasters had done their job to the maximum degree that meteorology and technology allowed them. Intense tornado activity

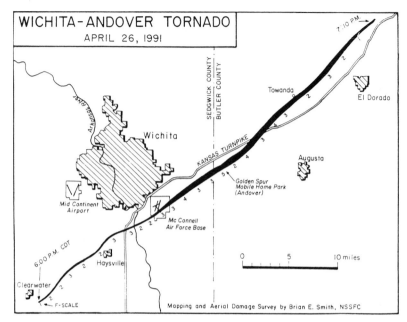

Fig. 5.9. A path map of the Wichita-Andover tornado. Drawn by Brian Smith of the NWS.

continued in other areas of southeastern Kansas and in Oklahoma until after midnight.

Had these tornadoes occurred in an era without forecasting, warnings, and good communications, the death toll might have been closer to that in and near Udall, Kansas, in 1955: 82. It is difficult to compare situations, and speculation on death tolls is just that. The Udall homes were sturdier than the Andover trailers, but the Udall tornado occurred in darkness at 10:00 P.M. If the 1991 tornado had occurred in darkness, with people still insisting on having their own visual sighting, the death toll might have been higher.

THE PLAINFIELD, ILLINOIS, TORNADO OF AUGUST 28, 1990

Forecasters confront many difficulties, and at times Mother Nature seems to conspire with humans to produce monumental problems. On August 28, 1990, one of those problems occurred at Plainfield, Illinois. Nature put the NWS tornado forecasting system to a major test.

Nature seemed to look for a place where communications might break down and the uniqueness of the situation might leave forecasters unprepared. She chose the Chicago suburbs, where two local NWS offices served the northern Illinois area, Chicago and Rockford. The situation would include a tornado track on the boundary between two forecast office jurisdictions, so as to test the communication between the offices. The track would be in the ground clutter of pre-Doppler radar at the Chicago NWS Office. Chicago would have to confer with a third office, in Marseilles, Illinois, for radar information. The tornado would move from northwest to southeast. Historically, there was no record of a violent tornado having moved from the northwest in the Chicago area in the past 130 years.

The tornado occurred near the end of summer vacation and the start of school, when spotter and storm chase groups are not likely to be as organized as they would be in April or May. The tornado was cloaked in clouds and rain so that, from a distance, no one saw it. The mesocyclone's hook echo was present but not easily identifiable on conventional (pre-Doppler) radar. The final outcome included twenty-nine dead as a tornado passed through Plainfield and Crest Hill, Illinois. Mercifully, the devastation of two large schools occurred a day before students would have arrived by the hundreds. Some deaths did occur in the schools, however. On August 26, 1993, two of the severely injured and the survivors of twelve of those killed at Plainfield filed suit in federal court against the NWS for $74 million, claiming that the NWS knew there were tornadoes in the area but did not issue any warnings. The suit was eventually dismissed.

In retrospect, communications were not good, warnings were late, spotters were not deployed, and radar information from Marseilles was received at Rockford but not at Chicago. One can be sure that forecasters will be tested again and again. These tests will be conducted unannounced, at random times, on random dates, by an unforgiving atmosphere.

TOUGH FORECASTING CHOICES

NWS personnel often face tough forecasting situations for which there are few guidelines. One combines strong wind shear and only marginal instability. Either there will be a significant outbreak, or there will be nothing at all. Forecast the outbreak, and you may be charged with crying wolf

when the sky remains sunny. Forecast nothing, and you may find that someone wants you held accountable for negligence in the deaths of many people.

There is no one set of ingredients that produces tornadoes. If there were,
forecasting them would be much easier. The atmosphere is a stew that
produces violent tornadoes by combining many ingredients in very subtle
ways. The July conditions in Colorado that cause afternoon tornadoes are
quite different from the March conditions in Mississippi that produce
tornadoes in the early morning.

Many of the tornado-producing ingredients do not show up on weather
maps, because they are of a size that fits between weather stations. Weather
stations are spaced 50 to 200 miles apart at the surface and 300 miles apart
for upper-air observations. Most upper-air parameters are measured only
once every twelve hours by World War II–style balloons. It is in the undocumented part of the grid that wind shears, outflow boundaries, and other
invisible ingredients can hide. The spacing of the measurements leaves
plenty of room for unpredictable supercell development.

Year after year the same general situations present themselves, but with
enough variations so that each forecasting predicament is unique. The jet
streak (or jet max) may not move through the jet stream as fast as expected.
It may catch up to the surface conditions at an unexpected time. A developing low-pressure area off the Texas coast may cut off Gulf moisture and
lower the tornado probability in Kansas while increasing the likelihood of
floods in Texas. Cool outflow from decaying thunderstorms in Arkansas,
hidden in satellite photographs by anvil cirrus clouds, may or may not
arrive in time to trigger thunderstorms over the Mississippi Delta. There
must be a constant search for hints of small-scale air mass boundaries.
Estimating the strength of all ingredients and parameters, their relationship to one another, and predicting how they will interact is immensely
challenging, and it is what severe storm forecasting is all about.

The legacy of Plainfield may live on in the minds of many forecasters
across the country. The memory of this event, called the "Plainfield syn-
drome," could influence a forecaster to make the prudent choice and issue
a warning, even if his or her intuition says that a tornado is unlikely.

Today most radar-based warnings are issued after a mesocyclone is
located by Doppler radar in a thunderstorm. Since fewer than half of all
mesocyclones actually spawn a tornado, this method guarantees many false

warnings. But it guarantees that on many occasions people will have 20 to 30 minutes to find cover. The average warning time is about 8 minutes, according to a study by Paul Bieringer and Peter Ray (1996).

During the outbreak of March 1, 1997, people in Arkansas had up to 45 minutes' warning. Some towns had several supercells pass overhead and received warnings each time. On average, towns had about 15 minutes' warning that a tornado was imminent or had already touched down. Still, 25 people died and some survivors claimed that there were no warnings. At Moore, Oklahoma, on May 3, 1999, people had so much warning from television meteorologists that one emergency management expert suggested that there was time to actually dig an underground shelter.

When Doppler radar picks up a midlevel mesocyclone 50 miles away, the forecaster issues a warning for one or more counties. The tornado that eventually touches down may not have been spawned by the particular mesocyclone that appeared on radar. It may not even have been spawned by the same convective cell. What the forecaster did was identify the storm as dangerous and potentially tornadic.

However, some tornadoes have almost no Doppler radar signatures at all and form very quickly. A VORTEX study by Wakimoto and Atkins (1996) revealed that funnels can form in just a few minutes, with no midlevel mesocyclone. This storm barely had any low-level mesocyclone, and although it hit only vegetation, it was very impressive and potentially devastating. The good news is that this storm had other detectable mesocyclones in other parts of the thunderstorm, so the storm had been considered dangerous for some time.

In addition, tornadoes will occur outside watches where supercells are unlikely. Squall line storms can change character rapidly. It is possible for them to develop supercell-like structures for a short while and spawn a brief tornado very unexpectedly.

The NWS does not put out a tornado watch each time there is a slight potential for a small tornado. If every set of parameters that could possibly produce a minor tornado were enclosed in a watch, the watches would be so frequent and cover such a large area that they would be routinely ignored by everyone, setting up an eventual catastrophe.

One of the biggest limitations on radar-based warning is that imposed by the curvature of the earth. The NWS has become very good at detecting mesocyclones but not from a great distance. Some tornadoes apparently are triggered by airflows too close to the surface for a fixed radar, tens of miles away, to detect. This curvature does not allow observations of low-level mesocyclones and convergence lines much beyond 35 miles. Radar horizon problems also occur with midlevel mesocyclones. The atmosphere does not bend radar beams at the same curvature as the earth. No matter how low the radar beam is aimed, it will eventually be far enough above the surface so that even a midlevel mesocyclone will be too low to detect. The beam overshoots most midlevel mesocyclones at a distance of about 110 miles (fig. 5.10). The range for detecting the position of the storm is about 200 miles.

SUMMARY

Tornado forecasting is an imperfect system, but people are constantly working to improve it. Technologically, we are a long way from the watchful eyes of the Larsons in 1928, and death tolls are down from an average of 322 per year in the 1920s to about 50 in the last few decades. We have also come a long way since the shaky start that forecasting had in 1953. The bad news is that the dream of a 20-minute warning is realistic for only a portion of all tornadoes. The good news is that a large percentage of strong and violent tornadoes, including most of those with the potential for massive destruction, are handled well by the current system, and advanced warnings for these are likely.

Not all solutions to keeping the death toll down are technological, however. Public awareness and attitudes toward seeking proper shelter, watching the sky, and understanding the meaning of watches and warnings may be just as important as the role of the forecaster. Without effort by the public to reduce their own risk, advanced warnings and more lead time might simply be making people who are already well informed that much more informed. Those who are in the dark may remain in the dark. It is hoped that the increased warning times will not give people so much time that they can get themselves in trouble. Tornado warnings are meant to give us time to find shelter, not to get across town and check on relatives and neighbors. Thirty minutes' warning could be just enough to get caught in a traffic jam in the path of a tornado.

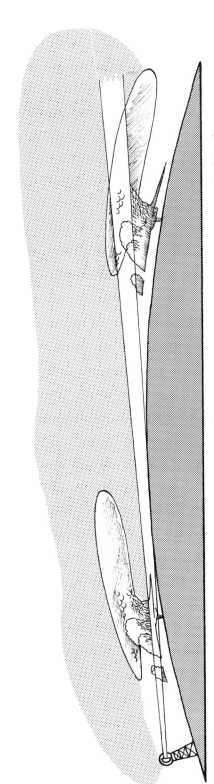

Fig. 5.10. This drawing illustrates how the curvature of the earth interferes with radar detection of a low-level mesocyclone at long distances.

The issues of tornado risk are much more complex than the lead time provided by an NWS forecaster or a community spotter. Modernization and training continue, but that still does not make a 100-death tornado impossible. Before I discuss that in chapter 15, many more topics must be covered. Risk includes the belief in myths, many kinds of safety considerations, and the actual wind speeds inside a tornado.

Forecasters will keep trying, but they are only a link in the chain. At the end of the chain is the individual, and each of us must accept responsibility for our own safety. We have no constitutional right to a precise forecast of one of nature's most complex phenomena or to a government that protects us from even the lowest probability natural hazards.

CHAPTER 6

Tornado
Wind Speeds

It is important to avoid fatalism with regard to tornadoes. Overblown wind speed estimates of 400 to 700 mph help to reinforce the myth that we cannot protect ourselves and our buildings against attack from tornadoes. If we have that attitude, then nothing will be done, and there will be unnecessary deaths and damage. Building an aboveground shelter to withstand 600 mph winds is a vastly different problem from building one to withstand 250 mph winds.

For most of the last two centuries, stories of tornado outbreaks included mention of extravagant wind speeds. An early experiment by Elias Loomis followed the 1842 tornado at Mayfield, Ohio. During his survey of the damage, he found boards driven into the ground to a depth of 18 inches. Soon after, he loaded similar boards into a cannon (these were probably the same cannons he used to defeather chickens) and shot the boards into a hillside. He concluded, by a means I have not been able to locate, that a speed of 682 mph was needed to accomplish the feat. These results added to the belief that extraordinary wind speeds were possible. Actually, there was no conclusive evidence on tornadic winds until 1958.

Direct measurement of tornadic wind is very rare. Tornadoes are uncommon, and relatively few buildings have survivable anemometers on the roof, although one recorded a 151-mph gust at the edge of a tornado at the Tecumseh, Michigan, airport on Palm Sunday, 1965. Most of our understanding of tornado wind speed comes from indirect evidence.

DOPPLER RADAR ESTIMATES

On June 10, 1958, neither C. O. Gatrell nor Denby Marshall was aware that meteorological history was being made above the remains of their homes. Gatrell had been scoffed at for years after building a steel-reinforced concrete tornado shelter under his backyard, but not anymore. Gatrell, his family, and fifteen neighbors were huddled in terror, but in safety. A few feet above them, houses were being ripped to shreds, cars were being hurled hundreds of yards through the air, fifteen people were losing their lives, and forty-five blocks of El Dorado, Kansas, were being torn apart by a violent tornado. A few blocks away, Marshall had packed twenty-seven people and two dogs into his new 6-foot by 8-foot underground shelter and bolted the door shut. As people spoke in whispers, he heard two more voices outside, begging to come in. He unbolted the iron door and two people who had found so much amusement in Denby's shelter were safe from winds in excess of 200 mph.

A year earlier, the U.S. Weather Bureau had parked a mobile laboratory full of experimental Doppler radar equipment 20 miles to the west-south-west, at Wichita. At 5:15 P.M. on this stormy June afternoon, the researchers in the trailer learned that a hook echo had been detected west of El Dorado on conventional radar. The experimental Doppler was pointed to the east-northeast, and radiowaves were sent streaming from the unit toward the tornado while it was tearing apart the west side of El Dorado.

Striking the debris inside the tornado, the wavelength and frequency of the signals were changed and scattered back to the Wichita receiver. The radiowaves were shortened on the left side of the tornado, as the tornadic winds swirled toward the transmitter/receiver. On the right side of the funnel, the radio waves were lengthened. The degree of change in frequency was measured, and it revealed winds of 206 mph. For the first time in history, we had actually measured the speed of the winds inside an active tornado. While there was some doubt about the accuracy of the reading, because of some equipment malfunctions, that Doppler radar measurement was satisfying to people who had insisted for years that estimates of 500 mph were absurd. In the 1960s Doppler radar was developed as a forecasting tool rather than just a "radar gun" speed-detection device. Burgess and Lemon (1990) provide excellent histories of that development.

It would be another twenty-three years before winds of 206 mph were reached again, this time at Binger, Oklahoma. Another ten years passed before that reading was exceeded by a large amount. It was on April 26, 1991, that a very excited and nervous Bluestein and his team of OU students set up a portable Doppler radar in the face of a half-mile-wide tornado near Red Rock, Oklahoma. Before this spectacular event became wrapped in rain and hail, the team received signals indicating wind speeds that were initially estimated to be as high as 287 mph. The number was later lowered to a more conservative 275 mph. This reading was 44 mph higher than the highest wind speed ever recorded on the earth's surface—231 mph on Mount Washington, New Hampshire, in 1934. Then on May 3, 1999, Josh Wurman recorded a 318-mph wind speed (plus or minus 9-mph error) in the Moore, Oklahoma, tornado, with the truck-mounted DOW. Both of these readings were taken near extremely violent tornadoes, at several hundred feet above ground level, which is about where the maximum winds in tornadoes probably occur.

Doppler radar wind speed values are not precise, because it is difficult to separate the radar signals from background noise. Only a small part of the tornado, with a small amount of debris or precipitation, is swirling with the very highest winds. The scattered signal from the few particles in those peak winds is very weak.

THE DISTRIBUTION OF WIND SPEEDS IN A TORNADO

A tornado is basically a fluid. It is not a solid cylinder or a cone, turning at a uniform rate. The tornado is always in the process of changing its structure. This makes the distribution of high winds in the funnel rather complex.

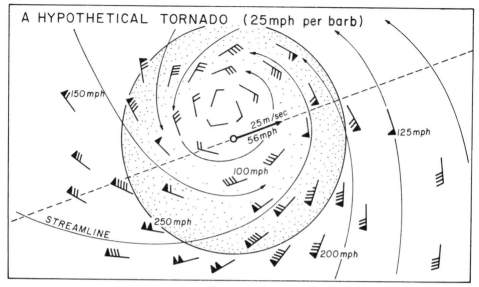

Fig. 6.1. The distribution of winds inside a single-vortex tornado is shown here as it appeared in Fujita 1981. Each of the flags on the wind direction indicator represents 125 mph. Each of the barbs (the small lines) is 25 mph.

    Figure 6.1 is Fujita's (1981) diagram of wind speeds in a rapidly rotating single-vortex tornado that is moving forward at 56 mph (25 meters per second). Had the tornado been standing over a single location, the wind speed at the outer edge of the vortex might have been the same on all sides, about 200 mph. The forward motion of the tornado is to the right and causes the wind on the right side of the tornado to increase by 56 mph. The wind on its left side would decrease by that same amount. This results in a 112-mph difference from one side of the tornado to the other. This movement also shifts the area of calm air, from the center of the tornado, to the left.

    Figure 6.2 (Fujita 1971b), shows the wind field in a tornado with three subvortices. I have added winds speeds at four points of reference. At point A the counterclockwise rotational speed of the tornado (100 mph) and the forward speed of the tornado (40 mph) add together, creating a 140 mph wind. At point B on the left side of the tornado, the 40 mph forward speed is subtracted from the rotational speed and the resultant wind is about 60

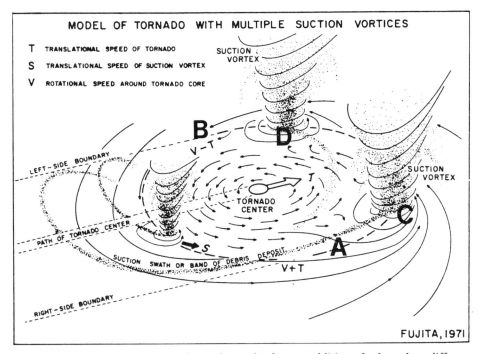

MODEL OF TORNADO WITH MULTIPLE SUCTION VORTICES

T   TRANSLATIONAL SPEED OF TORNADO

S   TRANSLATIONAL SPEED OF SUCTION VORTEX

V   ROTATIONAL SPEED AROUND TORNADO CORE

FUJITA, 1971

Fig. 6.2. The wind speeds in a tornado are the result of vector addition of at least three different horizontal wind speeds. Each of the vortices also has its own vertical component with air moving upward, adding to the complexity. Drawing by Ted Fujita (1971).

mph from right to left. The highest wind speeds would be at point C. This is a small area on both the right side of the main swirl and the right side of a suction vortex. There, all three speeds are added, giving a total of about 240 mph. At point D the suction vortex speed, is 100 mph to the right. The forward speed is 40 mph to the right. The tornado's rotational speed of 100 mph to the left is subtracted. The result is only 40 mph. It is no wonder that the damage patterns from tornadoes are so complex. Each building is constructed differently and each one is hit by a different wind speed. In figure 6.3 (Fujita 1981) there is a less detailed, overall view of winds in single-vortex and multiple-vortex tornadoes.

Multiple vortices may be the common way that 200- to 250-mph winds are produced. It as also likely, however, that a single-vortex tornado can spin at 200 to 250 mph. This probably happened at Pampa, Texas, in 1995,

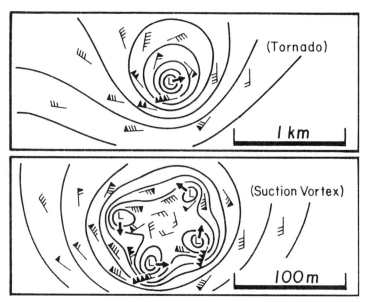

Fig. 6.3. Fujita's diagram of a hypothetical wind speed in both a single- and a multiple-vortex tornado. Each flag is 50 mph; each barb adds another 10 mph.

in the tornado shown in figure 6.4. Whether a tornado can rotate at 250 mph and also have multiple vortices in its walls is a speculation I will leave to others.

PHOTOGRAMMETRY

Doppler radar was not the first technique to give us a wind speed estimate in excess of 270 mph. Photogrammetry has indicated winds as high as 284 mph. This method uses motion pictures taken at a known distance from a tornado rather than an on-site measuring device.

In photogrammetry, the speed of debris is measured by comparing successive frames of motion picture film. Before this can be accomplished, an initial "scaling" determines the distance to the tornado, the size of the tornado, the exact location of the camera, and the filming rate of the camera in frames per second. The motion of cloud tags, bits of debris, and clumps of dust is then measured with as much precision as possible.

Fig. 6.4. The Pampa, Texas, tornado of June 8, 1995, had extreme horizontal as well as vertical wind speeds. A vast amount of debris was generated as it passed through the industrial area of town. Copyright Alan Moller.

In 1953 a film showing lots of measurable debris was taken at Warner Robins Air Force Base, Georgia. The distance between the tornado and the camera was unknown, however, so the size and speed of the debris cannot be determined with accuracy. Since we know that the individual frames were approximately one-sixteenth of a second apart, some crude photogrammetry is possible, as in figure 6.5.

In the 1970s, when most photogrammetry was done, the highest measured wind speed value was in the Parker, Indiana, tornado of April 3, 1974. Greg Forbes (1976), at that time a student of Fujita's, found a wind speed of 284 mph about 1,000 feet above ground level. The cumulative errors in his study may have been as high as 18 mph, so the maximum wind speed would fall within a range of 266 to 302 mph. It is likely, however, that some errors canceled each other, so that the resultant error is rather small. Trees and clouds of dust prevented a detailed analysis near ground level. Within the dust clouds, just above treetop level, the highest wind speed was 215 mph.

OVERESTIMATES

Most of us have experienced winds only as high as 50 to 60 mph, which is the range in which tree damage begins to occur. When one is walking through the debris of tornado-destroyed buildings, it is natural to think that only winds of 400 to 500 mph could have produced such destruction. It seems rational to suggest that a wind ten times greater than normal would be needed to create the catastrophe, but this is an erroneous calculation. Ten times the force is not the same as ten times the wind speed. What is not understood is that the pressure of the wind increases by the square of the speed. For instance, a doubling of wind speed increases pressure four times; a tripling of speed from 60 mph to 180 mph produces not three times greater wind pressure but nine times greater. One does not need a tenfold increase in wind to create a tenfold increase in the force of the wind. Just over three times will do.

In addition, most of us have no direct experience of winds blowing upward. High winds blowing vertically can hold objects aloft in a "weightless" state. Horizontal winds in a tornado can then accelerate these suspended objects laterally, doing great damage to anything that they happen

Fig. 6.5. At Warner Robins Air Force Base in Georgia, the tornado of April 30, 1953, produced debris whose size could be estimated. It is possible that the large piece of roof shooting upward to the right is about 16 feet long. Frames are 1/16 of a second apart, and the roof moved its own length in about two frames, or 2/16 of a second. This translates into a 90 mph wind speed. The roof accelerated from 0 to 90 in less than a second. Courtesy of NOAA.

to hit. Ignoring the presence of vertical winds increases the possibility that wind speeds will be overestimated. The upward component of the wind in some tornadoes may exceed 150 mph, well in excess of the speed needed to make cars and people essentially weightless.

The wind needed to create enough air pressure on a person's body to equal his or her weight is about 90 mph. At that point something akin to weightlessness begins to set in. The wind speed needed to create pressure on the side of a car to equal its weight is 100 to 120 mph, depending on the weight and profile of the vehicle. This speed is probably approached or exceeded in hundreds of tornadoes each year. A mobile home requires only a 60 to 80-mph wind for air pressure to equal its weight and make it vulnerable to overturning. The combination of 100-mph horizontal winds and 100-mph vertical winds can create spectacular damage.

On May 27, 1896, one of the deadliest tornadoes in U.S. history killed 255 people at St. Louis, Missouri, and East St. Louis, Illinois. It also drove a 2-inch by 10-inch wooden plank through the half-inch-thick wrought iron side of the east approach to the Eads Bridge across the Mississippi River. This was the first and last case of such a tornado-generated missile penetrating this much iron. The event was widely publicized because the Eads Bridge had been constructed to withstand tornado winds after a tornado struck the same area in 1871. At the time it was calculated that the board would have to be moving at 278 mph to penetrate the iron. Other estimates put the speed at up to 560 mph.

We suspect today that the speed was probably much lower. The wrought iron on the Eads Bridge could have had a weak spot, perhaps weakened by other debris a few seconds earlier. A likelier possibility is that something heavy was originally attached to the board and then broke off after impact. The added mass would have given the missile considerably more damaging "momentum." When the original calculations were made, only the mass of the board itself was used. In addition, the added material could have acted as a sail, providing more surface area to catch the wind and help accelerate the beam to high speed.

In a more recent case, engineers at Texas Tech University (Minor et al. 1977) studied 30-foot-long, 6-inch by 15-inch timbers carried 1,000 feet from the Westgate Elementary School at Omaha on May 6, 1975. Eyewitnesses reported that the beams were indeed attached to the roof, which acted as a sail. The beams and roof separated on impact, sending the beams deep into the ground and nearby cars. Engineers have found that often the most spectacular damage can be explained by a series of events like this; incredible wind speeds need not be present. Overestimates are usually made by observing just the end product of a chain of events rather than by considering the entire sequence.

The Oshkosh, Wisconsin, tornado of April 21, 1974, devastated thirty farms southwest of town and four hundred homes in town and produced spectacular multiple vortices. It was calculated that a 358 mph wind was needed to bend steel fence posts at Oshkosh. What was ignored in this estimate was the influence of the attached fencing itself and the debris that may have smashed into it. The calculation was based on a pole standing alone in the wind.

In 1953 engineers calculated the winds in the Worcester tornado at up to 335 mph (Booker 1954), based on damage to high-voltage towers. The engineers knew that the towers were near the edge of the tornado, but they assumed, incorrectly, that the tornado spins faster near its center. They estimated that the towers could withstand 170-mph winds, then extrapolated the 170-mph value to the center of the tornado and published that 335 mph estimate. Those engineers understood steel towers and vortices, but they did not understand tornadoes. In 1953 we had no knowledge of multiple vortices or that the highest wind speeds in a large tornado are in suction vortices, swirling outside of the tornado "eye."

Another factor that was not considered at Worcester was gust sensitivity. Wind gusts can make objects vibrate and perhaps destroy them at relatively low wind speeds. If winds gust at regular intervals, this regularity can induce a harmonic motion in objects of the proper size. In normal wind situations, low-frequency gusts may cause a poorly designed suspension bridge to sway. When wind gusts are in rhythm with the natural harmonic sway of the bridge, the bridge can be destroyed much more easily.

All objects, even telephone poles and power lines, have periods of harmonic motion. Power poles and transmission towers may break or collapse at a lower than expected wind speed; they may simply vibrate to the point of destruction. Also, when power lines are attached to towers, the lines can transmit stress from one falling tower to another. If the power lines were broken on only one side of the tower, the wires on the other side may have helped to bend the structure to the ground. Add to this the vibrating effect of high-frequency wind gusts, and even the most impressive towers can buckle and fall to the ground without the 200-mph winds that the tower was supposedly built to resist.

OF TOOTHPICKS AND STRAW

Experiments in the 1960s by Bernard Vonnegut and others at the State University of New York at Albany (Keller and Vonnegut 1976) shed light on a puzzling tornado oddity. It is not uncommon to see splinters and straws embedded in trees and telephone poles after a tornado has passed. Before the experiments by Vonnegut and colleagues no one had tried to determine just what wind speeds were needed to create these unusual pincushion effects. Toothpicks and broom straws were fired into various types of wood using a tornado gun that had a top speed of 694 mph. The conclusion was that "the driving of straws or splinters into trees, posts, or other targets does not necessarily mean the presence of extremely high winds." It was found that toothpicks can penetrate some softwoods at speeds as low as 67 mph. At speeds of 155 mph straw was able to penetrate fir plywood. Penetration into hardwoods was another matter. Toothpicks did not begin the first millimeter of penetration into solid (uncracked) maple until speeds of about 480 mph. The longer, and therefore heavier, the straw or toothpick, the deeper the penetration. Wet toothpicks penetrated up to four times deeper than dry. It was suggested that minimum wind estimates could be set by careful examination of straws on a tornado damage site survey, but no such estimates have been published to date. A variable that would be hard to duplicate in a laboratory is the degree to which the wood was stressed and cracked by the wind while being bombarded with splinters and straw. Survey teams have reported straws only in posts or telephone poles with preexisting cracks. Many fence posts and trees have had straws driven into the softer bark rather than into the wood itself.

Civil engineers at Texas Tech University Institute for Disaster Research have spent years studying countless damage situations involving uplifted roofs, empty foundations, overturned tombstones, snapped utility poles, airborne steel beams and pipes, flying school buses, and sliding railroad bridges (Minor et al. 1977; pers. com.). They have yet to find any examples of destruction that require a wind in excess of 250 mph to explain them. Neither Doppler radar nor photogrammetry have confirmed winds over 250 mph near the surface.

For centuries it had been thought that wind speeds are related to the degree of damage. But no system had ever linked the two in such a way that the interested amateur meteorologist could do his own wind speed estimates. In 1971 a system called the Fujita Scale (F-scale) was designed to do just that. It is frequently used to estimate a tornado's wind speed from the damage it produces. The F-scale has allowed us to determine that most tornadic winds are 100 mph or less and that even large tornadoes have only a relatively small area of extreme winds. Fujita's mapping of tornado paths leads us to believe that less than 1 percent of all tornadic winds exceed 200 mph. We now know that proper construction techniques can hold buildings together and provide safe shelter in the vast majority of tornadoes. The Fujita Scale is the subject of the next chapter.

CHAPTER 7

THE FUJITA SCALE OF TORNADO INTENSITY

Despite being a large target on the southwestern edge of tornado alley, the Texas Panhandle city of Lubbock, in early May 1970, had enjoyed the good fortune of having had no destructive tornadoes for the entire century of its existence. The one killer tornado in Lubbock County's history had done its deadly work at a frail rural home, 10 miles northwest of the city, on June 20, 1939. This freedom from disastrous tornadoes ended in the darkness of a late Tuesday evening, May 11, 1970, at 9:45 P.M. CDT. At 9:15 P.M. a supercell was located by forecasters on radar and seen churning in the southern sky by many residents. It appeared as if the storm would move to the north-east and pass east of the downtown area. But after half an hour of explo-sive cloud growth on the southwestern flank of the thunderstorm, a massive tornado touched down at the southern edge of the city. Moving north-northeast for 9 miles, it produced $135 million in damage. To that date, it was the most destructive tornado in history.

The funnel, seen by few people in the dim light, was up to a mile wide and was made incredibly destructive by its numerous suction vortices.

All along the track these tornadoes-within-a-tornado produced such extreme winds that anyone aboveground in their vicinity was in mortal danger. In one such vortex, an old pickup truck was hurled onto a woman as she ran to her storm shelter. Farther north, another suction vortex blew a father and son out of their car at a stoplight, killing the young boy. A man died as he waited at the door of a storm shelter. His family was to have followed him from the house but could not escape the building as it was being torn apart. Next door, another family raced into a heater closet. When they emerged they saw that the closet was the only part of the house left standing. Nearby, a woman died wrapped in sheet metal after being swept out of her house. Six people died in cars, 3 in the open, 19 in homes; 27 of the 28 deaths occurred in or near the path of suction vortices.

The tornado did more than merely level houses and hurl vehicles. Ten-inch-thick, steel-reinforced concrete lids were torn from grain storage bins. A 13-ton fertilizer tank was carried through the air for more than half a mile. The twenty-one-story Great Plains Life Building, asymmetrically built with large elevator shafts on one end of the structure, was twisted and distorted. This first high-rise building to encounter a tornado was abandoned and became known as "the Largest Pigeon Roost in the Panhandle." Years later it was repaired and declared safe for occupancy.

The 1970 Lubbock tornado marked the beginning of a golden age of tornado research. It provided a bonanza of information on how tornado damage occurs, what wind speed seems to be necessary to produce that damage, and what the deadliest part of the tornado is. The passage of the tornado within a few miles of the Texas Tech University Civil Engineering Department allowed study to begin within hours after the tornado passed. Texas Tech would soon rise to world leadership in the field of wind engineering research.

The Lubbock tornado also changed forever how we discuss tornadoes. From the bewildering array of damage came the Fujita Scale of Tornado Intensity, devised by Ted Fujita of the University of Chicago (Fujita 1971a; see fig. 7.1). We were no longer limited to counting all tornadoes equally, despite the forces they displayed. Every documented tornado since then has received a Fujita Scale rating from 0 to 5. The rating is based on the highest intensity level of damage that occurred along the path. Today terms like

Fig. 7.1. The official NWS Fujita Scale damage photographs were taken by Fujita at Lubbock, Texas, in 1970.

"F5" or "F2" are heard on every storm chase, are used in news reports on tornadoes, and are even found in movie scripts.

The F-scale is a classification system analogous to the Richter Scale of earthquake intensity. In theory, both the Fujita Scale and Richter Scale have no upper limits. In reality, however, we are not likely to experience a Richter-9 earthquake or a Fujita-6 tornado. The Fujita Scale changed the way we report, study, and count tornadoes. After the F-scale was used to rate all known tornadoes, it was used to organize data in ways that had previously been impossible.

FUJITA SCALE DAMAGE STANDARDS

The process of rating a tornado with the F-scale begins by observing the damage. The worst damage is then compared to the descriptions and the best guess for an F-scale number is made. A wind speed range can then be estimated for this tornado. There is nothing magical about the wind speed numbers; they are only rough estimates. The 318-mph top speed for an F5 tornado was an educated guess that Fujita made in 1971. Since that time most meteorologists and engineers have come to believe that maximum tornado wind speeds in the bottom 10 meters of the atmosphere are somewhat less than his original estimated values.

F-scale rating standards are listed below. Note that economic losses are not a consideration. Some weak tornadoes may hit expensive airplanes, marinas, and trailer parks, producing millions of dollars in damage. Some violent tornadoes may hit only a single house. A tornado is rated by the single most intensely destructive thing it does, at any single point along the path. If a tornado sweeps away just one well-constructed house along a 50-mile-long path, then that entire path is given an F5 rating. All other damage is of no relevance as far as the F-scale rating is concerned. The rating is assigned after the damage has occurred. A motion picture script such as *Twister* in which an F5 tornado is announced as about to touch down shows no understanding of the F-scale rating system.

F0 (40–72 MPH). Damage that is rated at F0 includes broken chimneys and awnings, broken tree limbs, bent TV antennas, and damaged signs. In F0 tornadic winds a few roof shingles may be removed from houses and some roofing may be removed from barns. Sheet metal garden sheds would be moved or buckled and garden furniture blown around. Recreational vehicles may be overturned. Any tornado that disturbs only dust should be ranked at F0 for actual damage done. However, many meteorologists are loath to give an F0 rating to a spectacular, potentially devastating tornado that touched down in some remote part of the western plains and stirred up little more than dust. This is a dilemma that will be addressed below.

F1 (73–112 MPH). A tornado is rated at F1 if it tears off part of the roof of a frame house or an industrial building. At F1 a mobile home that is not tied down will be pushed off its foundation, overturned, and destroyed but will still be recognizable. Automobiles will be pushed off roads. Attached garages will be torn apart, as will outbuildings and barns.

At F1 a poorly anchored frame house or lakefront cottage will be twisted or completely moved from its foundation, but most of its roof may still be intact. A frame barn that is blown over, and thus "destroyed," should be considered to have F1 damage if little of the structure is blown away. Barn damage is rated F2 only if the entire frame barn is ripped apart and much of it blown away. Complete destruction of pole barns, quonset barns, and irrigation systems are considered F1 damage. If a roof is cleanly and completely lifted from a frame house, or a house is rolled on its side, then poor attachment is likely and only an F1 rating should be applied. Shallow-rooted trees, or trees in wet or loosened soil, will be uprooted. Brittle evergreen tree species will snap. Straight line winds in this range have shown that F1 winds can level large amounts of forest, push over railroad boxcars, and blow down telephone poles. In many cases what some people proclaim as "amazing" damage deserves only an F1 rating.

F2 (113–57 MPH). An F2 tornado tears all or most (perhaps 80%) of the roof from a well-constructed frame house. Mobile homes are obliterated and rendered unrecognizable. Cars are tumbled in the funnel and left mangled along the road. Timbers become deadly missiles, and well-constructed barns are destroyed. High-voltage electrical transmission towers may be bent to the ground in an F2 tornado, even if supposedly built to withstand a 200-mph horizontal wind.

Fig. 7.2. This photograph of damage at Wichita Falls, Texas, on April 3, 1964, illustrates F1, F2, and F3 damage. The superimposed numbers are the appropriate F-scale rating. Another subdivision had F5 damage. Courtesy of the American Red Cross.

F3 (158–206 MPH). An F3 tornado tears the roof and exterior walls from well-constructed houses. It can lift and throw heavy cars hundreds of feet. Large swaths of forest trees can be ripped from the ground. Tree damage is dependent on complex factors such as species, age, health, soil moisture, root depth, and vertical wind velocities. An F3 rating is never given to mobile home damage or barn damage. My opinion is that an F3 tornado can throw a car 200 yards or more, although officially some tornadoes have been rated F4 after accomplishing that feat. Cars that were parked in front of houses with less than F4 damage have been carried that far. Figure 7.2 shows F-scale ratings for each house in a section of a Wichita Falls subdivision that was hit on April 3, 1964.

F4 (207–60 MPH). An F4 tornado completely destroys well-constructed houses, leaving only debris on the foundations. Cars, vans, trucks, and farm machinery can be thrown hundreds of yards. Individual well-anchored trees are often left as branchless and barkless skeletons. For an F4 rating, a frame house should have no more than a fragment of one wall standing.

F5 (261–318 MPH). An F5 tornado will obliterate a strong frame house and scatter the debris. The signature example of F5 damage is an empty, poured-concrete foundation, with sills ripped away from properly spaced anchor bolts and shredded studs, flooring, walls, and other remnants of the house extending in a swath away from the vacant foundation.

Judging whether an F5 rating applies is very difficult. The major difficulty is that the house no longer exists. To judge whether it was strongly built and well anchored one has to look for clues. The neighboring houses may be of similar design and construction, and these may have sustained only F2 to F3 damage. Damage to the foundation itself may indicate whether the house was well anchored. For an F5 rating to be appropriate, the house should have been bolted to a poured-concrete foundation. About once a year an F5 rating is assigned to a tornado after the damage has been surveyed.

Figure 7.3 shows damage rated according to the F-scale. The buildings at the extreme upper right have minor roof damage (F0). On the left of center is a house with slightly more serious roof damage (F1). Across the street is a house that has been completely unroofed (F2). Beyond that house, near the center of the photograph, is a house with only interior walls (F3). Just above that house is a house with a debris-filled lot but no walls standing (F4). Near the right edge of the photograph are empty foundations with just a streak of debris extending from them; an F5 rating would apply there if the homes were found to have been well attached to the foundation, which they were.

F6 (319–79 MPH). It is possible that an F6 tornado cannot exist. If one did occur, we would probably not be able to confirm it. The small area of F6 damage that might be produced would not be recognizable, even if we knew what to look for. It would be surrounded by the F4 and F5 winds that would also cause massive destruction. In F6 winds missiles such as cars

Fig. 7.3. This aerial view of Andover, Kansas, after the tornado of April 26, 1991, shows damage at every rating from F0 to F5. This was the only official F5 tornado of the year. Copyright Paul Bowen.

and refrigerators might do inconceivable impact damage that could not be
identified because of the F5 impact damage that came before and after it.
Winds in the F6 range may eventually be detected by a portable Doppler
radar unit or some other remote-sensing device. This would not necessarily constitute the identification of an F6 tornado, unless the winds were
detected within 10 meters (33 feet) of the ground.

Portable radar readings of wind speeds are irrelevant to the Fujita Scale,
since they are well above ground level. If a house was unroofed and portable
Doppler noted a 350-mph wind, the tornado should still be rated F2. Since
portable Doppler readings are not measured over a known time period,
they do not qualify as world speed records either.

Table 7.1 compares tornado numbers and deaths with F-scale ratings.
Note that violent tornadoes make up only 1.2 percent of all tornadoes (12
out of 1,000). But these dozen or so tornadoes each year cause about 70
percent of tornado-caused deaths. Weak tornadoes make up nearly 75
percent of all tornadoes but cause only about 4 percent of all deaths, with
most of those in mobile homes.

Table 7.1
A COMPARISON OF TORNADO NUMBERS AND DEATHS
WITH FUJITA SCALE RATINGS

Fujita Scale	Wind Speed Range	Percent of All Tornadoes	Percent of All Deaths
F0	under 73 mph	38.9	0.4
F1	73 – 112	35.6	3.6
F2	113 – 157	19.4	9.4
F3	158 – 206	4.9	18.9
F4	207 – 260	1.1	43.9
F5	261 – 318	0.1	23.8

It is important to note that the assigned wind speed values are an
educated guess made in 1971, without scientific testing, and should not be

taken as precise. In my opinion, and in the opinion of many colleagues, damage that has an F5 appearance may occur at wind speeds far below 261 mph, perhaps below 180 mph in poorly attached houses. The opposite kind of faulty estimate is also possible. Winds in excess of 157 mph may fail to remove the roof of a well-constructed home. Use of specific values in phrases such as "homes were unroofed by winds of 157 mph" or "homes were leveled by winds up to 316 mph" are unscientific, even if they emanate from NWS offices. A statement to the effect that homes were leveled by winds that may have exceeded 260 mph would be more accurate.

THE FUJITA-PEARSON SCALE

The process that brought the Fujita Scale into national use can be traced to 1969, when a deadly tornado touched down on January 23 and cut a long swath across Mississippi. Eleven of the deaths were at Hazelhurst. Both watches and warnings were issued for this tornado. The next tornado of the year, five days later, was a waterspout in the swamps west of Buras, Louisiana. It was insignificant compared to the massive Mississippi tornado, and no watches or warnings were posted. Allen Pearson was director of the NSSFC at the time. Both events counted equally in his database as one tornado. A colleague jokingly said to Pearson something like, "Well, Al, you got one out of two, 50 percent isn't bad." Suggesting that the minor waterspout was in any way comparable to the monster that killed thirty-two people a few days earlier made Pearson more determined than ever to find a means of separating minor events from major ones. In 1969 there was no easy-to-use rating system available.

When Fujita suggested his system in 1971, Pearson and he met for lunch to discuss its potential for use, how it might be tested, and how the state climatologists could be enlisted to do the ratings. Pearson also devised a scale of numbers for path width and path length, to complement Fujita's intensity rating (Fujita and Pearson 1973; table 7.2). This produced a shorthand notation for all tornadoes called the "F,P,P rating." This three-digit number records the Fujita Intensity Scale, the Pearson Path Length Scale, and the Pearson Path Width Scale. For instance, the Tracy, Minnesota, tornado (see fig. 1.3) was rated F5, had a path length of 13 miles, and a path width of 600 yards. Its full Fujita-Pearson rating would be FPP 5,3,4.

Table 7.2
THE FUJITA–PEARSON FPP SCALES

Rating	Fujita Wind Speed (mph)	Pearson Path Length (miles)	Pearson Path Width
–	0 – 39	< 0.3	< 6
0	40 – 72	0.3 – 0.9	6 – 17 yards
1	73 – 112	1.0 – 3.1	18 – 55 yards
2	113 – 157	3.2 – 9.9	56 – 175 yards
3	158 – 206	10 – 31	176 – 566 yards
4	207 – 260	32 – 99	0.3 – 0.9 miles
5	261 – 318	100 – 315	1.0 – 3.1 miles

Pearson decided that the Fujita Scale was sufficiently well designed and Fujita's reputation sufficiently strong that the F-scale rating should be included as part of the official NWS database, despite the fact that the many inherent problems would probably never be resolved. The F-scale had two important attributes. First, it was simple enough to be used by a wide variety of people having only a brief period to study the damage. Second, the guidelines approximated reality enough so that meteorologists and engineers could use the ratings and adjust mathematically for any shortcomings.

By 1973 the Fujita-Pearson Scale was the official NWS classification system for tornadoes. It did not undergo rigorous peer review but was simply incorporated into the new digital, 80-column tornado database at NSSFC. The NWS tornado database, incidentally, still has 80 columns of information. This is not because 80 digits are needed to contain useful information but because the old IBM paper cards that held the data had 80 punch holes.

The Pearson length and width ratings are still officially recorded but rarely used. They were a computer memory–saving means of recording data in the early 1970s. Computer memories are so large now that short-hand codes are no longer needed. Given the inaccuracies of the Fujita Scale, it would probably not have passed peer review and been accepted by the scientific community. Had Pearson not had the need, foresight, and courage to adopt the F-scale on his own, we might not be using it today.

FUJITA SCALE DEBATE

Controversy over using the Fujita Scale to rate tornado intensity continues. No damage-based tornado classification system can work perfectly, and the Fujita Scale is no exception. What follows are some examples of the controversial aspects of the Fujita Scale

Identically constructed homes can be damaged differently by identical tornadoes if they are attacked by wind from different angles. If winds hit broadside into a garage door, the damage may be extreme. The garage door is a weak point; and the destruction of the garage may start a sequence of failure that can spread to the whole house (Minor 1983). If the wind hits the back side of the house, which has no garage opening and fewer windows, or the end of the house with a smaller wind profile, the damage might be less severe.

Houses can be constructed in the same way but be aligned differently on various landscapes—in valleys, on hilltops, or on slopes. A house in a Pennsylvania forest, sheltered by 60-foot-tall oak trees, will be damaged differently than an identically built house on the open Kansas prairie. The Kansas structure might be swept from its foundation while its Pennsylvania counterpart is crushed by falling trees before it has a chance to be swept away.

Wind speeds can be estimated inaccurately, because of differences in construction. The specific F-scale wind speed values may be overestimated by 30 to 100 mph in some damage situations. A contractor may hurry a house to completion with just a few nails, fully expecting that gravity will hold the roof in place for the life of the house. Such a roof will be torn off by winds of less than 113 mph (the low end of F2), especially if the winds have an upward component.

If a house is not well anchored to a foundation, it will move from that foundation in winds of considerably less than 207 mph, the low end of the F4 range. Engineers have found that frame houses can be shifted off their foundations by winds of less than 100 mph if they are poorly anchored or, much to the surprise of the home owner, not anchored at all. Whether the

Fig. 7.4. One house at Belmond, Iowa, on October 14, 1966, was completely swept away, and the tornado was rated at F5. The tornado must have been very narrow, possibly in a shrinking stage, or the house was poorly anchored.

home in figure 7.4 deserved the F5 rating that it was given will never be known. Perhaps the funnel was very intense and very narrow, or perhaps the house was poorly anchored, or perhaps the garage door was open. The presence of so much of the house in a pile just a few hundred feet away from the foundation suggests to me that the F5 rating was too high.

In the opposite situation, above-average construction might result in an underestimate of wind speed. If houses are bolted strongly to their foundations and the roofs hurricane-clipped in place, they may withstand 150-mph winds with relatively little damage. This might lead one to think that a mere F1 tornado passed through the area when in reality it had winds in the F3 range.

An abnormal time of passage of a tornado can cause wind speeds to be either underestimated or overestimated. A slow-moving tornado could produce an overestimate of wind speeds just as poor home construction can. In slow-moving tornadoes, lower wind speeds may sweep away a house that is subjected to their forces over a longer period, perhaps for a full minute rather than just a few seconds. For instance, on May 31, 1947, a tornado was about 8 miles west-southwest of Leedey, Oklahoma. It moved slowly (about 15 mph) to the east-northeast. Sirens were sounded and warnings were spread from house to house. The half-mile-wide funnel reached town about 30 minutes after it was first spotted. It took 5 full minutes to chew its way across the northern half of the unfortunate community. A large residential section of Leedey was left completely barren of walls or any standing structures. Little or no personal property from the houses could be found. Yards were stripped of lawns and all vegetation. People who had seen the devastation at Woodward a month earlier (107 dead on April 9) noted that at least there were piles of debris at Woodward. Most of the 7 fatalities were elderly or hearing-impaired.

The problem posed by the Leedey tornado was whether it truly deserves its F5 rating and the associated 261 to 318-mph wind speeds. Surely the damage was F5 in appearance. The question arises whether a slow-moving tornado with only F3 level winds (158–206 mph) could do F5-appearing damage. The F3 winds would have less immediate impact. However, if they were imposed on a house for a full minute, the building might vibrate to pieces. Weak points might appear in even the most well built frame house. Normally the highest winds in a tornado pass in only a few seconds. The F5 rating is valid because the destruction appeared to be F5, and the F-scale is a damage scale first and a wind speed scale second.

Another school of thought suggests that fast-moving tornadoes are the ones that do extreme damage. The onrushing tornado may not be spinning that fast, but it hits the house like a solid sledgehammer, producing great destruction. Which idea is correct? No one knows; there is much we do not know about tornadoes, and no easy way to study them.

A well-formed, long-track tornado, capable of leveling hundreds of houses, may not encounter any homes at all and may receive only an F1 rating. That rating may be based on the destruction of a single pole barn or downed trees and power lines. We are forced to assume that the tornado did its worst destruction at its time of maximum intensity. This is not a good assumption. It could have done its worst damage at the time of its lowest wind speeds, right at its touchdown point, for instance. This necessary reliance on building damage means that many tornadoes on the Great Plains will not be rated at anything close to their potential maximum intensity.

The dilemma of the nondamaging tornado has been the subject of much discussion. Should future tornadoes be rated on the basis of damage done, or should they be rated on the best estimate of the wind speed by someone who actually saw the vortex? I believe that a rating system of wind speed based solely on visual observations invites more inconsistencies and inaccuracies than a damage-based system. With consistency, one can at least understand the problems with the data.

Another solution was proposed by Doswell and Burgess (1988). They suggested that the source of the rating be included with each F-scale rating. The source could be a visual estimate by an experienced observer or a damage-based estimate. The official NWS guide to damage survey techniques (Bunting and Smith 1993) suggests that no matter how the rating is arrived at, the method and rationale should be listed in an accompanying description. My experience is that that advice is not always followed in practice. Another suggestion is to list a confidence level, a ranking of how sure we are that the F-scale reflects the actual maximum wind speed. Events with a high confidence rating could be used for research in tornado risk. Tornadoes with a lower confidence rating would be used for general climatology.

I favor keeping the system as it is but overlapping the wind speed ranges. For instance, F4 damage might range from 150 to 250 mph and F5 from 200 to 300 mph. This would better reflect the realities of home construction and our own uncertainties.

The media will continue to focus their reports on the top of the wind speed range rather than on the middle or bottom of the range. They will probably continue to exclaim about the incredible devastation and total destruction of the weakest and most poorly constructed buildings that lie in the wake of F1 tornadoes. One can only hope that such exaggerated reports will not be the sole basis for the F-scale rating. However, as the NWS trims its staff and becomes more automated, it has less personnel time available to do accurate surveys; media reports may come to have a large impact on the ratings.

For all its flaws, the Fujita Scale is better than no scale at all. There is no way to resolve all of its problems. For more than two decades it has provided a focus for dialogue, elevating the discussion from pure speculation to discussion within the framework of a classification system.

CHAPTER 8

TORNADO
MYTHS

In 1851 several hundred Pottawatomie Indians traded land in their native territory (now part of Michigan) for land near present-day Topeka, Kansas. Legend has it that soon after their arrival some Pottawatomies were camped along the Kaw River and killed by a tornado. They were buried at the base of the largest hill in the area, and the Great Spirit was called on to protect the place from tornadoes forever. One of the Indian leaders was a 400-pound, colorful, well-educated cattle trader and doting father who took the name Abram Burnett. He had moved to the Topeka area in 1848 and settled near that hill at the southwestern edge of town. Since then it has been called Burnett's Mound. Burnett was about fifty-nine years old when he was rolled into his grave at the base of the mound. The eight-foot-tall headstone reads "May His Spirit Rest in Peace."

The legendary mound has a storied history of Indian rituals and buried gold, but its most lingering myth, until 1966, was its ability to protect the city of Topeka from tornadoes. The prominent hill supposedly would divert or split the winds of any tornado, saving Topeka from destruction. Others, however, said that the Great Spirit had been angered by the construction of houses on the slope of the mound. In 1966 one more myth about tornadoes was laid to rest, and the Great Spirit had his (or her) revenge.

On June 8, 1966, at about 6:56 P.M., the National Weather Service alerted the Topeka police that there were many funnel sightings in eastern Kansas. Policeman David Hathaway headed up Burnett's Mound on his weather-watch duty. He topped the hill at 7:02 P.M. and spotted the tornado that would become the most destructive to touch down on earth until then. His sighting was reported, and two minutes later warning sirens began to shriek across Topeka. Hathaway stayed at his post until the last minute, providing continuous updates on the funnel's movement. His final report, at 7:14 P.M., stated, "I'm getting the hell out of here." He was injured and his car destroyed as the tornado passed directly over him a few seconds later.

The funnel swept into town at 29th and Gage streets, leveled the houses at the base of Burnett's Mound, and cut a $100 million destructive swath across Washburn University and residential Topeka. Sixteen people were killed and more than four hundred were injured. The mound did protect Topeka indirectly, however. As a vantage point for an early sighting and warning, the mound undoubtedly saved many lives. The Topeka tornado was typical of storms that, before the advent of awareness and watch-warning programs in the mid-1950s, might have killed as many as two hundred people. Five miles northeast of the mound, about fifty people were attending a music recital in MacVicar Hall on the Washburn University campus. Aware that the area was included in a severe weather forecast, they started for the basement when they heard the sirens and the roar of the huge funnel. Someone shouted, "To the southwest corner." In the confusion they sought shelter in the southeast part of the building. They were very fortunate in making this mistake, since it saved their lives. The southwest section of the basement was immediately filled with tons of stone and debris.

The story of the Topeka tornado brings to the forefront the first two of the ten tornado-related myths that are addressed here.

MYTH #1: SOME TOWNS ARE PROTECTED

Native American tribes perceived tornadoes in different ways. Some saw them as a cleansing agent, sweeping away the ragged and negative things of life. Others saw them as a form of revenge for dishonoring the Great Spirit. Today only the myths about the protection of towns by rivers and hills linger in modern American culture.

The Osage Indians, native to Kansas, Oklahoma, and Missouri passed on tornado legends to the early settlers. One such legend has it that tornadoes will not strike near the point where two rivers join. In the past one hundred fifty years, this idea has provided a false sense of security for some towns. Emporia, Kansas, for instance, had sat "protected" between the Cottonwood and Neosho rivers, in native Osage territory, for more than a century. Emporia was free of damaging tornadoes until June 8, 1974, when one killed six people. (Part of the path of the 1974 tornado was also crossed by a deadly twister on September 29, 1881, but the area was farmland then.) Another tornado hit the west side of Emporia on June 7, 1990.

The idea that one's town is protected is a combination of wishful thinking, short memory, the rarity of tornadoes, and a distorted sense of "here" and "there." Protection has been justified by oversimplifying the facts. One can argue, correctly, that a particular town has never been hit by a tornado, but ten tornadoes may have touched down outside town in the past thirty years.

The belief that tornadoes do not hit "here" but always seem to hit "north of town" or "south of the river" ignores some very simple mathematics. "Here" may be a small town with an area of one square mile. "There" may be anywhere within visual sighting from the water tower, perhaps 10 miles in all directions. Therefore, if the town has an area of one square mile, "there" has an area of more than 300 square miles. A tornado touchdown would be three hundred times more likely "outside" town than in town. "Protection" does not come from hills, or mounds, or the joining of two rivers but from the same source as protection from falling comets, meteors, or asteroids—the laws of probability, the very low probability of rare events.

There is no reason to think that rivers have any effect on tornadoes. We are not sure just what effect steep ridges and deep valleys have on mature tornadoes. Tornadoes passed seemingly unaffected over mountain ridges 3,000 feet high during the "Super Outbreak" of April 3, 1974. Dozens of tornadoes have crossed the Mississippi River, from near its source in Minnesota to its mouth in Louisiana. Both sides of the river, including its confluence with the Missouri near St. Louis, have seen devastating tornadoes.

MYTH #2: THE SOUTHWEST CORNER OF A BASEMENT IS THE SAFEST LOCATION DURING A TORNADO

The part of a building facing the approaching tornado (often the southwest) is the least safe part of the basement, not the safest. This is also true of the aboveground portion of buildings. In most tornadoes more houses will be shifted off their foundations than blown completely away. That movement can cause, and has pushed, chunks of the concrete foundation onto people and killed them.

The misconception that the southwest corner of a building, both above and below ground, afforded the best protection did not originate in scientific comparison and testing. The faulty logic was that when the house blew away, falling debris (boards, cars, dead pigs, etc.) would be propelled over the southwest corner and carried to the northeast corner of the basement.

The advice to seek shelter on the side of a house facing the oncoming tornado dates at least to the nineteenth century and Finley's book *Tornadoes*. Finley italicized the following incredible piece of misinformation: *"Under no circumstances, whether in a building or in a cellar, ever take a position in a northeast room, in a northeast corner, or an east room, or against an east wall."* He also added the time-wasting suggestion that furniture should be removed from the west-facing room. Although relatively few people probably read the book, the advice was quoted in many newspapers. It is possible that in one of his damage surveys Finley came upon the scene of fatalities that occurred in the northeast portion of a poorly constructed house. However, the house may have simply fallen over, which influenced his thinking. Today houses are better constructed. Trailers may flip, roll, or disintegrate, but even they do not just fall over.

Finley's assumptions went largely unchallenged until 1966, when Joseph Eagleman (1967) of the University of Kansas undertook a survey of destroyed houses after the Topeka tornado of 1966. Eagleman's study showed that the south and southwest corners of houses, the direction of approach for the Topeka tornado, were the least safe areas and that the north side was the safest, both on the first floor and in the basement. He repeated the study in Texas after the Lubbock tornado of May 11, 1970 (Eagleman and Muirhead 1971). The results were even more striking. The southwest portion was unsafe in 75 percent of those damaged homes, double the percentage of unsafe areas in the northeast part.

Ignorance of Finley's suggestions, combined with common sense, has saved lives in the past. In Georgia, at the Pacolet Mills near Gainesville, 550 people ran to the northeast corner of the building as the tornado approached from the southwest on June 1, 1903. That corner was the only part of the building that was not destroyed. At least 50 people died in other Gainesville fabric mills on that day, and more than 40 more died in frail houses near the mills. Clearly, the parts of a building that face the oncoming tornado are the least safe.

MYTH #3: OPENING WINDOWS TO EQUALIZE AIR PRESSURE WILL SAVE A ROOF, OR EVEN A HOME, FROM DESTRUCTION BY A TORNADO

The idea that moving one thin pane of glass protects a roof or a house from one of the most violent natural forces on the planet has a certain absurdity. Like Myth #2, it is probably born of wishful thinking and faulty logic, from people's need to do something, anything. In reality opening windows is a dangerous and useless waste of time and could actually be harmful to both the occupants and the house itself.

To get to the very center of a mature tornado, where the pressure may be low enough to cause some explosive effects, the windows would have to endure 100- to 200-mph winds in the outer walls of the vortex. Those winds would be laden with boards, stones, cars, trees, telephone poles, and the neighbor's roof shingles as well as wind pressure of more than 100 pounds per square foot. This barrage would blow more than enough ventilation holes in the building to allow any pressure difference to be equalized.

Even with the windows closed, most houses and commercial buildings have enough openings to vent the pressure difference in the time that it takes for a tornado to pass. Engineers at Texas Tech point out that the pressure drop inside a tornado with 260-mph winds is only about 10 percent, or 1.4 pounds per square inch (Minor, McDonald, and Mehta 1977). A violent tornado would blow apart a house before this 10 percent pressure drop ever arrived. Venting of air to relieve air pressure would not be an issue, although most buildings can vent this difference through its normal openings in about three seconds.

If the home owner opens the wrong window, air can rush in and blow up the building like a balloon. There are many unknowns. A resident probably does not know where the construction weak points are. In addition, the wind fields in a passing tornado are very complex and constantly changing. It is not possible to predict the strongest direction of attack. The best advice, from every engineer with whom I have discussed this, is to leave the windows alone and get to shelter as fast as possible. One should not think first of the house roof but of the impact of one's death on one's family, or of oneself unnecessarily crippled or scarred for life.

MYTH #4: A TORNADO WILL SUCK WATER FROM A SWIMMING POOL OR A WELL

Even a 10 percent (100 millibars, or 3 inches of mercury) lowering of air pressure is not enough vacuum to suck large amounts of water into the funnel in a short time. If a tornado with a central pressure of 26.92 inches of mercury (about 10% lower than the normal air pressure of 29.92 inches) were to remain in one location over a lake, the water would rise only about 3 feet inside the funnel (Minor, McDonald, and Mehta 1977). The actual pressure drop inside most intense tornadoes is probably less than 10 percent. The largest drops measured are only about 0.7 inch, or about 2 percent. A 2 percent drop in air pressure would cause only about an 8-inch rise in water level.

In each studied case of a tornado emptying a swimming pool, it was found that the pool had been emptied beforehand. In 1975, a year of serious research into this idea, tornadoes passed directly over several swimming pools without removing a measurable amount of water. On December 5, 1975, a tornado at Tulsa, Oklahoma, completely destroyed a motel adjacent to a swimming pool. The pool remained completely full. A widely reported incident of a pool being sucked dry occurred at Omaha on May 6, 1975. The report originated with someone who observed a dry pool after the tornado had passed. He was unaware that the pool had been drained for cleaning. The true story, unlike the original version, was less interesting and was never broadcast nationally. Like so many tornado-related myths, this one is perpetuated by reporters in search of a good story.

To empty a pool of water, the tornado would have to be of a smaller width than the pool and stay directly over the pool spraying water into the air (fig. 8.1). Crossing a lake, a tornado can spray water to heights of several hundred feet and blow water into an advancing wave 6 feet or more in height. However, the low pressure in the funnel raises the level of the water in the funnel just a matter of inches.

A considerable amount of water can be blown from the surface of a pond or pool in just a few seconds, and shallow rivers may have had their bottoms exposed very briefly. Some people have insisted that the level of water in wells dropped during a tornado passage. This has never been documented, but the water certainly was not sucked out.

MYTH #5: MOBILE HOMES ATTRACT TORNADOES

Perhaps the most persistent of all myths is that mobile homes somehow attract tornadoes or that the orderly rows in mobile home parks promote the formation of tornadoes. The degree to which the alignment of mobile homes can influence convergence and rotation of air is probably very small. It is large enough to trigger formation of a dust devil but not large enough to have any influence on tornado formation. The largest and most intense dust devil that I ever witnessed was on a 100°F day outside Des Moines, Iowa. It remained stationary in a large trucking terminal, at the intersection of several lanes of parked trucks. The airflow between the trucks was undoubtedly the controlling factor in its formation. But the energy of this system is minor compared with that of thunderstorms. A mere gust of wind and the shade of a passing cloud interrupted the system and the truck terminal dust devil disintegrated.

There are two explanations for the supposed propensity of tornadoes to hit mobile homes. The first is the self-fulfilling prophecy of the news media. News personnel, aware of the belief that mobile homes attract tornadoes, report the occurrence and end up reinforcing the myth. Dozens of destroyed barns and thousands of uprooted trees are rarely mentioned, for that is not deemed to be newsworthy.

The second explanation lies in the fact that mobile homes are ideal detectors of small tornadoes. They are lightweight enough to be destroyed by even the weakest tornadoes, yet expensive enough to make news when

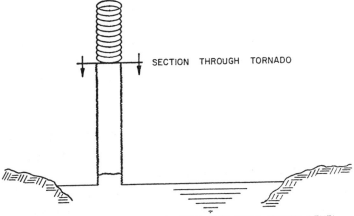

SECTION THROUGH TORNADO

(a) SMALL TORNADO OVER A POND CAN RAISE WATER LEVEL ONLY A FEW FEET AT MOST

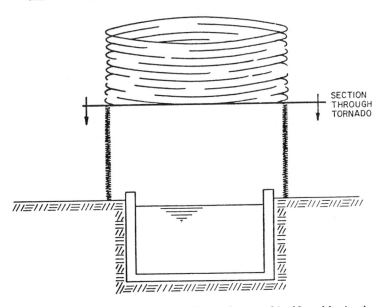

SECTION THROUGH TORNADO

Fig. 8.1. Only a small tornado, smaller than the pool or pond itself, could raise the level of water in a pool. A large tornado cannot "lift" water out of a pool, but it could blow some water out of it. Drawing courtesy of Texas Tech University Institute for Disaster Research.

they are. Unanchored mobile homes may be overturned by winds of only 60 to 70 mph. Many small, weak tornadoes may go unreported, unless they hit a trailer. The number of mobile homes hit by tornadoes seems destined to increase, given their expanding use as affordable single-family housing.

Several times a year meteorologists at government laboratories are approached by people who believe that they have discovered the answer to the question of why mobile homes attract tornadoes. Often the idea is that, in rotating, the tornado turned itself into a generator of electricity and therefore into a powerful electromagnet, despite the lack of any copper wire. Thus the tornado becomes attracted to the metal in mobile homes. These amateur theorists ignore the fact that magnetic anomalies have never been recorded near a passing tornado. They ignore case after case in which tornadoes have bypassed trailer parks, railroad yards, and truck terminals, and continued their nearly straight-line path uninterrupted. When I have pointed this out, they have replied, "Only some tornadoes are magnetic." Myths die hard.

MYTH #6: TORNADOES FOLLOW RIVERS

There are two possible explanations for the popular myth that tornadoes follow rivers. The first is that there is no direction of tornado movement that is not roughly parallel to a stream. If the tornado path is perpendicular to the main stream, then it is parallel to some tributary. Suggesting that the stream influences the path of the tornado is a convenient observation made in search of a simplistic answer. Second, those tornadoes that follow rivers are more likely to encounter large numbers of buildings, receive wider publicity, be remembered longer, and be well documented. Human habitation has always clustered along rivers. The chances of encountering a series of farms or small towns would be greater for tornadoes that do happen, by pure chance, to follow rivers.

MYTH #7: TORNADOES CAN PRODUCE WINDS THAT APPROACH OR EXCEED THE SPEED OF SOUND (738 MPH)

Sometimes it takes only one widely read story, with a "logical" explanation, to enhance, spread, or even begin a myth. Captain Roy Hall's (1951) story in *Weatherwise* magazine is one such example.

On May 3, 1948, Hall, a retired U.S. Army captain, made a detailed set of observations as he looked up into a tornado at McKinney, Texas. (See chap. 12 for additional details of this account.) His house was unroofed, and he stared directly up into the base of the funnel as it hovered overhead. He noted,

> During pistol practice in the Army, when light was favorable, I have seen bullets from a .45 pistol flash from gun to target. The bullets have a known velocity of 825 feet a second (563 mph). The white planks from the house moved at a speed equal to, if not greater than, those of the bullets, which would establish the velocity of the tornado's rotation at close to 600 miles per hour. This, I believe, is conservative. My own conviction is that the funnel was spinning faster than the speed of sound, accounting, in some way beyond my knowledge, for the total lack of noise within it.

Captain Hall's conclusion concerning the speed of funnel rotation was vastly overstated. He may not have known, in 1948, that objects exceeding the speed of sound produce loud shock waves, or sonic booms, not silence. His eagerness to interpret and explain tornadoes, based on limited experience, is shared by many people. Such observations, devoid of measurements and documentation and yet often repeated, give rise to myths that may spread more readily than the truth, largely because they are easier and more entertaining.

MYTH #8: IF TREES AND HOMES ARE TWISTED, IT MUST HAVE BEEN DONE BY A TORNADO

The shifting and twisting of a house on its foundation by high winds has nothing to do with the rotating winds of a tornado. A poorly anchored house can rotate on its foundation in strong straight-line winds. Houses are often asymmetrical, with added rooms and a garage. One corner might be anchored better than the others. The house rotates in a straight-line wind when the weaker corners give way and the stronger one holds tight. A bathroom drain could be the strongest anchoring point. If an added garage has a large surface area, the wind pressure may be much greater on one end of the house than the other.

The typical house or tree is far smaller than the diameter of most tornadoes. Houses experience winds from opposite directions on opposite ends at the same time. They will experience nearly straight-line winds as one side of a tornado passes over. Trees often appear to twist, even in straight-line windstorms. Most trees have more branches on one side than the other. The wind will apply more of a force, or torque, to the side with more leaves, and the tree will indeed twist. A twisted tree should never be used as evidence of the passage of a tornado.

MYTH #9: IF FALLEN TREES ARE POINTED IN THE SAME DIRECTION, THE EVENT WAS NOT A TORNADO

Normally tornadoes leave a debris pattern that shows rotation and/or convergence. Fallen trees often point inward toward the center of the vortex. However, a tornado can leave straight-line damage patterns, despite the rotation and convergence. For instance, if a cyclonically rotating tornado is moving forward at 50 mph and rotating at 100 mph, it can produce straight-line damage on one side of the path. On the right side the tornado damage will be caused by the forward-moving 150-mph winds. This is the sum of the 50- and 100-mph air movements. On the left side of the tornado the components would effectively subtract, to produce a 50-mph wind, which is not damaging at all.

Since 1950 only a few killer tornadoes have missed being officially counted. On February 1, 1955, the deadliest of these "unrecorded" events occurred at Commerce Landing, Mississippi (Lee 1955). What was seen as a well-defined, cone-shaped funnel formed over the Mississippi River and killed at least twenty people, most of them students at an elementary school. The teacher lost her life trying to get the children into ditches along the road. Her car was carried 300 yards. The body of one dead child was carried about half a mile. Although a funnel was seen and heavy objects were thrown long distances, the event was not officially called a tornado. A Weather Bureau survey team noted that since all debris was thrown in one direction and trees were pointed in one direction, the events should not be listed as a tornado.

The reverse situation is also a myth. That fallen trees are pointing in different directions does not guarantee that a tornado was involved. Successive,

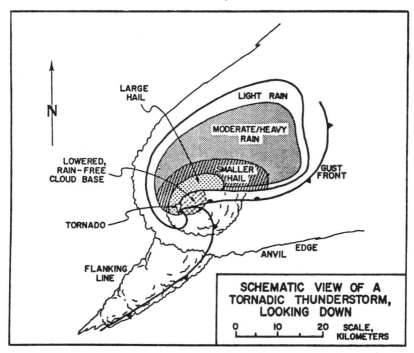

Fig. 8.2. This cross section shows the distribution of precipitation in a supercell. Hail can be swept around the mesocyclone and fall either in front or in back of the tornado. Drawing by Charles Doswell.

overlapping microbursts blowing down trees from different directions can create confusing damage patterns. Microbursts move down and outward from thunderstorms, producing roaring sounds like tornadoes. They can unroof houses and cause narrow, tornado-sized damage swaths. It is very difficult to determine what kind of windstorm blew down a narrow swath of trees in a forest, even when the event was witnessed. Most such treefall events are not documented as tornadoes.

MYTH #10: TORNADOES ARE ALWAYS PRECEDED BY HAIL

Hail can both follow and precede a tornado (fig. 8.2). Hail can be expected ahead of a tornado, because most of the precipitation is on the front side of the storm. But the falling hail can also be swept around a mesocyclone, as part of the hook echo on radar. That hail would fall primarily behind a tornado rather than in front of it. Therefore, hail before a tornado is common but not a reliable tornado warning.

Myths are difficult to dispel, and new ones appear unexpectedly. People hold tightly to them, just in case they might be true. A single suggestion by a respected but careless television anchorperson to open windows when a tornado is approaching might undo a decade's worth of preaching by the NWS and local civil defense officials. The degree to which a belief in such myths affects safety is unknown. The next chapter, on safety, includes a few other ideas that might be considered myths.

CHAPTER 9

TORNADO
SAFETY

On Sunday, August 10, 1924, 4 miles east of Thurman, Colorado, the Garrett, Yoder, and Kuhns families gathered at Henry Kuhns's ranch after a Mennonite service. Twenty-seven people had just finished a harvest celebration dinner. Just after 1:00 P.M. one of the men spotted a tornado to the north, moving in the direction of an adjoining ranch. In the Mennonite tradition of assisting people after disasters, Henry Kuhns and eight other men left to see whether help was needed. When they saw that no buildings had been hit, they returned to the ranch to witness the most tragic moment of their lives. It was also the deadliest tornado disaster in the history of Colorado. What may have been the next member of that tornado family was bearing down from the west, directly at the ranch house. Eighteen women and children inside were apparently unaware of the approach of an intense, 100-yard-wide funnel. The men drove south as fast as possible, but, as they came to within 200 yards of the front gate, the structure was ripped apart and its occupants hurled into the air. Ten of the eighteen people died; nine of the ten were children.

On Sunday, March 27, 1994, the congregation of the Goshen United Methodist Church near Piedmont, Alabama, had gathered at 11:00 A.M. for Palm Sunday services. The area had been under a tornado watch since 9:30 A.M. Thunderstorms along a stalled cold front were expected to produce destructive tornadoes in Alabama all day. At 10:49 A.M. a tornado warning was issued for Calhoun County and extended to Cherokee County at 11:27 A.M. The Goshen church is in Cherokee County, near the Calhoun County line. The tornado that was to hit the church touched down at 10:51 A.M., near Ragland, and headed toward the Piedmont-Goshen area, 32 miles to the northeast. More than eighty calls to the 911 emergency line were placed, warning of a tornado to the southwest of Piedmont. It seems that none of this information reached the Goshen church.

At 11:39 A.M. an inflow jet at the south edge of the tornado blew in the 18-foot-high, 60-foot-wide south wall of the Goshen church sanctuary during the musical pageant part of the service. The heavy timber and steel gable roof lifted and shifted. No longer supported and connected, the roof and walls of the sanctuary fell onto the 147 people inside (fig. 9.1). Twenty of them were crushed to death, and ninety others were injured. Victims ranged from a 6′8″, 300-pound sergeant in the Alabama National Guard to the four-year-old daughter of the minister. The twenty deaths at the Goshen church were not the result of some unpredicted, unseen, rain-wrapped tornado that swooped down on a well-constructed church and leveled it. Early news reports on the day of the tornado hinted that such was the case.

The tornado hit the church 48 minutes after it had touched down and 12 minutes after the county had been put under a tornado warning. The 60-foot-long wall was unreinforced concrete masonry, with no intervening columns or lateral braces. The long hallway leading to the sanctuary remained virtually untouched and would have provided a safe haven during the storm.

TORNADO AWARENESS AND THE DECLINING DEATH TOLL

The Goshen and Thurman disasters occurred seventy years apart, yet they have important things in common. Tornado forecasts and warnings were not factors in either case. They were nonexistent in 1924 and irrelevant

Fig. 9.1. A heavy, poorly supported roof fell on the congregation at the Goshen United Methodist Church during Palm Sunday services on March 27, 1994. Copyright Tim Marshall.

to the situation at the Goshen church in 1994, since no one was listening, even though both a watch and a warning were in effect. Both tornadoes would have been seen by anyone standing watch outside the buildings. The deaths occurred because of a lack of awareness or a lack of the occupants' willingness to act. For much of the population, lack of awareness was the rule in 1924. Today it is the exception.

Despite an increasing U.S. population, the number of annual deaths caused by tornadoes began to drop after reaching a peak in the decade 1920–29 (fig. 9.2). Conventional wisdom suggests that this number should have risen along with the population as there was no tornado forecasting at this time. However, societal changes that occurred in the United States between 1920 and 1940 may have had a role in the declining death toll. One factor may have been the migration to cities in the North and in California that began as people abandoned farms on both the Great Plains and in the

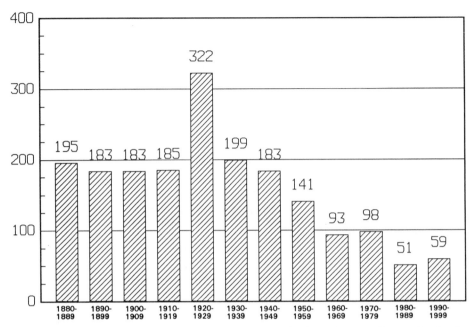

Fig. 9.2. This graph of the average annual tornado-related deaths in the United States, by decade, shows that the decline in fatalities began in the 1930s.

rural South during the Depression. During this time also, awareness about disasters and hazards began to increase, even among the illiterate part of the population. The 1920s saw the birth of radio; the late 1940s witnessed the beginnings of television. The massive manufacturing effort in World War II was accompanied by storm safety programs in factories and by the creation of more than two hundred spotter groups.

I am suggesting that the number of deaths is greatly influenced by the overall change in public awareness of hazards, as well as forecasting technology. Both are absolutely essential. When improved tornado forecasting and federally organized awareness programs came on the scene in the 1950s and 1960s, an accelerated decline began again, despite an ever-increasing population. As of this writing, the last one hundred-death tornado was in 1953, the first full year of forecasting. Awareness and warning technology continued to improve in the 1970s as supercells became better understood. In the 1980s and 1990s television meteorologists in tornado-prone areas stepped up awareness efforts. Stations acquired their own Doppler radar units and produced their own tornado specials with the latest videos. Competition among stations became fierce, with more information as a selling point. Some stations began to compete for the chance of getting a tornado on live television by hiring chasers and outfitting them with remote links back to the studio. The result has been a gradual decline in the annual tornado death toll through the 1980s, after which it seems to have leveled off at about twenty-five to sixty per year.

GENERAL SAFETY

Awareness is the key to tornado safety. Personal and family safety begins with awareness of local weather conditions and proper safety procedures for a variety of places and situations. Ideally, one should know where the safest shelter would be if you had 10 minutes' warning and where it would be if you had just 10 seconds' warning.

Each household and business should develop a tornado safety plan, well ahead of time. This includes determining where the most up-to-the-minute weather information would be available. During any severe thunderstorm or tornado watch, that media outlet—whether it is commercial radio, NOAA Weather Radio, television, a police scanner, or all four—should be monitored closely.

You should not depend on sirens. They may not be sounded in time or sounded at all. This could be due to a power outage caused by the storm or failure of the siren itself. Tornadoes are rare enough so that a community can gradually become complacent and fail to test and maintain the sirens. Be sure you understand what the siren means in your community. Is it a warning to take immediate shelter or an alert to get better prepared? Different communities have different philosophies about the use of a siren. City or county emergency management coordinators can give you that information.

Your first response should be to get to shelter. It should not be to grab the camcorder or run to a window. This may be very hard for some people, given that the most spectacular thing they will ever witness is getting closer and more impressive every second. But the flying glass and incoming debris could make it the last thing that you ever witness.

Be aware but not panic-stricken. Tornadoes are extremely rare events. Even in the most tornado-prone areas, any given frame house probably will not be destroyed totally, on average, more than once in 100,000 years (see chap. 14). In much of the country that number is less often than once in 1,000,000 years. But awareness is especially necessary during times of predicted or actual severe weather. Just as with a lottery, there will be a few winners (or losers in this case) somewhere, despite the overwhelming odds against it. Having a plan and rehearsing it can make a big difference. Many states have a Tornado Awareness Week aimed at getting people to develop individual safety plans.

SAFETY IN A FRAME HOUSE

The first rules for safety in a frame house without a basement is to get to the lowest level of the structure, avoid windows, and put as many walls as possible between you and the tornado. Objects like boards and branches become spears in tornadic winds.

Go to an interior closet or bathroom with no windows. The short-span walls may provide a life-saving additional degree of strength. Cover your body with a sleeping bag, cushions, or blankets. Protect your head as much as possible. Placing a metal trash can over your head may mean the difference between having a headache and being dead. The southwest corner of the house, or whatever part is facing the oncoming tornado, is the least safe. That area will probably have direct penetration of high-speed debris carried by the wind.

It is not uncommon to see only the bathtub remaining on the lower floor of a house in the aftermath of a tornado. The tub can be a planned destination if you have only a few seconds' warning. A bathroom often has extra bracing used to hold the various fixtures. In a frame house without a basement, the tub and commode will be anchored into the ground. In that type of house, an aboveground shelter can be built into the house. The civil engineers at Texas Tech recommend that the designated safety area be windowless and reinforced with four layers of 3/4-inch plywood in the walls and ceiling. The floor *must* be anchored directly to a concrete slab.

The safest place is in the basement, but you still need something sturdy under which you can hide, like a work bench or a staircase. A small room designed as a shelter is even better. Be sure that the entire family is aware of the location of the safest area ahead of time. Also be sure that the area is not below a piano or another heavy object on the first floor and not in a path likely to be taken by a falling chimney.

Tornado-related deaths in basements are rare. They total only about 20 to 30 out of more than 11,000 deaths since 1880. None was under a stairwell or heavy table. To my knowledge, there is only one recorded instance in which someone was killed by large debris (a wooden beam) blown into a basement. This took place on June 8, 1953, in Washtenaw County, Michigan. The other fatalities were under collapsed chimneys or under concrete basement walls that were pulled over as the house shifted.

SAFETY IN SCHOOLS AND OTHER PUBLIC BUILDINGS

No warning sirens were sounded on August 28, 1990, at the high school in Plainfield, Illinois. More than one hundred students and coaches were on the junior varsity and varsity football fields. About thirty girls were in the gym preparing for a volleyball game, and about thirty teachers and administrators were preparing for the next day's opening of school. When intense lightning approached the school from the northwest, the football coach ordered everyone into the gym. With the onset of hail, the players began running at full speed. They were completely unaware that churning toward them, hidden in rain just a few miles away, was the most violent and deadly tornado in the area's history.

The exact sequence of events in the next few minutes was never completely sorted out. Debris flying from nearby houses was seen by several people, including the principal, who rang the fire alarm. The coaches, reacting to the alarm and the storm, rushed all the students out of the gym into the corridors. With students screaming and crying, and ceilings collapsing behind them, they ran and huddled next to the lockers and walls, as they had been trained to do every year that they were in school. No student was seriously injured. As winds of 200 mph ripped across the school, the other people in the building were too far from interior corridors. They scrambled for shelter wherever they could find it. The track coach, a custodian, and a volunteer worker did not find shelter in time; they were among the twenty-nine fatalities along the 16-mile path of the tornado.

It is not the purpose of this book, nor should it be the purpose of any book, to provide a detailed and specific list of individual school safety rules. Schools and other public buildings are built so differently that each one needs its own unique set of emergency plans with designated shelter areas. This plan should be drawn up by local emergency management officials.

Generally, students should first be moved into a sheltered hallway on the lowest floor of the building as fast as possible. Auditoriums, gymnasiums, cafeterias, or any other rooms with large unreinforced walls and/or wide-span roofs should be avoided. The safety plan should include procedures that deal with every situation, including morning arrival on buses, classroom and lunch situations, special events in the auditorium and on school grounds, and school bus loading in the afternoon. Planning for problems during the morning arrival of students is especially important in the southeastern states, where strong or violent tornadoes have occurred at almost every hour of the day and night.

Each school should have designated safe areas with steel-reinforced concrete. The safest corridors are those with no potential openings (doors or windows) to the outside at either end. The least safe are those with openings to the south, southwest, or west—the likeliest directions for a tornado's approach. Any hallway with lots of glass is unsafe. Corridors that open to the direction of the tornado's approach can turn into wind tunnels full of debris, with glass, stones, and metal becoming dangerous missiles. If the school has no interior corridors in which to hide, those with potential openings to the north and east would be the least dangerous. Students should crouch down with faces to the floor in a protective position, on knees and elbows, with hands covering neck and head. If there is no time to get to the hallway, they should get under tables and chairs. No one should open or close the windows.

Texas Tech has developed relatively inexpensive guidelines for school design and construction. They have shown that schools need not be constructed to look like concrete bunkers to provide adequate protection against the most violent tornadoes. Typically, a media center or other room near the middle of the school can be strengthened so that it can protect against even F5 tornadoes. The protected area is surrounded by corridors and contains 8 inches of steel reinforced concrete in the walls and roof.

Such reinforcements of a central area add only about 4 percent to the cost of a school if they are part of the initial construction.

The Plainfield High School story is not the only example of lives being saved in corridors. Students survived in the halls of Xenia High School in Ohio while the rest of the building was being ripped apart by an F5 tornado on April 3, 1974. The high school at Pleasant Hill, Missouri, was hit by a tornado on May 4, 1977. Some 550 students crouched in the halls of the north wing while another 100 found shelter in the basement-level kitchen and storage area. It took three minutes to get students to designated safety areas.

In Pleasant Hill, twenty-five homes were destroyed (F3) and two people died. The high school and elementary school sustained several million dollars in damage. A few students sustained minor injuries. The school gym was a good place to avoid. Its destruction appears to have been due to the weak, freestanding-wall design. This type of wall is often blown inward under the influence of what is called "stagnation pressure" on the side of the building toward the wind, the windward side. On the leeward side, away from the wind, the wall blows outward, as an area of low pressure forms on the far side of the building. The removal of any wall could cause the roof to collapse. If the roof is torn off, the walls may become vulnerable to even F0 winds.

A school should have an evaluation by knowledgeable people who were not involved with the original building design and construction or with its current administration. Independent observers will be more objective in determining whether a building was designed with safety as a high priority.

Many states have a Tornado Awareness Day, during which schools practice tornado drills. As has been found in virtually every human condition, practice makes the difference. Students who ridicule the drills as silly and a waste of time will, through enforced practice, know immediately what to do in an emergency. This was proven at Plainfield when the corridors were filled and proper positions were assumed with little instruction.

School buses should not leave school grounds during a tornado or severe-storm warning. If the bus is caught on the road in the path of a tornado or other extreme winds, the rules for cars should be followed. School buses have a high center of gravity and large surface area. They are even more likely than cars to be overturned in high winds, even in non-tornadic high winds.

Schools, emergency management officials, and the NWS should have well-established links of communication, even at odd hours of the early morning. What follows is an example of why this is necessary. At 6:30 A.M. on November 23, 1992, school buses from Elizabeth City, North Carolina, fanned out into the path of an approaching tornado. The tornado, or tornado family, had been on the ground for three hours. Neither emergency management nor school officials responded to an NWS tornado warning for counties southwest of town. The warning for Elizabeth City came at 6:48 A.M. All buses were on the road, without radios. The tornado hit at 7:24 A.M. Fortunately, there were no injuries when one bus was thrown from the road. The driver and twenty-one children were watching safely from a ditch as their 28,000-pound school bus was hurled 75 yards. There are so many different situations that can develop, it seems inevitable that tragedies will occur occasionally.

In general, the rules for most public buildings such as hospitals, nursing homes, and office buildings are similar to the rules for schools: stay away from glass, such as at windows or entrances; get into the innermost portion of the building on the lowest floor; protect your head and make yourself as small a target as possible by crouching down. Do not use elevators, which may stop when power is lost.

Long-span buildings such as factories, gymnasiums, warehouses, auditoriums, churches, department stores, indoor pools, and theaters can be especially dangerous. Most or all of the roof structure is supported by outside walls. The wind pressure can cause the failure of the windward wall, with catastrophic results for the occupants of the building as walls and the roof collapse. Restrooms are among the safest areas. Their plumbing, short-span walls, and metal partitions add strength. The corner of the building might be safer than the middle of a long wall.

If there is no time to go anywhere, get up against heavy shelving, under seats or heavy counters, anything that will support falling debris or deflect flying debris. Protect your head, and do not go to the parking lot.

SAFETY ON THE ROAD

On June 10, 1938, a large dusty tornado was clearly visible 8 miles northwest of Clyde, Texas, as it moved slowly to the southeast, heading for the center of town. The half hour the funnel took to move only a few miles seemed like an eternity. It looked like a vast column of brown earth sitting in a big brown bowl. As it neared the town, and the end of its path, the column swung to the west and into the west side of Clyde. Most residents were alerted, and at least one family headed west in a car, to avoid the funnel.

Just as the family was fleeing the tornado from the north edge of town, the tornado entered its shrinking stage. It made a rapid turn to its right, rather than to its left, which is more common. The tornado overtook the car, with tragic results. Four of the six occupants were killed. The two children who survived were found near the car engine, half a mile from the other bodies. Ten other people died as nine houses in one development literally vanished, with bodies carried up to a half mile. Railroad cars were tossed like toys. More than fifty thousand sightseers jammed the town the next weekend. This sequence of events has been repeated many times since.

One the most dangerous places to be in a strong or violent tornado, short of standing up and facing it in the open, seems to be in a motor vehicle. Every year they have proved to be steel coffins. The standard safety guidelines for cars are to stop the vehicle and get away from it and other vehicles so that they do not roll over on you; lie flat in a gully, a ditch, or a low spot; and protect your head. The ditch should be on the side of the road away from the approaching tornado and not close to large trees. Beware of flash flooding. Do not go to a grove of trees, where even peripheral winds can cause a multiton tree to fall on you.

It may be suicidal to try to outrun a tornado in urban or suburban areas where clogged intersections, downed trees, and power lines can block traffic. The occupants of the car may find themselves helplessly stranded, unable to drive in any direction, with no time to find a ditch before the air becomes filled with debris. Entrance ramps to limited-access highways become hopelessly congested.

One of the most lethal examples of collective poor judgment in the face of a tornado occurred in Texas on April 10, 1979. On that afternoon a violent tornado passed across the south side of Wichita Falls, destroying more than 3,000 houses and damaging about 1,000 others. About 10,000 people were in those houses at the time, but of the 43 traumatic deaths, only 5 were in houses (Glass et al. 1980). Twenty-six were in cars trying to drive out of the storm's path. Eight of the families with deaths in cars had abandoned homes that had only minor damage or no damage at all.

In personal conversations with Wichita Falls survivors, I have heard stories of traffic backups that might have been death traps had the tornado's path been slightly different. Traffic on Kell Boulevard, parallel to and a half mile north of the tornado track, was moving at 80 mph. Cars on limited-access U.S. 287, which crossed the track of the tornado, were leaving the area at a reported 110 mph, with pickup trucks going at high speed in the grass median. Attempting access to these roads might have been as dangerous as facing the tornado itself.

In rural areas people have devised their own rules for decades and will probably continue to do so. Many have left their homes (fig. 9.3) and driven at right angles to the path of the approaching tornado. Others have had an experience more like that of a family in Lyon County, Iowa, on April 26, 1986. Their pickup truck was still in the driveway when a fence post pierced a window and killed a young girl.

Other high tornado death tolls in automobiles had nothing to do with efforts to escape the tornado. On November 15, 1989, twelve of the twenty-one deaths at Huntsville, Alabama, occurred as people were going about their daily business. All were trying to get home from work in rush hour traffic.

Ideas about the danger of being inside a car while in a tornado are based on common sense and observations of mangled cars and mangled car occupants. They are not based on controlled scientific tests. Tom Schmidlin of Kent State University has suggested to me that getting out of a car at a crowded intersection, as at Huntsville in 1989, might have been more dangerous than staying put. However, I cannot envision any way in which research could be done to test this speculation. This is a perplexing public safety issue for which there may never be any hard and fast rules that guarantee survival. To date, there has been no conclusive scientific research indicating whether a parked car is safer than a parked mobile home. Changing the rules about whether or not to leave a car or a trailer might not significantly change the overall death toll. It is possible that with different rules, different people will die under different circumstances.

SAFETY IN MOBILE HOMES

About 100 miles to the east-northeast of the Goshen church on that same day in 1994, six members of the Turner family were huddled in the

Fig. 9.3. A tornado is seen passing across the Thomas farm near Beaver City, Nebraska, on April 23, 1989. Merrillee Thomas photographed her daughter, Audra, standing about a mile from the funnel. Copyright Merrillee Thomas.

central hallway of their double-wide mobile home on top of Henderson Mountain in Pickens County, Georgia. They were apparently aware of the approaching tornado. Perhaps they had seen the funnel. It was said to have looked like a rotating fog bank, filled with exploding trees. Perhaps they had heard the roar or felt the ground shake. The mile-wide tornado was moving through dense forest at 60 mph. According to survey team member Tim Marshall (1995), about 1,000 trees per second were uprooted or snapping, assuming a 20-foot tree spacing with 60,000 trees per square mile.

Perhaps the Turners did not consider their house to be a true mobile home, since it was not expected to be moved. Whatever the reason, they chose not to follow the rules for residents faced with an imminent tornado.

The unanchored mobile home was lifted from its block supports. It flew 300 yards, the length of three football fields, to the north before hitting the ground. Five members of the family were killed. One teenage boy apparently survived the impact. He bled to death from a neck wound inflicted by a tree branch before rescue workers could clear a path through downed trees. The next night it was possible to stand on a hill in northern Georgia and see the track of the tornado extending to the horizon. The path was marked by bonfires built to help clear the fallen trees that blocked roads.

In any given year between 25 and 70 percent of all tornado-related deaths will occur in mobile homes. They may simply overturn, or they may disintegrate into a deadly mass of flying appliances, furniture, and sheet metal. The standard rules, given in innumerable government pamphlets, are as follows. Do not stay in a mobile home during a tornado. Even those with a secure tie-down system cannot withstand the force of tornadic winds. Plan ahead; make arrangements to stay with friends or neighbors who have basements and go there if a tornado watch is issued. If a tornado warning is given, leave your mobile home and seek shelter nearby. Lie flat in a ditch or ravine and put your arms over your head. Do not take shelter under your mobile home. Encourage your mobile home community to build a tornado shelter if you live in a tornado-prone area.

Some people may find it odd to advise mobile home residents to leave their home in the face of a tornado. The reason for that advice is apparent, however, when one sees the twisted wreckage of a mobile home park after it has been hit by a tornado. Telling someone to run out of a building into the face of a tornado, into what might be an enormous blender of debris from nearby mobile homes, seems as suicidal as having them stay indoors. The choice is obviously between two very poor options. For mobile home dwellers, there is no substitute for a plan and a steel-reinforced concrete shelter.

The relatively low tornado death toll in the United States is, of course, not a miracle or an accident. The NWS, local media, emergency management officials, and schools have been dispensing tornado safety advice for decades. As a result people do head for basements, closets, and bathrooms just as they are supposed to. In the future the growing elderly population may result in a gradually increasing death toll, but the greater dangers may be apathy and greed.

Apathy is a product of the rarity of tornadoes. Any given town, even one in tornado alley, may be hit by an intense tornado only once in several centuries. That large span of time can breed indifference and complacency. The 1938 tornado at Clyde, Texas, was the first killer tornado in Callahan County in sixteen years and only the second in its history. That a major tornado has not hit your area within anyone's memory should not inhibit the creation of a personal safety plan and discussion of it with family, congregation, or fellow workers.

Greed, in the form of shortcuts in construction, can play a part in building failures. Tornadoes need not be involved. But the growing population of the United States is gathering in larger groups more often than ever before. The unwillingness to cancel a sporting event during a severe situation could lead to a major catastrophe (see chap. 15). The NWS and emergency preparedness coordinators will need to intensify their educational efforts. They must walk a fine line between letting down their guard and crying wolf too often.

Tornado safety can be summed up in very few words. Get as low as possible. Get behind as many walls as possible. Forget the windows. Have a plan. Use the media to get watches and warnings. Watch the skies.

CHAPTER 10

APPROACHING THE
UNAPPROACHABLE

One might think that the exact opposite of a tornado safety program would be a program whose object is to arrange a tornado encounter. Storm "chasing" is dangerous, but the most serious threats do not come from tornadoes themselves.

THE FLIGHTS OF STIRLING COLGATE

On May 19, 1982, sirens wailed across Pampa, Texas, for two and a half hours. As many as twenty-seven people crowded into a single basement. The next day, the front page of the *Pampa News* was devoted to coverage of the six tornadoes that had plagued the area. Many cattle were killed, and both farm and industrial buildings were destroyed.

The newspaper reported that a storm-related mystery remained unsolved. Shortly after 7:00 P.M., as the most threatening of the funnels were forming over Pampa, a single-engine plane was sighted, apparently in trouble. Airport and law enforcement officials attempted to reach the pilot and aid in an emergency landing on the west side of town but could not make radio contact. The airplane appeared, according to witnesses, to regain power but then disappeared into the heavy clouds.

Those distant sounds of an airplane over Pampa signaled the life and death struggle between Stirling Colgate, an astrophysicist from Los Alamos National Laboratory, and an unpredictable and dangerous inflow into one of the tornadoes near the base of a supercell thunderstorm. Instead of a Cessna 210 that he had flown before, Colgate and a student assistant were flying a Centurion 210, designed "for acrobatic stress" (Davidson 1996). It was a life-saving choice.

For several years, Colgate had been trying to perform one of the most challenging scientific experiments in the history of meteorology. The goal was to fire an instrumented rocket, at the speed of sound, into the core of a funnel. This was the only way anyone could measure the physical conditions inside a tornado. Here at Pampa, Colgate actually may have flown through one of the tornadoes in its organizing stage. His brush with death ended the air-launched rocket experiments that had taken years to prepare and seemed so feasible just a year before. This supercell at Pampa was not as well behaved as the Alfalfa, Oklahoma, storm he encountered just a year earlier.

On May 22, 1981, Colgate successfully flew his Cessna to within half a mile of two tornadoes. As at Pampa, under the wings were ten instrumented rockets. On these chases he would try to receive telemetry of the temperature, pressure, wind speed, and, most important, data on ionization and electrical field measurements from inside the tornado. All rockets went astray in these first face-to-face tornado encounters as the fins sheared off in the rapid acceleration away from the airplane.

In the 1960s Colgate became interested in electrification of thunderstorms and what effect, if any, it might have on the life cycle of tornadoes. A direct sampling of conditions inside a tornado would be one way to test whether a relationship existed. Having found support from the National Science Foundation, he practiced on waterspouts off the Florida Keys and refined the instrumentation.

By 1982 he had ironed out many of the bugs. All that was needed would be a well-behaved, predictable tornadic supercell, like the ones at Alfalfa, with little or no turbulence near the tornadoes. Fifty dummy rockets and twenty-five electronically equipped rockets had been test-fired during the previous three years. Experience at Alfalfa in 1981 had shown that a tornado could be approached from the air. But the storm at Pampa amazed chasers on the ground with its turbulence, rapid changes, and multiple funnel clouds. After fighting a horrendous inflow, a powerful downdraft plunged the plane close to the ground. Before gaining altitude, Colgate swore he saw a television screen in someone's living room (Davidson 1996). Rockets were fired at Pampa, but no tornadoes were hit. There would be no more rocket-launching flights in the distinguished career of this most adventuresome of scientists, who had barely escaped alive.

Colgate's efforts to study the temperature and electrical fields inside a tornado had been saddled from the beginning with almost insurmountable technical and bureaucratic problems. The restrictions were so severe, and the task so inherently dangerous, that a less adventurous scientist would have retreated from the challenge long before the first rocket was strapped under a wing.

Many of the restrictions had nothing to do with either meteorology or electronics. The rocket had to be made of paper. This was a limitation set by the Federal Aviation Administration (FAA). Military restrictions insisted that the rockets weigh less than one pound each and that the propellent be less than 80 grams each. Exceeding these values would classify the rocket as an airborne "lethal weapon" that could be fired only over a military test range. Yet the rocket had to carry miniaturized instruments and still achieve a speed of about 600 mph, nearly the speed of sound. That high speed was needed to penetrate the tornado circulation into the core. Otherwise the instruments would be centrifuged out or carried aloft with other debris. The nature of electrical fields in the core of a tornado remains a mystery.

STORM CHASING

Storm chasing can be a religious experience—the power of the Creator revealed in the spectacle of the thunderstorm. Chasing can be a cosmic experience, with the primal forces of the universe on display right here on earth. There is no need to imagine the energy in a supernova or a comet collision on Jupiter. Nature is truly up close and personal, especially when a 30-million-volt lightning bolt hits just a few yards away. For a few fortunate scientists, it is an opportunity to explore one of the last frontiers, the interior of a supercell thunderstorm.

Storm chasers from many walks of life converge on the plains of Texas and Oklahoma, north to Nebraska and eastern Colorado, mostly from mid-April to mid-June. They are an eclectic group on vacation from their jobs as bakers, engineers, postal employees, carpet installers, computer programmers, and, of course, meteorologists. Storm chasers may be storm spotters as well, helping to protect their communities by watching for storms from the edge of their towns. Many are amateur or "ham" radio operators. Some chasers work for very competitive television stations in midwestern or Great Plains cities. For them, the "holy grail" is to get a tornado on the air, live. These television station employees, both permanent and seasonal, are among the few who actually make any money storm chasing. For the vast majority, chasing is an expensive hobby. For all of them, it is a very dangerous one. Moreover, even those who have spent a lifetime studying tornadoes rarely see one during a chase.

A few people have made a meager living by leading "tours" that take novice chasers in search of a tornado. The profit is minimal because of the unavoidable expenses of automobile wear and tear. It is possible to put 30,000 miles on a rented van in a single chase season. A few make a living taking and selling storm photographs. But storm chasing is largely a hobby, not a profession. Chasing contains none of the glamorous heroics that are portrayed in the movies.

While many chasers have degrees in meteorology, many others do not. Some have educated themselves through years of study and field experience on their own or with other chasers. Those meteorologists who study storms as part of their research do a lot more indoor work than chasing. They spend fifteen weeks analyzing data and assembling equipment in an office for every week in the field. The data gathered in three weeks may take two years to organize and publish. The expertise to conduct storm-chasing research requires six to ten years of college training, with as much emphasis on electronics and mathematics as meteorology.

Storm chasing does provide the chance to see some of the planet's great natural wonders, but it is not a sport for thrill seekers. It may look that way in Hollywood movies, which seem to locate tornadoes at will, but this is strictly fantasy. Thrill sports such as bunjee jumping or extreme skiing guarantee excitement. Storm chasing guarantees disappointment and the promise of $1,000 in hail damage to your car.

Storm chasing is very much an intellectual challenge. It is a big-game hunt of sorts, and if you are successful, you will take genuine pleasure in knowing that you understood nature well enough to be in the right place at the right time when the storms developed. But outsmarting Mother Nature is not easy. If taken casually, your chances of seeing a tornado on a chase are only slightly better than sitting at home and looking out the window—near zero. You need strategy, experience, and a sense of what goes on in the atmosphere as the weather is occurring, not how it appears on a television weather map several hours later. A lifetime of watching television weather on a daily basis and buying every tornado video on the market does not prepare you for actual storm chasing.

The ultimate goal is not to race after a tornado but to be in position when it forms, letting it parade majestically by while every second is caught on film. Only a few hundred people do this annually, and not all of them excel at it. One might ask why more people don't do it. If it is so cosmic, so religious, and so spectacular, all from the inside of a car, why aren't thousands of people out chasing storms every year?

The reason is obvious to anyone who has tried it. Driving along a lonely road, miles from the nearest telephone, trying to see through blinding rain, hail, blowing dust, and vivid lightning is more of a nightmare than a dream come true. This is something most people avoid, especially after a 400-mile drive and a three-hour wait in the hot sun. It is common to drive several hundred miles to the area where you think tornadoes will form, then drive hundreds of miles in another direction, the one in which the storms actually formed. It can be grueling, exhausting, dirty, hot, frustrating, and aggravating to the digestive system. Tornadoes, if encountered, can be unpredictable, and a few chasers have become the chased.

Even if you have studied the weather from textbooks for many years, it will still take thousands of miles of driving before you get a real-world sense of how storms develop and decay and of how an outbreak of severe weather actually progresses. For the best chasers, perhaps nine of ten chases will be busts. You must be ready to appreciate a prairie sunset and a distant lightning show and to drive another 400 miles the next day.

Storm chasing does not fit most people's schedules. By the time school is out for the summer, much of the chase season may be over. Few bosses give employees free time to chase clouds. If you plan your vacation around chasing, there is no guarantee that Mother Nature will cooperate. Unless you chase regularly, you are not going to become good at it.

A state-of-the-art chase vehicle can cost from $30,000 to $100,000 to outfit. Along with computers, mounted videocameras, cellphones, CB radios, police-band scanners, standard AM/FM receivers, and amateur radio receivers, a fully equipped chase vehicle will have tripods, still cameras, an electronic automotive compass, a GPS satellite link with moving-map navigation software, a satellite television dish, and emergency gear. Several radios are needed to cover the full amateur radio spectrum. Success is more likely if you can pick up SKYWARN spotter reports, local television and radio broadcasts, fire and police reports, and NOAA weather radio. Is all this absolutely necessary? Of course not. But if you expect to look at the sky, drop a stream of dirt into the wind, and let intuition guide your path, you might as well stay home.

Storm chasers prefer the prairie states, because the relatively flat landscape gives them good views of the sky. In addition, the roads in the West have more of a gridlike system. This road pattern is easier and safer to navigate when you are trying to get closer to a promising storm, or move away from a dangerous one. It is also the area where the dryline forms.

THE DRYLINE

The dryline is often mentioned when thunderstorm formation is anticipated on the plains. While present in many tornado outbreaks, the dryline is not a continuous triggering mechanism that guarantees the formation of tornadic thunderstorms. The dryline develops during the spring and summer over the Great Plains. Oriented roughly north-south, it is the boundary between warm, dry air to the west (from the deserts of Mexico and New Mexico) and warm, humid air (of ocean origin) to the east. It is common over the Texas Panhandle in May, making that area and that month a favorite of storm chasers. Chasers may spend the day sunning themselves in dry desert heat or sweating in Gulf of Mexico humidity, depending on which side of the dryline they are positioned. They may be waiting for the dryline to "bulge" or the "cap" to weaken.

The humid air to the east may be very unstable but is often capped by an inversion, which inhibits the growth of clouds. The sounding in figure 5.8 showed a bend in a temperature line. That bend, the inversion, can bottle up energy and release it all at once, or it can suppress storm growth all day.

On the dryline the dry air to the west is not capped, but it does not have the latent heat energy, locked in the air's water molecules, needed for super-cell formation. The dryline, therefore, is often a critical zone where the moist, unstable, but capped air to the east is in direct contact with uncapped air to the west. Irregularities, such as bulges, in the dryline are a favorite haunt for storm chasers. During May and June, storm chasers stay close to the dryline, often starting their chases from Amarillo, in the Texas Pan-handle. They try to monitor its largely invisible perturbations and bulges and the growth of any clouds near it. With ample wind shear, dryline storms can be prolific tornado producers. Isolated dryline supercell thun-derstorms can become among the most magnificent natural features on the planet. Only in a very few special places on earth do slowly spiraling, multicolored, "breathing" objects larger than Mount Everest appear almost out of nothing and then vanish, at sunset, into thin air.

CHASE DAY

A perfect chase day is one that concludes with an entire supercell and all its features being visible, the tornado perfectly lit with lots of rotation and perhaps a suction vortex or two, and no rain between you and the tornado to hide the detail. First you have to keep track of the upper-air fore-casts days in advance. Many things need to happen at just the right time. Among the most important is an upper-air trough that must move from over the Pacific Ocean or the Gulf of Alaska to a position just west of tornado alley. At the same time, enough moisture must be moving north-ward ahead of the trough so that the energy for storms is present.

On the day before the chase, you might fly or drive in to the Day-2 outlook area, staying at a motel with cable access for local and national weather information. The chase day starts by watching for the NWS severe weather Day-1 outlook map. This map will contain irregularly shaped areas that identify the low, moderate, or high thunderstorm risk areas (see chap. 5).

In the past, a morning visit to a National Weather Service office would find serious chasers looking for small-scale weather features that are not usually plotted on typical weather maps. Now information gathering is done via the Internet, and on-line surfing starts early in the day. Among the features that chasers will look for is the leading edge of the cold outflow from yesterday's thunderstorms and bulges in the dryline. Any air mass boundary, no matter how indistinct, is a potential area for severe thunderstorm growth. Each weather station and balloon launch is examined for clues such as changing wind speeds and directions, changing temperatures—any changes that might be a tip-off as to what the day will be like. A good chase day starts out with terms such as "moderate risk," "surging dryline," "favorable shear profiles," and "good CAPE," mentioned in the technical forecasts available on-line.

Chasers then head off to the target area, often in opposite directions. They turn on their radios and watch the sky. One group might head north, to where the highest wind shear is going to be. Another group may head west, to where several frontal boundaries come together, an area called the "triple point." Another group might head south, where the moisture is greatest, guessing that the lack of moisture might be a big problem that day. The groups are constantly experimenting with the art and science of short-range forecasting. This is not thrill seeking, but for some people, the challenge, the spectacle, the camaraderie of other chasers, is the lure.

The National Weather Service provides weather data to anyone but does not provide specific chase suggestions. It is not its mission to promote dangerous hobbies and to be part of individual lawsuits if a chaser makes a tragic mistake in judgment. It is important that the forecasters on duty not be bothered with any questions. They will be busy with myriad responsibilities in severe storm situations. They are not tornado-intercept instructors. The individual chaser must assume all responsibility for every eventuality.

After a target area is selected, the order of the day is waiting, watching, driving, interpreting, driving, listening, watching, making cellular phone calls to other chasers, and then more driving. One scans the horizon, watches for convective development, and listens for tornado and severe thunderstorm watch box positions and possibly even for tornado warnings.

Ideally, a chaser predicts which growing cumulus cloud will become a tornado-spawning supercell. Its growth and movement is then projected forward in time. The storm-intercept team then tries to position itself on the side of the storm offering the best view. The most spectacular tornadoes tend to form on the right rear flank of a supercell. If the storm is moving east or northeast, as most do, the best view will be had from the southeast side of the supercell. If all goes well, the team will witness the growth of a supercell tower, the spreading of an anvil with mammatus clouds underneath, the development of a striated updraft, a "beavertail" inflow structure, a wall cloud, and an RFD-induced clear slot. Just as the cameras are in place, the tornado will form under the rotating wall cloud. The funnel will then majestically parade in front of the camera, displaying both interior and exterior multiple vortices, and ending as a mile-long rope. A trophy photograph or video is then taken home and displayed and the chase described many times to anyone who is willing to listen. The chase ends as the dying supercell is bathed in the light of the setting sun and the decaying storm provides a jaw-dropping lightning display.

A scientific chase team may have recorded wind direction, speed, temperature, and dew point measurements from points all around the storm, especially in the RFD and along the inflow-RFD-FFD occlusion. Instrumented balloons might have been launched. A tornado might have been recorded on Doppler radar from two different directions at the same time. Back at the lab there will be three-dimensional airflow analysis in and around the tornado for the next four or five years. Perhaps a probe was deployed to record seismic (earthquakelike shock waves in the ground) readings (Tatom, Knupp, and Vinton 1995).

THE "BUSTED" CHASE

Successful tornado or supercell intercepts are often difficult. There are so many unseen and unmeasurable elements, all changing minute to minute. Chasers do not always arrive in time to see a tornado, even if their forecast was precise. They may have been delayed by downed trees, police blockades, flooded roads, or deep mud and slippery Oklahoma red clay on a soggy back road.

Impatience can work against the chaser. After waiting for five hours in the hot sun, the temptation is to chase the first cloud buildup, but that is usually a mistake. One may find oneself heading in the wrong direction. Start out heading west, and the best storm may develop to the south. To get to the south side of that supercell, it will be necessary to drive directly through its core, a dangerous move called a "core punch." This means encountering high winds, torrential rains, and large hail while endangering one's own life and the lives of others. Storm chasers have driven blindly out of the thunderstorm's precipitation core and almost into the path of a tornado.

The day can be very stormy and still be a bust. A squall line of thunderstorms may form instead of individual supercells. The disorderly nature of storms in a squall line does not produce ideal conditions for long-lasting tornadoes. A continuous line of severe weather may produce a few short-lived, hard-to-see tornadoes whose location would be impossible to predict. The best chance to see a tornado may be near the last storm on the squall line, what chasers call "Tail-End Charlie." But that might be 300 miles away.

After a 400-mile drive, and reading the clues just right, a chaser may arrive at the spot where and when a tornado touchdown may be imminent. But then the entire mesocyclone may become rain wrapped just as the tornado is beginning to form. In such a case, the classic supercell has evolved into a high-precipitation, or HP, supercell, and one sees only rain and hail. The next day the supercell might be ready to "tornado" but crosses into drier air and evaporates into nothing, right in front of you. That might be a great sight, but it is not why you drove from Boston to Amarillo. On both days a tornado might have touched down in plain view, but after a 10-hour (600-minute) drive you were 20 minutes (and 20 miles) late.

It may be the last day of vacation, and you approach the southwest edge of a striated supercell with a rain-free base. You see a lowering wall cloud and know that this may be the big day. Then suddenly the hopes and dreams of twelve months are dashed. A storm farther to the south releases a torrent of rain-cooled air that cuts off the inflow to "your" supercell. The wall cloud evaporates and the chances of the big show disappear once more. You feel the cold blast of the RFD as the clear slot passes overhead. Next year you will be more patient, and you won't charge north so quickly.

Consolation can often come as a dying supercell puts on a spectacular lightning show and you understand the drama that you spent the afternoon witnessing. But, as for seeing a tornado, there may be a long wait until next year (similar to the waiting I did in my youth as a Red Sox fan).

STORM CHASE HIGHLIGHTS

Below is a list of ten special days in the brief annals of storm chasing. They are of my own choosing, and, unfortunately, I was not present for any of them. They are given in chronological order and are chosen to illustrate the variety that storm chases have taken.

#1. SOMETIME IN SUMMER 1755

While being entertained by Colonel Tasker at his Maryland estate, Benjamin Franklin saw a "small whirlwind" in the valley, blowing up dust along the road. While the rest of the household sat and watched as it moved up the hill, Franklin mounted his horse and gave chase. Noting the common belief that a cannon shot would break a waterspout, he frequently tried to break the whirlwind with his whip "but without any effect." Eventually, "it took to the woods growing every moment larger and stronger, raising instead of dust the old dry leaves and making a great noise with them and the branches of the trees." Franklin chased the vortex until he felt endangered by "some limbs of dead trees broken off by the wind." Leaves were carried "to a great height," and he followed as they fell for three miles. Franklin asked his hosts whether whirlwinds of this intensity were rare in Maryland. The answer was yes, "but . . . they had got this one on purpose to treat Mr. Franklin." Franklin noted that "a very high treat it was, too" (Ludlum 1970). One has to wonder whether what Franklin saw was a dust devil or a small landspout.

#2. MAY 4, 1961

For decades, perhaps even centuries, people have driven or ridden on horseback in the direction of large thunderstorms. By chance they may have seen a tornado. But the honor of being the first chaser using scientific equipment to set out in search of a tornado and actually finding one went to Neil Ward on May 4, 1961 (see chap. 3). His radar-assisted storm intercept showed that field research within sight of a tornado was a possibility rather than just a dream. Figure 10.1 is Ward's own photograph of the Geary, Oklahoma, tornado.

#3. JULY 6, 1962

Although for decades amateur severe-storm enthusiasts have gotten into cars and headed in the direction of a growing storm, the first to successfully intercept a tornado using forecasting parameters was David Hoadley. That first successful chase was on July 6, 1962, just a year after the first professional chase. The teenaged Hoadley plotted dew point and lifted index data at the Bismarck, North Dakota, Weather Bureau office. He predicted the area of storm development and drove south toward the South Dakota border. In the distance was a tornado. Hoadley did not see the tornado lift sixty-eight head of cattle high into the air and dash them to their deaths on the ground, but that is not what he came for, or would have wanted to see. Hoadley continues to chase today, taking his vacation days on short notice, flying to Texas, Montana, or wherever his instincts tell him that photogenic storms are likely.

#4. MAY 24, 1973

The life cycle of the Union City, Oklahoma, tornado of May 24, 1973, was discussed in chapter 3. This first great scientific team chase surrounded the tornado to a degree that has rarely been exceeded.

#5. MAY 6, 1975

At Omaha, Nebraska, a policeman's actions gave new testimony to the effectiveness of warnings. On May 6, 1975, Patrolman David Campbell "rode with the devil," keeping just ahead of an F4 tornado that was causing a new record toll in damage. The funnel "flung power poles like match sticks into the path of the battered cruiser. With the tornado at times only 100 feet to his side, flying debris smashed the windshield as he raced up

Fig. 10.1. The Geary, Oklahoma, tornado of May 4, 1961, was the first one photographed on a scientific storm chase. Photograph by Neil Ward. Courtesy of the Neil B. Ward Collection, History of Science Collections, University of Oklahoma Library.

72nd street, microphone in hand . . . warning the city as he veered from side to side avoiding flying power poles and power lines with everything lit up blue for a hundred feet around" (Ivey 1976). Seventeen houses were destroyed, and three people were killed. In 1913 a similar tornado destroyed two thousand houses at Omaha, with no warnings, and killed ninety-four people.

#6. MAY 22, 1981

May 22, 1981, may have been one of the best chase days in Oklahoma history. Stirling Colgate fired rockets at a tornado near Alfalfa. Near Arapaho, film of a tornado was taken from a news helicopter for the first time. A tornado at Binger was videotaped from several different directions. It was large enough so that the NSSL Doppler radar at Norman was able to record evidence of a 196-mph wind speed. The tornado circulation of the Binger tornado was detected to an altitude of 7.5 miles (Purrett-Carroll 1982). Howard Bluestein and his University of Oklahoma students just missed dropping TOTO, the Totable Tornado Observatory, into the path of that tornado (Bluestein 1983). It was dropped directly in what seemed to be the future path of the funnel, but the tornado turned to the left and missed TOTO by about half a mile. TOTO was not very far from the spectacular "Wizard of Oz" rope-out of the Cordell tornado (fig. 10.2). It would be another ten years before a day with similar video opportunities would develop. Bluestein would eventually put TOTO aside and turn instead to portable Doppler radar (Bluestein and Unruh 1993; Bluestein 1999), which he brought to a tornado in 1989 (fig. 10.3).

#7. APRIL 26, 1991

On April 26, 1991, storm chasers put on a remarkable display of short-range, tornado forecasting accuracy. The first tornado of the outbreak (see chap. 5) was photographed as it touched down near Washington, Kansas, by a team of chasers led by Jack Hales, an off-duty forecaster at the NSSFC. The touchdown of the first and second member of the Andover tornado family was videotaped by longtime storm chaser Jim Leonard. Tim Marshall and Carson Eads taped the early stages of the Andover tornado itself. John

Fig. 10.2. The graceful rope-out of the Cordell, Oklahoma, tornado of May 21, 1981, just missed the instrumented probe called TOTO. Courtesy of NSSL.

Fig. 10.3. It was at Hodges, Texas, on May 13, 1989, that Bluestein and his students first set up a portable Doppler radar in front of a tornado. Copyright Howard B. Bluestein.

Davies watched the touchdown of the fourth member of the tornado family, the one in the famous underpass video. In Oklahoma, Bluestein and his portable Doppler radar were in perfect position for recording a 275-mph wind in the Billings, Oklahoma, tornado (fig. 10.4). Television meteorologist Gary Shore broadcast a live play-by-play back to Tulsa.

#8. JUNE 2, 1995

This was an exceptionally successful VORTEX chase day in the Texas Panhandle. For the first time a tornado was literally surrounded, not just by cameras, but by instrumented vehicles. They were in proper position to sample the RFD and the baroclinic zone (see chap. 4). Portable Doppler radar was less than 2 miles away from the Dimmitt, Texas, tornado. Radar-equipped aircraft circled the storm at the same time as surface instruments measured the storm environment. VORTEX video was supplemented by video of the tornado taken by a dozen other storm chasers not formally involved in the project. The Dimmitt tornado was to that date the most studied tornado in history. It will take a decade to sort through and understand the relevance of all the data that were collected.

#9. JUNE 8, 1995

Near Allison, Texas, student volunteers in VORTEX Probe Two had just outraced the Kellerville tornado when they felt the car moving in directions a car should not be moving. The instrumented sedan was a fly speck compared to the milewide tornado it was following. The driver turned sharply to the left, facing west, perpendicular to the road, just as the car was hit by an 87-mph wind. As the storm chasers peered overhead, a small funnel was passing. This was a satellite vortex revolving around the giant parent tornado, 2 miles to the north. There was no time for celebration or reflection. Their job was to follow the Allison tornado northward, maintaining an assigned distance from it. The reward for risking their lives was a very valuable set of data and the words, "Good job, Probe Two," from the project director's voice on the car radio.

On the other side of the huge funnel, 3 miles northwest of Probe Two, Matt Biddle, Charles Edwards, and John Weeks sat in the equally small and

Fig. 10.4. DeWayne Mitchell captured the Red Rock, Oklahoma, tornado of April 26, 1991, shortly after a horizontal subvortex had formed. The videographer was Robert Prentice. This photograph was taken just a few minutes before Professor Bluestein recorded a wind speed of at least 275 mph.

well-instrumented Probe Three. They were blinded by torrential rain under the mesocyclone's hook. The group drove slowly to the east, as the gigantic vortex moved relentlessly to the northeast. This was potentially a collision course. Now out of the rain, the Allison "wedge" (as chasers call tornadoes that are wider than they are tall) nearly filled the horizon. Suddenly a mile-long rope funnel spun out of the clouds from behind them and swung around in front of the car and into the massive main funnel. It was another satellite vortex. Biddle reported in: "FC, this is Probe Three. The main tornado is just to our northeast. It has emerged from the rain. There are other tornadoes revolving around it. Here is our telemetry. This thing is huge. Request local search and rescue this location." Linked to a GPS satellite, the vehicle's instruments gathered more data that flowed smoothly into computer memory.

This could easily have been a narrative from a science fiction movie. It was in fact the last encounter with the last tornado, on the last chase of VORTEX. Field coordinator Erik Rasmussen's orchestration of the effort to surround tornadoes would have fit nicely in the script of *Twister*. For the two dozen storm chasers who witnessed the milewide Allison tornado up close and personal (from half a mile away), the word *big* now has a new meaning.

In *Twister,* the final scene had Jo and Bill near a similar digital tornado. They placed the truck, with the DOROTHY probe, in cruise control and allowed it to carry their version of TOTO directly into the funnel. Probe Three was now in a similar position, but they had no onboard probe and no spare vehicle to feed to a tornado. It was Mark Herndon and Matt Biddle who, just a month later, would take a *Twister* photographer on that movie's only successful search for a real tornado.

Earlier that afternoon, on his day off, VORTEX lead forecaster Charles Doswell and his chase partner, Allan Moller, witnessed what may have been the most violently rotating tornado ever caught on film (see fig. 6.4).

#10. MAY 3, 1999

This was a tragic day in Oklahoma. The largest outbreak in the state's history and the most destructive tornado in U.S. history tore across the state. But it also occurred with two scientific chase teams deployed in the field. On this remarkable day the VORTEX units and many amateur chasers saw fifteen or more tornadoes. One long-lasting storm spawned twenty-one tornadoes, the unofficial record for any one supercell. The huge DOW mobile radars were so close that debris was literally overhead. Wurman and his student crew recorded a wind of 318 mph in the walls of the funnel. All this within just a few miles of the fixed Doppler radar and NSSL research facilities in Norman.

CLOSING THOUGHTS

Scientific storm chasing holds great potential for the future as more sophisticated remote-sensing equipment is developed. The future of amateur storm chasing is less certain. It might take only a single careless incident involving the death of a pedestrian to turn law enforcement officials against storm chasers. Unless one is totally committed to accepting responsibility and respecting private property, is truly fascinated by storms, not merely curious, and thoroughly enjoys the unique beauty of the plains, it is best to stay home and enjoy the video that responsible chasers have shot. If you ever do join a tour or get to ride with an experienced storm chaser, my best wishes to you for that perfect chase. I hope when you arrive at just the right spot, I will have been there for ten minutes already—and will have gotten nine minutes of time-lapse photography. It is also my sincere hope that a future historic chase may include, as chief scientist, some young reader of this book.

CHAPTER 11

Tornado Records and Numbers

At 1:01 P.M. on March 18, 1925, trees began to snap near Ellington, Missouri, and for the next three and a half hours more people would die, more schools would be destroyed, more students and farmers would be killed, and more deaths would occur in a single city than from any other tornado in U.S. history. The tornado maintained an exact heading, N 69 degrees E, for 183 miles of its 219-mile path (fig. 11.1), at an average 62 mph, following a slight topographic ridge on which a series of mining towns had been built. These towns were the primary victims of the devastating winds. Between Gorham and Murphysboro, Illinois, the tornado's forward speed was an unusually fast 73 mph, more than double the "normal" speed, which is about 30 to 40 mph. No distinct funnel was visible through much of its path, yet for more than 100 miles the path width held uniformly at about three quarters of a mile and seems to have been continuous from eastern Missouri. Once out of the Ozarks and onto the Missouri farmland, the storm killed 13 people, including a child who died in a rural wooden school. That was the first of 72 children killed in or on the way home from their schools.

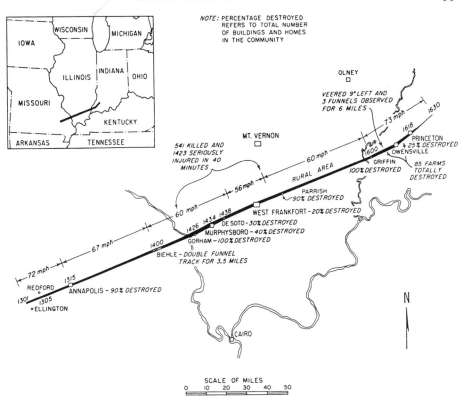

Fig. 11.1. The path map of the Great Tri-State Tornado of March 18, 1925. From Wilson and Changnon 1971.

In Illinois the devastation was at its worst, with at least 600 deaths. At Gorham 37 people died as virtually all of the town was destroyed. More than half of the town's population was either killed or injured. Seven of the deaths were at the school. Murphysboro had the largest death toll within a single city in U.S. history: 234 fatalities, including at least 25 in three schools. All of the schools were brick and stone structures, built with little or no reinforcement, and students were crushed under falling walls. Another 69 people died in and near Desoto (fig. 11.2); the death toll of 33 at the Desoto school is the worst in U.S. tornado history. Parrish, Illinois, was devastated, and 22 people died. At West Frankfort, about 800 miners were 500 feet down in a mine when the tornado struck. They knew there had been a storm, for they had lost electrical power. The only way to get out, and find

Fig. 11.2. Desoto, Illinois, was devastated by the Great Tri-State Tornado of March 25, 1925. It is likely that some cleanup took place before this picture was taken. Courtesy of the National Archives.

out how their families had fared, was to go up a narrow escapement. Most of the demolished homes were miner's cottages, and most of the 148 dead and 410 injured were their wives and children.

Also unprecedented were the 65 rural deaths in Hamilton and White counties in Illinois. There were single deaths in three rural White County schools. At least 20 farm owners died in southeastern Illinois and southwestern Indiana, a total not matched by any other four tornadoes in U.S. history combined. The normally weatherwise farmers were apparently unaware of what was bearing down on them. With its great forward speed, and appearing as a boiling mass of cloud, dust, and debris rolling along, rather than a widely visible funnel, the tornado gave these people too little time to react. Only in the tenant shanties of Mississippi and Alabama have rural death tolls approached this magnitude.

In Indiana multiple funnels were occasionally visible, as the three-quarter-mile-wide path of destruction continued and curved slightly to the left (northeast). The best estimate, by John Wilson and Stanley Changnon (1971), is that 76 people died in Indiana. The town of Griffin lost 150 houses, and children were killed in the open, on their way home from school. Two other deaths were in a school bus. Another swath of rural devastation occurred between Griffin and Princeton and passed near Owensville. About eighty-five farms were devastated in that area, and half of Princeton was destroyed. The funnel mercifully dissipated about 10 miles northeast of Princeton. The tornado was hidden from view during most of its path, and there are no known photographs of it. The all-time records of the Great Tri-State Tornado of 1925 are still unbroken: the highest death toll from a single U.S. tornado (695), the greatest number of deaths in a single state (606 in Illinois), the longest time on the ground (3 hours, 29 minutes), and the longest continuous path (217 miles). Only rarely has its average forward speed of 62 mph been exceeded.

However, the accuracy of these and all other so-called tornado records is not good. Rainfall is commonly measured to within a hundredth of an inch, and temperature is measured to within a fraction of a degree. Tornado measurements have accuracy problems measured in yards and miles and in some cases have 1,000 percent errors. There are officially recorded path widths that are ten times wider than any actual funnel that happened to touch down that day. Here we will look at seven important types of tornado

data, their averages and their possible all-time records. Precise and definitive numbers cannot be given in any category; when it comes to tornadoes,
there are no such things.

DEATHS

It is likely that the "official" fatality number for every major killer
tornado (over 25 deaths) before 1965 is incorrect. The actual death toll for
the Tri-State Tornado will probably never be known. The Red Cross certi-
fied a total of 695 deaths (Root 1926). Several years later, for unknown
reasons, the Weather Bureau changed the number to 689. My own best
guess is about 710, for many people were still hospitalized in serious condition when the 695 total was announced. In previous years, before modern
medicine, some tornado victims suffered for months or years before finally
succumbing to their injuries. The events recounted below show the kind
of errors that exist in death statistics.

John O'Toole (1993) concluded that the death toll for the 1953 Worcester,
Massachusetts, tornado was 94, rather than the official 90. He was a history
teacher who walked door to door along the entire path of the tornado,
reviewing family histories and death records. He tracked down people who
had moved and investigated every rumored death in the most comprehensive study of its kind ever done for a tornado. He also located
photographs indicating that the Worcester tornado should have been rated
at F5. In 1975 the NWS gave that tornado an F4 rating, a rating that I
concurred with in my NRC-funded official review of pre-1971 ratings. We
all make mistakes, and for me this was a painful one. The great tornado of
my youth will forever be denied its rightful place among elite tornadoes.

The fortieth anniversary issue of the *Wichita Eagle* listed the names of 77
fatalities for the May 25, 1955, tornado in the town of Udall, Kansas. These
77 in town, plus the 5 children who died in a frail oil field shack south of
town, give a final total of 82 deaths, rather than the 80 that are officially
listed.

The toll at Woodward, Oklahoma, on April 7, 1947, is officially 95,
recorded shortly after the event. Meteorologist Don Burgess (pers. com.)
reviewed death records, comparing them to the published injury list, and
identified 107 fatalities in Woodward and 181 for the entire tornado.

The official toll for the Lubbock, Texas, storm in 1970 is 26 deaths, yet Fujita (1970) found 28 deaths. The official total for the Wichita Falls, Texas, disaster in 1979 is 42 deaths; however, a detailed cause-of-death study for the Center for Disease Control (Glass et al. 1980), listed 45 deaths.

Even smaller fatality numbers get confused when abnormal circumstances surround an event. The conflicting accounts of the Kansas killer tornado of October 31, 1984, intrigued me for quite some time until a visit to the Kansas State Historical Library allowed me get the facts in order. The official Weather Service documentation of this tornado reads as follows: "A tornado dropped to the ground about a mile and a quarter north-northwest of Carbondale, Kansas, and moved northeast across Old Highway 75 for about a mile. One woman was killed when the twister destroyed her mobile home and two-car garage." This account was both incorrect and very limited in its portrayal of what must have been a horrific series of events involving five people. In its coverage of the event, some national newspapers stated that five people died. Clearly there was a discrepancy here. The entire story, which I relate below, brings to the forefront both the problems and successes of advising people about tornado safety in mobile homes and aircraft safety near a tornadic thunderstorm.

A tornado did indeed touch down near Carbondale, Kansas, shortly after 6:00 P.M. on October 31, 1984. There were no warning sirens, and the tornado, surrounded by rain, was barely visible. The relatively weak funnel "skipped" to the northeast for 6 miles. The last touchdown was a mile and a quarter north-northwest of Carbondale at about 6:18 P.M. Two people, not one, were killed by the tornado.

One woman was killed in her mobile home across the street from the trailer court. At the trailer court, a man ran from his home and took shelter in a frail metal shed. The shed was destroyed and the man was killed. His trailer was not destroyed. As the tornado passed across the court, it destroyed the trailers that were not tied down, yet barely damaged those that were.

At 6:12 P.M. a single-engine, four-seat airplane was west of Ottawa, Kansas, heading for Topeka. By 6:17 P.M. it was 10 miles south of Topeka's Forbes Field, heading north. A retired navy pilot with six thousand hours of flying time was talking with air traffic control about landing. If the plane was 10 miles south of Forbes Field at 6:17 P.M., then it was just northeast of

Carbondale, within a mile of the tornado's path, about one minute before the tornado's arrival at that point. The pilot was apparently unaware of the tornado when he last spoke to air traffic control. At 6:18 P.M. people in a frame house a half mile northeast of the trailer court heard a crash in a nearby field. The funnel was approaching the trailer court at this time, and the family thought that it was debris from the trailers. The wreckage was ignored until the next morning, when it was seen to be the small plane. The pilot and two passengers died instantly. The plane was clearly traveling in a south-southwest direction when it crashed. Just a minute earlier it had been heading north for a landing. A tornado warning was issued at 6:28 P.M.

What happened to the veteran pilot and his two passengers in that last minute will always be a mystery. Was he caught in a strong inflow jet moving into the tornado at the base of the clouds? Did he turn to watch the tornado and lose control in a wind shear downdraft? Since we will never know, the deaths in the plane cannot be counted as tornado related.

There is considerable reluctance on the part of the NWS to change death totals once they are entered into the official database and widely disseminated and quoted all over the world. Changing the data probably causes more confusion than having slightly inaccurate numbers. (See the Appendix for a list of the deadliest U.S. tornadoes.)

INJURIES

The all-time injury record of 2,027 also belongs to the Tri-State Tornado. Precise injury statistics are the exception rather than the rule. In a minor tornado, if two people are cut by flying glass and are treated at home, those injuries might be officially recorded. In major storms with large injury totals, many cuts and other injuries treated at home will be ignored. The official injury list will count only those who were treated professionally in hospitals or by emergency field units. All of the twenty-seven tornadoes that caused more than five hundred injuries are included in the Appendix.

PATH LENGTH

My research in Missouri suggests that the first 60 miles of the Great Tri-State Tornado of 1925 involved two or more tornadoes, probably on parallel paths. Newspapers also hint at a break in the intense damage and possible downburst activity over a 5-mile-wide front, west of Biehle, Missouri. From Biehle, the path seems to have been continuous for the remaining 157 miles. Either the official 217 miles or the above-noted 157 miles for the Tri-State Tornado would be ranked as the all-time record path length. In my opinion, there are no other viable candidates for first place. Naming the tornado path lengh that ranks in second place is much harder.

As of this writing, the official National Weather Service records for modern times (since 1950) list twenty-eight tornadoes with a path length of more than 100 miles. Whether any single tornado can actually be sustained by its parent supercell for that long has been questioned by many people, most notably Doswell and Burgess (1988).

My selection for second-longest path is actually ranked twenty-first on the official list. My choice is the 103-mile-long Guin, Alabama, tornado of April 3, 1974. It was surveyed by Fujita and confirmed by him (pers. com.) as the longest of the 148 tornadoes that day. The funnel cut a swath across the Bankhead National Forest that could be seen from earth-orbiting satellites. I consider the twenty others that are officially listed as longer to be just carelessly linked tornado families rather than single tornadoes.

The longest "officially" recorded tornado path, on the Storm Prediction Center database, is a long-forgotten 218-mile path across southern Georgia on April 18, 1969. It was probably a family of six insignificant tornadoes. This rather weak event caused no deaths and only a few widely scattered injuries. It was accompanied by damaging downbursts. The quickest way to handle a complex multiple-tornado path was to draw a straight line through the damage and call it one tornado.

Doswell and Burgess (1988) listed a 98-mile path length for the Woodward, Oklahoma, tornado of 1947, which is a suitable choice as the third-longest track. Officially, that track is 198 miles.

Flora's *Tornadoes of the United States* and many other books (which probably derive their information from Flora) list the longest tornado path as the 293-mile track of the Charleston/Mattoon, Illinois, tornado of May 26, 1917. The path of this supposedly continuous tornado ran from Missouri across Illinois to Indiana, about 100 miles north of the 1925 Tri-State path. Damage surveys at the time, and my examination of about thirty newspapers, clearly revealed that the 1917 tornado was probably four, and perhaps as many as eight, separate tornadoes. The two Illinois towns in which most of the 101 deaths occurred, Charleston and Mattoon, are 8 miles apart and were probably hit by the same tornado. The longest track for a single member of this famous 1917 tornado family was about 45 miles.

Flora (1953) noted that the average tornado path was 13 miles long. More tornadoes are now counted each year, and these additional tornadoes are mostly of the short-path variety. As expected, the average path length for a modern tornado database (Schaefer et al. 1986) is considerably shorter, especially for all tornadoes. The data of Schaefer and his colleagues suggest that the average tornado path is about 1 mile long. So many brief touchdowns have no documented path length that it is impossible to calculate an accurate average. As I have said before, definitive answers and accurate numbers are not available.

I intend no criticism of the NWS in mentioning inaccuracies in tornado data. The primary mission of the NWS staff is forecasting. While it is important to verify forecasts by documenting tornadoes, the local offices are not given time and resources to determine the precise beginning and end points for each tornado. Not every worthwhile and interesting activity can be supported by limited federal tax money. Some of these tornadoes might have damaged a single tree on a farm, 120 miles from the office. Tracking down details about a storm that broke a tree branch seems to be a waste of resources. Yet how is forecasting going to improve if we do not have accurate "ground truth" occurrence data to compare with forecasts and the radar observations that were the basis of a warning?

PATH WIDTH

The search for the widest tornado begins with the official database. On that list of more than 35,000 tornadoes, 73 have path widths of 1 mile or more and 7 have path widths of 1.5 miles or more. Unfortunately, many of these data do not relate to tornado width: the recorded value is either the width of downburst damage that accompanied the tornado or the distance between two small funnels that formed at the same time and traveled together. Damage points may have been a mile apart, with no damage in between and no actual funnel more than 100 yards wide.

Another problem arises here. Just what do we mean by "path width"? A tornado's width is quite variable. Does "width" mean the maximum width or the average width? Since about 1982, many Weather Service offices have recorded the maximum path width. Before that time the average path width was recorded. Therefore, most of the widest paths have occurred since 1982.

Despite the inaccuracies and changing policies, the tornado with the widest official width, 9,990 feet (1.9 miles), turns out to be a worthy first choice. The actual maximum width of this tornado was 2.2 miles, and it may have been one of the great tornadic events of the century, although no one may have seen it. It cut a continuous 69-mile-long path, mostly across the Moshannon State Forest in Pennsylvania, on May 31, 1985. The actual 2.2-mile (11,600-foot) maximum width cannot be recorded in the official database. The largest three-digit number that the data file can handle is 999, or 9,990 feet.

There are other worthy candidates for the widest tornado. The official description of the Red Springs/McColl, North Carolina, tornado of March 28, 1984, notes a maximum width of 2.5 miles, but its official database lists it as just 1.5 miles. Another choice is the Gruver, Texas, tornado of June 8, 1971, listed as 1 mile wide and tied for fifty-third place officially. As it occurred before 1982, it was the average width that was listed. The Gruver tornado is different in that its 2-mile width was actually seen by experienced storm spotters, so there is some direct evidence that the event was actually a tornado. It seems that just over 2 miles is the maximum tornado width.

In the long history of tornadoes that occurred before 1950, there are a few interesting candidates. The widest of all, if judged by press reports, was the 7-mile-wide-tornado at Blair, Oklahoma, on June 16, 1928. That was the same day as Will Keller's tornado near Greensburg, Kansas, described in chapter 1. The destruction across eastern Jackson County was immense, with 7 people dead and more than 1,000 head of cattle and 100 horses killed. The town was entirely engulfed as the storm moved to the southeast. There was F4 damage on the right side of the storm. It seems likely that most of the 7-mile-wide, 40-mile-long storm area was affected by straight-line downbursts. The path of the Woodward, Oklahoma, tornado of April 9, 1947, was estimated to be just under 2 miles wide. Given the difficulties in identifying the outer edge of circulation, it might have been wider than that. So the Woodward tornado is a definite candidate for the widest.

DAMAGE

Accurate estimates of the damage done by a tornado are rare. The actual economic loss cannot be determined until all repairs have been done, but by then there is little or no interest in counting. An initial damage estimate is made within a day or two of the event, as part of the local appeal for federal and state aid. Once the money has been disbursed, there is little incentive to keep track of expenses. In addition, insurance companies, for reasons of privacy and competitiveness, do not make public everything that they know about losses. It is also difficult to compare losses from year to year. Inflation is one factor in the rising loss figures but not, in my opinion, the most significant. Inflation may have increased values by a factor of five or more since the 1950s, but the cost of what is in a home or a business has risen by a much larger factor. A high-tech automated factory may be valued at one hundred times the cost of a similar-sized factory just a few decades ago. Moreover, in years past a farmhouse may have had a pen and pencil set and a mechanical calcu-lator on the desk, and the farmyard may have contained only a fenced-in pigpen and a well-worn tractor. That desk today may contain a computer with a satellite uplink for weather radar and up-to-the-minute reports on grain-futures trading. The pigpen is now a climate-controlled, hog-containment facility. The tractor now has an air-conditioned cab, 10 feet off the ground, capable of doing the work of ten old tractors and costing as much as the entire farm did just a few decades ago. Today there are fewer farms, but they are larger. Fewer tornadoes will hit any farm build-ings. Those that do may encounter the larger agribusiness enterprises, which have very expensive equipment.

Table 11.1 lists record-breaking damage estimates since 1680, not adjusted for inflation. Each event broke the damage record of the previous one. The listed values, before 1950, represent either my best estimate or the average of several estimates made at the time. Table 11.2 lists tornadoes that have caused at least $200 million in inflation-adjusted 1999 dollars. Some esti-mates place the dollar amount of damage caused by the Omaha tornado of 1975 at $500 million (unadjusted) or more than $1 billion (adjusted to 1999 dollars). This is a wildly inflated number, published the day after the tornado and used in an effort to get federal disaster assistance. The February 1, 1976, issue of the *Omaha Sunday World-Herald* placed the final damage

Table 11.1
RECORD-SETTING TORNADO DAMAGE IN THE UNITED STATES THROUGH 1999

Date	Damage in Dollars (unadjusted)	Location
July 8, 1680	20	Cambridge, Mass.
June 10, 1682	1,000	New Haven, Conn.
Aug. 3, 1724	5,000	Chester County, Penn.
June 22, 1756	20,000	West Orange, N.J.
May 4, 1761	200,000	Charleston, S.C.
June 19, 1835	300,000	New Brunswick, N.J.
May 7, 1840	1,260,000	Natchez, Miss.
June 17, 1882	1,300,000	Grinnell, Iowa
Mar. 27, 1890	3,500,000	Louisville, Ken.
May 27, 1896	12,000,000	St.Louis, Mo., and E. St.Louis, Ill.
June 28, 1924	12,500,000	Lorain and Sandusky, Ohio
Mar. 18, 1925	16,500,000	Tri-State Mo., Ill., Ind.
Sep. 29, 1927	22,000,000	St. Louis, Mo.
May 11, 1953	41,000,000	Waco, Tex.
June 9, 1953	52,000,000	Worcester, Mass.
June 8, 1966	100,000,000	Topeka, Kan.
May 11, 1970	135,000,000	Lubbock, Tex.
Apr. 10, 1979	400,000,000	Wichita Falls, Tex.
May 3, 1999	1,200,000,000	Oklahoma City, Okla., area

estimate at a more realistic $111,234,732. I use that number in table 11.2, which eliminates the Omaha tornado from consideration in table 11.1.

OUTBREAKS

According to Galway (1977), to have an "outbreak" of tornadoes, there must be six or more tornadoes from a single weather system. To determine a "record" outbreak, we must also define when a tornado outbreak begins

Table 11.2
INDIVIDUAL TORNADOES CAUSING $200 MILLION OR MORE IN 1999 INFLATION-ADJUSTED DAMAGE

Date	Location	Deaths	Unadjusted Damage (in millions)	Adjusted Damage (in millions)
May 3, 1999	Oklahoma City, Okla., area	38	1,200	1,200
Apr. 10, 1979	Wichita Falls, Tex.	45	400	902
May 11, 1970	Lubbock, Tex.	28	135	569
June 8, 1966	Topeka, Kan.	16	100	504
Oct. 3, 1979	Windsor Locks, Conn.	3	200	451
May 27, 1896	St. Louis, Mo.	255	12	388
May 6, 1975	Omaha, Neb.	3	111	337
Apr. 3, 1974	Xenia, Ohio	34	100	332
May 31, 1973	Conyers, Ga., area	1	89	327
June 9, 1953	Worcester, Mass.	94	52	317
June 3, 1980	Grand Island, Neb.	4	140	278
Dec. 3, 1978	Bossier City, La.	2	100	251
May 11, 1953	Waco, Tex.	114	41	251
May 20, 1957	Ruskin Heights, Mo., area	44	40	233
Sep. 29, 1927	St. Louis, Mo.	79	22	207
Aug. 28, 1990	Plainfield, Ill.	29	165	207

and ends. Some stormy periods can go on for five consecutive days, with tornadoes every day but with long breaks in the tornado activity. My definition holds that if activity stops for six or more hours and then begins again, the activity is considered as two separate outbreaks rather than one. With this definition, we can construct a ranking of outbreaks (see table 11.3).

COUNTING TORNADOES

Tornadoes are among nature's most enigmatic creations, hiding, shifting, retreating, and re-forming. They do not automatically become recorded

Table 11.3
TEN OUTBREAKS WITH THE GREATEST NUMBER OF SIGNIFICANT TORNADOES, 1880–1998

Date	Significant Tornadoes	Killer Tornadoes	Deaths
1. Apr. 3–4, 1974	95	48	307
2. Nov. 21–23, 1992	43	9	26
3. Apr. 11–12, 1965	38	21	256
4. Feb. 19–20, 1884	37	28	167
5. Mar. 21–22, 1932	36	27	330
6. Apr. 29–30, 1909	35	24	132
7. June 5–6, 1916	34	23	112
8. Apr. 15–16, 1921	34	17	90
9. May 8–9, 1927	32	17	217
10. Mar. 28, 1920	31	19	153

in databases the way earthquakes (through seismometers) and some floods (through stream gauges) do. Many brief touchdowns of small tornadoes go completely unseen, obscured in darkness or embedded in rain. The only legacy of some tornadoes may be a few conflicting observations and a pile of debris. Some form no visible funnel at all and are only strong enough to break tree branches and stir up dust.

The number of annual deaths from tornadoes is relatively well documented and is probably 90 to 95 percent accurate. The number of tornadoes that touch down annually remains something of a mystery and may be counted with only about 50 percent accuracy. In broadly rounded numbers, the weather over the United States annually produces about 100,000 thunderstorm cells. About 10,000 of them become severe, producing various combinations of high winds, large hail, heavy rain, and frequent lightning. About 1,000 of these thunderstorms produce tornadoes, although this does not mean that there is one tornado per storm.

During the past few decades, the number of recorded tornadoes has risen as efforts to verify forecasts have become a priority. Chaser and spotter activity has also increased. The annual total of tornadoes recorded has risen from 200 in 1950 to 1,000 in 1973 to more than 1,400 in 1998. That increase has nothing to do with how many actually touch down.

Although the annual number of counted tornadoes has soared, the number of significant tornadoes (F2–F5) has not (see fig. 11.3). We obviously are counting a lot of small tornadoes that were previously ignored. The answer to the question, How many tornadoes hit the United States each year? depends on the years we choose to count and on a "missing tornado" factor. The farther back in time we start counting, the smaller the average is going to be. The 1953–98 average is 836 annual tornadoes. A more recent average, 1990–98, is 1,201 tornadoes annually. But what about those that might have missed being counted?

The idea that fewer than half of all tornadoes are reported was first expressed by Eshelman and Stanford (1977) of Iowa State University, based on a study of reported Iowa touchdown sightings in 1974. The official Iowa tornado count for 1974 was 27. They confirmed 81 touchdowns by tracking down details of every windstorm in the state that year.

I estimate that only 53 percent of tornadoes are actually counted (see table 11.4). To make this estimate we must assume that in larger cities, where the population is more dense, all tornadoes are counted. In rural areas, small vortices are either missed or ignored. I have found that the concentration of counted tornadoes in some cities is three or more times the concentration in rural areas (Grazulis 1993).

To create a valid estimate, I do not simply handpick cities. That would bias the result. The cities must be chosen either at random or by some method that has nothing to do with climatology. As tornado data are available by county, my method is to choose the county surrounding the state capital in the most tornado-prone states. For example, consider Marion County, Indiana, the location of Indianapolis, the capital. The National Weather Service has recorded 26 tornado touchdowns in Marion County between 1959 and 1994. The year 1959 is used because it was the first year of *Storm Data,* the official book of records. Those 26 tornadoes are listed in column 2 of table 11.4 along with the concentration of 66.3 tornadoes per 1,000 square miles of county area. Column 3 in Table 11.4 shows that the actual counted number of tornadoes in the state of Indiana is 737, just 20.4 tornadoes per 1,000 square miles. If the entire state had the Marion County

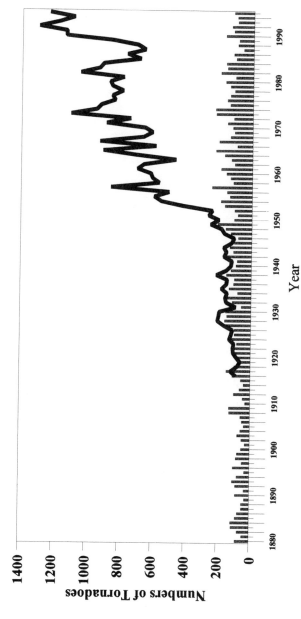

Fig. 11.3. A graph showing the rapid rise in the number of all tornadoes compared to the more gradual variation in the number of significant (F2–F5) tornadoes.

Table 11.4
DATA FOR ESTIMATING THE PERCENTAGE OF UNCOUNTED TORNADOES, FOR YEARS 1959–1994

1	2	3	4	5
County, State (Capital City)	Counted Tornadoes in County/ Tornadoes per 1,000 sq. mi.	Counted Tornadoes in State/ Tornadoes per 1,000 sq. mi.	Estimated Tornadoes in State	Estimated Percent of State Tornadoes Counted
Marion, Ind. (Indianapolis)	26 / 66.3	737 / 20.4	2393	31%
Oklahoma, Okla. (Oklahoma City)	50 / 71.4	1902 / 27.7	4911	39
Ingham, Mich. (Lansing)	15 / 26.8	617 / 10.9	1523	41
Shawnee, Kan. (Topeka)	27 / 49.3	1678 / 20.5	4032	42
Pulaski, Ark. (Little Rock)	23 / 30.1	680 / 13.1	1564	44
Franklin, Ohio (Columbus)	17 / 31.6	589 / 14.4	1295	45
Polk, Iowa (Des Moines)	28 / 48.4	1306 / 23.3	2708	48
Sangamon, Ill. (Springfield)	34 / 38.7	1051 / 18.9	2157	49
E. Baton Rouge, La. (Baton Rouge)	23 / 45.3	1020 / 22.7	2035	50
Hinds, Miss. (Jackson)	36 / 41.1	964 / 20.4	1944	50
Franklin, Ken. (Frankfort)	3 / 14.2	331 / 8.3	564	57
Travis, Tex. (Austin)	32 / 32.4	5184 / 19.8	8489	61
Dane, Wis. (Madison)	27 / 22.5	775 / 14.2	1225	63
Burleigh, N.D. (Bismarck)	26 / 16.0	724 / 10.5	1108	65
Davidson, Tenn. (Nashville)	8 / 15.7	446 / 10.8	649	69
Ramsey, Minn. (St. Paul)	2 / 12.9	784 / 9.9	1023	77
Lancaster, Neb. (Lincoln)	15 / 17.8	1435 / 18.8	1361	105
Montgomery, Ala. (Montgomery)	10 / 12.5	795 / 15.7	644	123
Cole, Mo. (Jefferson City)	5 / 6.94	1000 / 14.5	478	209

Note: South Dakota was not used because its capital city, Pierre, has a population of less than 25,000 and it is considered rural.

concentration, 2,393 tornadoes would have been recorded in Indiana (column 4). The actual count, 737, divided by the estimated count, 2,393, provides the estimate that only 31 percent of Indiana's tornadoes were counted (column 5). That is the lowest percentage of any state in the sample.

The three states with the most extreme values in column 5 of table 11.4 were thrown out as unrepresentative. Indianapolis may be in the part of Indiana that has the highest concentration of tornadoes. Cole County, Missouri, may be in the least tornado-prone part of that state. After the extremes are discarded, the average for the thirteen remaining states is 53 percent. If only 53 percent of tornadoes were counted nationally, then our estimate for the true annual tornado total would be the 1959–95 average of 902 divided by .53, which is 1,806 (rounded to 1,800) tornadoes per year.

The "missing tornadoes" probably fall into two categories: (1) well-formed tornadoes that form in very rural areas and are unseen and unreported due to remoteness, darkness, rain, or other visibility problems; and (2) minor tornadoes that do not form enough of a visible funnel or stir up enough dust to be noticed, even with adequate visibility.

We do not know what percentage of reported tornadoes are gustnadoes, small vortices at the leading edge of outflow from a storm. Thousands of them form each year. In practice, damaging gustnadoes are probably documented as tornadoes, regardless of whether they reach up to cloud base (see chap. 4). Few people in the process of losing a garage roof or a recreational trailer are going to go outside to check whether the offending vortex has a full ground-to-cloud base connection. If a person watches a small rotating vortex rip shingles from his house, he is going to report it as a tornado. I will not confuse the issue of the actual number of tornadoes any further. Counting them accurately is impossible.

SPEED AND DIRECTION

Data are not collected on the forward speed of tornadoes, for we rarely know the exact time of touchdown and dissipation. The upper limit on forward speed is probably about 70 mph, and the average is probably about 30 mph. Most tornadoes probably last just a few minutes. The Tri-State Tornado of 1925 may have lasted three and a half hours. Many tornadoes have remained virtually stationary for their entire lives.

A tornado generally moves along with its parent thunderstorm. Those storms are often moving in a southwest-to-northeast airflow, on the east side of an upper-air trough and surface low-pressure area. Consequently, most tornadoes, about 60 percent, move from southwest to northeast. The upper-air flow can also be from the west, moving the thunderstorm/ tornado system to the east (18%). Another 11 percent move to the southeast or south, under the influence of a northwesterly flow aloft. About 9 percent move to the north or northwest, and only 2 percent move to the west or southwest.

The Jarrell, Texas, tornado family of May 27, 1997 (see fig. 3.9), was an interesting case in which the upper-level airflow was moving to the northeast but the tornadoes moved to the south, opposite the upper-level flow. In a somewhat oversimplified explanation, the parent thunderstorm grew so rapidly, as tropical humidity was flowing into its south side, that it developed backward (called back-building) toward the south and southwest faster than it moved forward to the northeast. Consequently, the tornadoes moved to the south and southwest rather than to the northeast. Given enough time, the atmosphere seems to be able to create even the most unlikely scenarios. We have only to wait for the next tornado season for the next unprecedented event.

Tornadoes that move to the west are often weak and may be driven westward by outflow from a stationary parent thunderstorm. Intense westward-moving tornadoes are rare. However, hurricanes moving to the west and making landfall on the Texas coast have spawned westward-moving tornadoes of considerable intensity. Along the north coast of the Gulf of Mexico and along the Atlantic coast, hurricane-spawned tornadoes often move to the north or northwest. Tornadoes are spawned by the thunderstorms that make up the hurricane's spiral bands. These bands are moving westward on the north side of the hurricane, as the storm rotates cyclonically. The path of a tornado can have drastic twists and turns if the parent storm is nearly stationary for most of its life while continuing to produce multiple mesocyclones, tornadoes, and downbursts.

Among the most frequently asked questions is, What is the worst tornado? I will choose five candidates, for different reasons. "Worst" can mean the most damaging, the deadliest, or the one with the highest wind speeds. This category "worst" is subjective and inaccurate and based on

Fig. 11.4. The Jordan, Iowa, tornado of June 13, 1976, produced F5 damage to farmhouses. It made an unusual U-turn after encountering downburst winds and was accompanied by an anticyclonic companion (not shown). Courtesy of Holly Filson.

interpretations of actual damage. Conversations with Fujita on this subject have led me to mention the Xenia, Ohio, tornado of April 3, 1974, where incredible damage was done to steel-reinforced concrete schools. Also prominent in those discussions was the Jordan, Iowa, tornado of 1976 (fig. 11.4) in which prosperous, seemingly well-built farms literally vanished. Based on my own observations of more than five hundred tornadoes on video, the Pampa, Texas, tornado of June 8, 1995 (see fig. 6.4), was the fastest-spinning vortex I have ever seen. Among its many feats of tornadic strength was the lifting and movement of a 35,000-pound lathe.

Statistics can be used both to illuminate and to confuse an issue. Because tornado data are so subjective, they are ready-made for conflict and confusion. In chapter 14, I use these statistics cautiously to create maps that illustrate the distribution and frequency of tornadoes across the eastern two-thirds of the United States. The maps are, of course, just approximations. But first I want to provide the broadest perspective on tornadoes, in both time and space.

CHAPTER 12

TORNADOES BY DECADE

The story of tornado activity, research, and the people involved was only touched on in the preceding chapters. This potpourri chapter picks up some interesting pieces. Much of the information is drawn from the work of David Ludlum (1970).

1643–1779

The known history of tornadoes in what would become the United States began just twenty-three years after the Pilgrims landed at Plymouth Rock. An early windstorm, described as a "sudden gust," felled trees and killed a Native American on July 5, 1643. It probably was not a tornado, although some books list it as such. The earliest recorded tornado snapped trees near Rehobeth, Massachusetts, in August 1671, fifty-one years after the first landing at Plymouth Rock. The first confirmed tornado-related fatality occurred on July 8, 1680, when a small tornado killed a servant at

Cambridge, Massachusetts. That funnel was filled with "stones, bushes, boughs, and other things."

In Europe a survey report of the tornado at Rheims, France, on August 10, 1680, numbered 169 pages. A 342-page report on European tornadoes was published in 1694. Both of these reports preceded similar American studies by about one hundred fifty years. This was not an enlightened age. In 1650 the geographer Varenius made the outlandish suggestion that large ocean storms rotate. That idea was rejected or ignored for nearly two hundred years.

In 1702 Cotton Mather, preacher, philosopher, and student of the weather, put into print the feelings of many people in America at this time. He felt that tornadoes and other storms were "the voice of glorious God" working through the underworld. "Satan, let loose by God, can do wonders in the air; he can raise storms, he can discharge the great ordnance of heaven, thunder and lightning; and by his own art can make them more terrible and dreadful, than they are in their own nature."

On June 11, 1749, a waterspout went inland at Rome, Italy, and moved eastward for 20 miles, destroying property. This event drew the interest of Benjamin Franklin. Franklin's 1752 experiments with kites and atmospheric electricity are part of American folklore. In addition, Franklin speculated and wrote about waterspouts and tornadoes. He theorized, correctly, that there were both ascending and descending whirlwinds and that the descending variety were more common. He was correct in his theory that the visible funnel of a waterspout was due to condensation rather than surface water being carried aloft. That idea would not be universally accepted for more than one hundred years, as many people believed a waterspout was a column full of liquid water. He also concluded that circulation could be present without a visible funnel or column. Many of his writings displayed a scientific logic that would be absent from many discussions of tornadoes until the mid-1800s.

One of Franklin's correspondents, Cadwallader Coldren, also believed that a waterspout "contained a solid wall of whirling wind, and this could be broken by firing a cannon ball through the core, thus giving horizontal vent for the winds to escape from the whirl and cause it to collapse." This meteorological version of bloodletting has a certain twisted logic to it. Other writings debated the role of lightning and atmospheric electricity in

tornado formation, but there was still little understanding of the basic principles of storm movement, condensation, and evaporation.

The first multicolony outbreak of tornadoes hit Maryland, Pennsylvania,
New York, and New Jersey on June 22, 1756. Rumors of many deaths, especially in Maryland, circulated throughout the colonies. The first multiple-
death tornado occurred near Charleston, South Carolina, on May 4, 1761,
as a "stupendous thick black pillar of clouds seemed to impel the water to
a mountainous wave about 12 feet high." Dwellings were destroyed, as were
three ships ready to sail for England. Eight people died, four each on ships
and in houses. Some time later word reached Charleston that other tornadoes had struck on May 4, in Indian Territory 300 miles to the west, probably in present-day Alabama. Before the American Revolution about twenty
tornadoes were documented in the colonies.

1780–1799

During the period that included the American Revolutionary War there
were only rumors of tornadoes. Then, beginning in 1782, they were
reported in unprecedented numbers in the northeastern states. There were
three New England outbreaks: 1782, 1786, and 1787. All three caused deaths.
The outbreak of August 15, 1787, was a "four-state tornado swarm" that
produced a record, up to that time, of five confirmed tornadoes. The
formation of a tornado in 1787 at Northborough, Massachusetts, occurred
when "a black fuliginous vapour instantly ascended from the point of
coalescence." The year 1794 witnessed an outbreak in New York and
Connecticut. At Branford, Connecticut, multiple vortices were described
as the tornado "appeared to divide into a number of whirls yet all complete
in one. . . . [T]he herbage of the field, the fowls of the heavens, fences,
leaves, boughs, and trunks of trees filled the atmosphere, and whirled in
every direction."

Tornadoes even found their way into early American history. On August
20, 1794, 1,100 warriors from an alliance of six Indian tribes tried to ambush
2,000 American soldiers. The strategy was to attack the soldiers after drawing them into a maze of trees, blown down by a tornado, near present-day
Toledo, Ohio. The ambush turned into an Indian defeat known as the Battle
of Fallen Timbers.

1800–1809

Westward expansion brought the first definitive reports of tornadoes from west of the Appalachian Mountains. On March 14, 1801, two soldiers were killed by a tornado at a remote outpost in Mississippi. The nation's first double-digit death toll for an outbreak (11 deaths) occurred on April 5, 1804. What was undoubtedly a family of tornadoes moved east-north-east from Macon, Georgia, to near Meriwether, South Carolina, crossing the Savannah River, 15 miles north of Augusta, Georgia. In Hancock County, Georgia, the funnel was described as "black as the smoke from burning tar, but its front glimmered with a strange light." At least eleven people were killed. A "huge branch of a tree" was driven into the ground south of Warrenton, Georgia, and was still visible during the survey of a later tornado outbreak by the Army Signal Corps in 1875. The 1804 track was "still distinguishable at some points, both from decayed logs and the different growth of timber which has since sprung up."

On June 5, 1805, a tornado crossed the Mississippi River, 20 miles south of St. Louis, Missouri. Fish were "scattered all over the prairie," and clothing from a pioneer house was carried 8 miles. The tops of pine trees were said to have been carried 50 miles from the Ozark Mountains in Missouri and dropped on the rich alluvial plain of the Mississippi River known as the American Bottom. In central Illinois the three-quarter-mile-wide swath of downed trees became a major obstacle for early pioneers for many years.

1810–1819

In South Carolina on September 10, 1811, a hurricane-spawned tornado moved to the northwest across downtown Charleston, destroying sixty houses and killing eleven people. For the first time a single U.S. tornado had killed more than ten people.

The deadliest tornado of this decade hit near Beaufort, South Carolina, on June 30, 1814. The funnel moved out over Port Royal Sound and struck the schooner *Alligator,* drowning at least twenty-three of the forty people on board. The funnel hit land again, and "thousands of trees on Parris Island were torn off and carried in the air like feathers."

On August 25, 1814, during the War of 1812, a probable tornado killed British soldiers as they burned the White House and the Capitol in Washington,

D.C. "Roofs of houses were torn off and whisked into the air like sheets of paper."

1820-1829

Only five killer tornadoes were reported in the 1820s. Before the great Worcester tornado of 1953, New England's most devastating tornado struck on September 9, 1821. It cut a wide swath across mountains and forest in sparsely populated central New Hampshire, killing six people near Lake Sunapee. One cluster of seven houses was "lifted from the earth into the bosom of the whirlwind, and anon dashed into a thousand pieces." A Massachusetts tornado, on a parallel track 50 miles to the south, killed two people and carried a half-inch-thick, 14-inch-x-5-inch account book from Warwick to Groton, a distance of 45 miles.

1830-1839

In the 1830s the tornado phenomenon finally came under serious study by the growing scientific community in the United States. The first of these intensely studied tornadoes turned Shelbyville, Tennessee, "into a heap of ruins" on May 31, 1830, killing five people.

The most important tornado of the decade touched down on a New Jersey farm on June 19, 1835, and moved eastward through the village of Piscataway and the city of New Brunswick, killing five people and wrecking 150 buildings. This event brought into heated debate three of the most renowned scientists of the time: Robert Hare, William Redfield, and James Espy. Hare said that the "parched and scorched" nature of the vegetation supported his ideas on the role of electricity in the production of tornadoes. He also stated that houses exploded in the rarified air of the tornado, a myth that still persists today.

Espy surveyed the damage patterns and found ample evidence to reinforce his idea that tornadoes do not rotate but that the air only rushes inward and upward. Espy was one of the nineteenth century's most renowned scientific lecturers. He traveled across the United States and Europe with pumps and jars, demonstrating atmospheric processes and occasionally promoting his ideas about rain making. He drew more than one thousand weather maps with temperatures and wind arrows but no isobars. In 1841 he wrote a 552-page book, *The Philosophy of Storms,* and was called "Storm-breeder" and "Storm King."

Espy created conceptual models that were advanced for his time. They involved storm formation based on dew point temperatures and the idea that air rises, expands, cools, and condenses out moisture, releasing latent heat and causing it to rise further. He added ideas about the thunderstorm life cycle that would not be significantly improved on for many years. His model included the more refined, but not exactly correct, idea that air was rising within the interior of the storm and descending along the edges. But after surveying nine tornado damage tracks, he still insisted that tornadoes were nonrotating storms with a central vacuum.

Espy's bitter intellectual rival, William Redfield, was a less public man, a genius in engineering and business who believed that tornadic winds do indeed rotate. Redfield wrote extensively on hurricanes and the general circulation of the atmosphere. He wrote about "rotating discs" of air above the surface that are part of larger rotating areas. In direct contrast to Espy and Hare, Redfield believed that unusual electrical phenomena are a consequence of tornadoes and not the cause. He theorized that upper-air conditions are as important as surface conditions in storm development and that midlatitude storms do indeed rotate. He wrote that the motion of storms is caused by "the predominant current in which they were imbedded." Redfield concluded that local storms are part of a worldwide weather system and that they must be understood in the context of larger phenomena. While Espy dispensed his thoughts directly to the public, Redfield worked in private, responding to Espy's public insults only by letter.

Redfield was named the first president of the now-prestigious American Association for the Advancement of Science. Most of Espy's tornado theories eventually were rejected. He spent his last years in religious contemplation and died in seclusion.

1840–1849

The 1840s saw, for the first time, the destruction of a large part of a city by a tornado and a single-tornado death toll that has been exceeded only once to this day. That event occurred in and near Natchez, Mississippi.

Natchez was a flourishing port on the Mississippi River, a prime cotton and lumber trading center, surpassed in wealth and volume of trade only by New Orleans. Flatboat and steamboat traffic was always heavy in the middle of a workday. At about 1:00 P.M. on Friday, May 7, 1840, a tornado touched down at least 20 miles southwest of Natchez and moved northeast, straddling the entire Mississippi River, "stripping the forest from both shores" and devastating both the town and river traffic. We have no way to judge the accuracy of the published human death toll of 317. Fatalities on the river were reported to be 269, with 48 additional deaths in the city. The tornado was wide enough to have caused deaths on the opposite shore, in Louisiana. Whether this on-land total includes deaths of slaves on plantations is not known. In my opinion, the death toll may have been considerably higher than 317. A newspaper reported that "a large number of transients and itinerant boatmen" were probably on the river, of whom city officials would have known nothing. It is likely that many boatmen drowned and that their bodies floated downriver, uncounted. It was rumored that hundreds of people were killed on plantations in Louisiana, but those reports were never confirmed. Even fifty to eighty years later, in the early part of the twentieth century, the deaths of African Americans were not counted in the rural South. The Natchez tornado's $1,260,000 in damage (1840s dollars) was an immense sum for those days, a total not exceeded in any tornado for fifty years.

The much-studied Mayfield, Ohio, tornado of February 4, 1842, inspired Elias Loomis to compile the first known list of previous American tornadoes with a summary of their characteristics. Loomis is remembered best for his tornado wind speed experiments, using a cannon and, on occasion, a chicken.

What was thought to have been a family of intense tornadoes leveled thousands of acres of forest across 100 miles of sparsely populated Upstate New York on September 20, 1845, without producing a single known human fatality. The Great Adirondack Tornado was actually a family of tornadoes that probably originated in Canada. The first tornado crossed Lake Ontario as a waterspout. Others produced immense tree damage all the way to the edge of Lake Champlain. "Large trees and roofs of buildings, boards, hay, [and] grain were carried and whirled about in the air like straws and twigs in a whirlpool, presenting an awfully sublime and appalling sight. Large and well cultivated farms [were] covered with trees and the wrecks of the forest." A hemlock tree, 2 feet in diameter, was said to have been carried a distance of 2 miles.

Also in the 1840s, weather data began to be transmitted via telegraph to Washington, D.C., and the first crude weather maps could then be drawn on a daily basis. The Smithsonian Institution was in charge of weather observations.

1850–1859

In 1851 William Blasius drew a detailed path map of a tornado at Cambridge, Massachusetts. The following year he proposed the revolutionary idea that advancing cold air "pushed humidity" into the upper atmosphere to form cumulus clouds.

After the New Harmony, Indiana, tornado of April 30, 1852, Professor Chappelsmith meticulously measured the bearing and position of seven thousand fallen trees in a 1-square-mile area. After the Knox County, Ohio, tornado of January 20, 1854, O. N. Stoddard of Miami University mapped out the spiral ground markings with such perfection that it could have been mistaken for the work of Fujita, 110 years later. Both Chappelsmith and Stoddard concluded that tornadoes rotate.

In the 1850s ten of the fifteen killer tornadoes occurred in either Illinois or Ohio, but the deadliest was at Louisville, Kentucky, on August 27, 1854. The vortex seemed not to be especially intense, but it hit the downtown area. At least eighteen people died in the collapse of the newly built Third Presbyterian Church.

1860–1869

The Civil War and Reconstruction interrupted tornado documentation. The press and the armies of the North and the South were preoccupied with much greater tragedies. It is unlikely that the decade was as free of tornadoes as the record indicates. Twenty-one tornadoes were documented in 1860, but only seven were counted during the entire five-year period from 1861 to 1865.

The decade began with one of the deadliest tornadoes in history. On June 3, 1860, a complex family of tornadoes moved across central Iowa and northern Illinois. Entire farm communities of newly arrived settlers were wiped out. One tornado killed 111 people, including 16 on one Iowa farm and 23 of 26 people on a raft on the Mississippi River; the three survivors found themselves on the Illinois shore with no memory of how they had arrived there. At Camanche, Iowa, "the air, darkened by the immense moving cloud, was charged with death and the shrieks and groans and prayers for help were heard even above the din and roar of the tempest. Forty-one persons were instantly killed and more than 80 lacerated and mutilated in every conceivable way. Trunks, clothes, beds, carpets, furniture, and even stoves absolutely vanished. The hotel could not have more effectively been destroyed had a barrel of gunpowder been exploded within its walls." After the Camanche event, interest in tornadoes was so high that the Smithsonian Institution prepared a circular on tornadoes, requesting that information on any sightings be sent to Washington, D.C.

Just a few days later, on June 8, a family of six died as their house was swept away by an intense nighttime tornado in Miami County, Kansas. That was the first documented killer tornado in a Great Plains state, although it is possible that Native Americans were killed in earlier years. Just how many Native Americans were killed by tornadoes is unknown. Not all tribes considered tornadoes to be evil. Some looked on them as cleansing entities.

It was during the 1860s that the work of a Tennessee school teacher and self-taught mathematician named William Ferrel became prominent. It was he, building on the ideas of Redfield, who would bring the study of severe storms into the modern era. During the period 1856–89, Ferrel led the meteorological community out of the wilderness of speculation into the realm of genuine science. He was the first to link mathematically the rotation of the storm and the rotation of the earth. Ferrel also wrote that the rotation of tornadic winds was induced by the parent thunderstorm and that thunderstorm rotation was ultimately linked to the rotation of the earth. While the concepts of horizontal and vertical wind shear were decades away, the genius of Ferrel's scientific vision pointed us at last in the right direction. He also suggested that the highest wind speed in a tornado was probably 140 meters per second (313 mph), just 5 mph from the top of today's F5 level on the Fujita Scale.

1870–1879

The reported number of tornadoes for the decade 1870–79 reached twenty-three per year as western expansion and development was proceeding rapidly. After the Civil War the spread of railroads, the telegraph, and newspapers greatly improved communications. Reporting was also enhanced by the presence of numerous army posts in the South during Reconstruction.

The decade saw at least 136 killer tornadoes, more than in all previous decades combined. Most of these occurred in the latter half of the 1870s. It was on January 1, 1874, that weather observations and tornado damage surveys were taken over by the newly established Weather Service of the U.S. Army Signal Corps. It is my opinion that as of 1875, we have a record of at least 80 percent of all tornado deaths. I suspect that before 1875 there were many unrecorded tornado deaths on plantations in the rural South and in remote pioneer settlements on the western frontier. In this era the popular press published hundreds of tornado, waterspout, and storm-related illustrations in magazines all over the world.

The March 20, 1875, outbreak across Mississippi, Alabama, Georgia, South Carolina, and North Carolina produced a record eleven killer tornadoes. A second outbreak, with seven killer tornadoes, occurred in the same area just six weeks later. The decade's deadliest tornado took thirty-four lives at Wallingford, Connecticut, on August 9, 1878.

In 1879 army private John Park Finley was sent to Kansas, Missouri, and Iowa to survey damage and prepare a report of the tornado outbreak of May 29 and 30. The 116-page report (Finley 1881) was a landmark effort and the most detailed survey of its kind on any outbreak until Fujita's study of the Palm Sunday tornadoes of April 11, 1965 (Fujita, Bradbury, and van Thullenar 1970). In the next decade Finley would become the father of serious tornado climatology and forecasting.

The Tornado Memorial Park is situated 4 miles from Brussels in Door County, Wisconsin, at the site of the former town of Williamsonville, near Peshtigo. The sixty people (out of 77 residents) who died in an open field on October 8, 1871, were killed not by a true tornado but by a "tornado of fire," a vortex generated by one of the most destructive forest fires in U.S. history. October 8 saw enormous fires that burned millions of acres in Wisconsin and killed at least eighteen hundred people. It was also the date of the Great Chicago Fire.

1880–1889

This decade of rapid development of the western United States was also the first to record an average of more than one hundred tornadoes annually. The years 1880–1884 were the most violent periods of tornado activity in this country's history: there were five outbreaks with ten or more killer tornadoes each. No other five-year period has seen so many. The first major outbreak was on April 18, 1880; two parallel long-track tornadoes, on the ground at the same time, passed across southwestern Missouri. The northernmost of the pair passed through Marshfield, killing at least 99 people. The second killed 31 people in rural areas.

The tornado seasons of 1883 and 1884 were relentless. Those two years produced a total of 126 killer tornadoes, the all-time record for the largest number of such events over two consecutive years. One of the last in 1883 occurred on August 21 at Rochester, Minnesota. *The History of Olmsted County, Minnesota* provides this description in splendid nineteenth-century prose:

> A roar was heard that caused stern faces to blanch and brave hearts to throb with terror. With a roar like ten thousand demons it swept down upon the beautiful city. Like a great coiling serpent darting out a thousand tongues of lightning, with a hiss like the seething, roaring Niagara, it wrapped the city in its hideous coils. Trees bent down as wax candles in a furnace; barns and houses sunk before its awful force as men sink down in battle. The work of the storm-fiend is complete. He gave no quarter to man, woman or dimpled child. The death-angel was enthroned above his dusky form, and together, with a wild, hideous roar, they swept down upon our beautiful city like a devouring demon. The expression of sadness on every face told more plainly than fluttering crepe or tolling bells the tale of mourning, desolation and death.

The most publicized tornado outbreak to that date hit the United States on February 19, 1884. A record twenty-eight killer tornadoes struck in rural areas of Alabama, Georgia, and the Carolinas. That single-day killer-tornado total would not be exceeded, or even matched, for ninety years, until April 3, 1974. The national press spread rumors that more than two thousand people had been killed. An Army Signal Corps survey team counted 182 deaths.

Fig. 12.1. On April 26, 1884, A. A. Adams took the first photograph of a tornado at Garnett, Kansas. Photo from Snowden D. Flora, *Tornadoes of the United States* (Norman: University of Oklahoma, 1953), courtesy Kathryn Mitchell.

The first photographs of a tornado were taken in 1884 on the cumbersome glass plate negatives of the day. That first photographer was A. A. Adams (fig. 12.1), who captured the shrinking stage near Garnett, Kansas, on April 26. The second was F. N. Robinson, who photographed a mature and violent tornado from Howard, South Dakota (fig. 12.2). No other known photographs were taken for twelve years. I suspect that Robinson's photograph was taken at a great distance and thus occupied only a small part of the original glass plate. That portion may then have been enlarged and enhanced. Following nineteenth-century practice, the edges of the wall cloud may have been enhanced to create the pendant funnel clouds. The huge dust cloud may have been added on the basis of the photographer's beliefs rather than his observations.

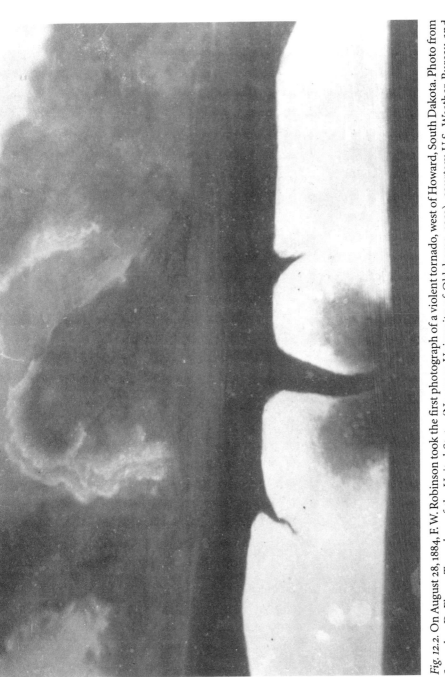

Fig. 12.2. On August 28, 1884, F. W. Robinson took the first photograph of a violent tornado, west of Howard, South Dakota. Photo from Snowden D. Flora, *Tornadoes of the United States* (Norman: University of Oklahoma, 1953), courtesy U.S. Weather Bureau and F. W. Robinson.

In 1884 J. P. Finley, now a lieutenant in the Army Signal Corps, completed an account of all 600 tornadoes "known" to have occurred through 1882 (Finley 1884). His count of 107 tornadoes for 1880 made it the first year in which more than 100 tornadoes were recorded.

In 1889 Indian Territory was opened for general settlement. It paved the way for eventual Oklahoma statehood in 1907 and more complete documentation of this tornado-prone state. Finley's (1887) records showed Oklahoma as a virtually tornado-free area. It was free of documentation, perhaps, but most certainly not free of actual tornadoes.

1890–1899

The decade 1890–99 opened with the century's second-worst outbreak, on March 27, 1890. The worst of its sixteen killer tornadoes crossed the Ohio River from Indiana and passed through downtown Louisville. Multistory buildings collapsed, and damage totaled a new record of $3.5 million, a record that would stand for only six years. More than half of the deaths (44 out of 76) were at what was called Falls City Hall. When this popular meeting place collapsed, about 200 people were in the building—75 at a lodge meeting on the upper floor and 125 children and their mothers at dancing lessons on the lower floor. This was perhaps the highest tornado-related death toll ever in a single building.

On July 13, 1890, a tornado killed six people near St. Paul, Minnesota. Most of the dead were thrown into lakes along with their cottages. An hour later what was probably the same storm system passed over Lake Pepin, 40 miles to the southeast. The gust front or a downburst related to the storm overturned the excursion boat *Red Wing*, drowning at least 110 people.

In the previous decade Iowa's Gustavus Hinricks, the first official State Climatologist, blasted Finley's documentation of Iowa tornadoes. Hinricks claimed that many of Finley's events were not tornadoes at all and insisted that Iowa tornadoes do not occur in the summer months. History does not record his reaction to the July 6, 1893, tornado that killed seventy-one Iowans, mostly at Pomeroy. On June 3, 1894, three people died in a house near Long Creek, Oregon, the first known tornado-related deaths west of the Rocky Mountains.

The year 1896 was the first with more than 500 tornado-related deaths. Its 537-death total would be exceeded only twice, in 1925 and 1936. Individual tornadoes killed 20 or more people on five days in May. This is a record that is unlikely to be broken in a modern, aware society. In the latter part of the twentieth century, individual tornadoes causing 20 or more deaths occur, on average, only once a year, if that often.

Also in 1896, for the first time a single tornado caused more than 100 deaths within the limits of a single city. Remarkably, that same tornado inflicted the toll in two separate cities. On May 27, 1896, the funnel passed across St. Louis, Missouri, and blew down or swept away houses, factories, saloons, hospitals, mills, churches, and buildings in railroad yards. At least 137 people were killed and damage set a new record. The list of fatalities probably did not include those living on shanty boats, whose bodies were washed downriver. The tornado was apparently at maximum intensity and in its shrinking stage when it crossed the Mississippi River into East St. Louis, Illinois. Buildings along the river were completely swept away, killing an additional 118 people. The $12 million damage total for the storm was a property loss five times greater than any previous tornado had inflicted and a record that would not be broken until the Great Tri-State Tornado in 1925.

The *Engineering News* published a photograph of what appears to be the shrinking stage of a tornado north of Oklahoma City, Oklahoma, on May 12, 1896. It was the first reproduction of a tornado photo in a magazine.

The decade ended with the deadliest tornado ever to occur in the northern tier of states. On June 12, 1899, a spectacular tornado touched down on Lake St. Croix, Wisconsin, and moved to the northeast. The funnel passed through New Richmond, Wisconsin, on Circus Day, when about one thousand additional people had crowded into the small town. In the center of town the tornado produced massive amounts of flying debris, resulting in multiple deaths in at least twenty-six families. The good visibility of the funnel may have helped keep the death total from being even higher than 114.

In the 1890s the newly formed Weather Bureau was made part of the Department of Agriculture. Tornado documentation and research were a very low priority. In 1897 the priority dropped to zero and national documentation ceased altogether.

In the mid-1890s balloons were carrying weather instruments as high as 11 miles, and the English physicist W. H. Dines was experimenting with the first laboratory models of tornadoes.

1900–1909

This was the only full decade of the twentieth century with no organized tornado documentation. Despite the poor record keeping between 1897 and 1915, there is newspaper evidence that tornadoes were as active as ever. The year 1909 produced seventy-six killer tornadoes, a record tied only once (in 1917) but never exceeded. Only two consecutive years in history recorded more than four hundred deaths each, 1909 and 1910.

The year 1908 marked the beginning of a twenty-nine-year period of what might be called a tornadic reign of terror in the United States. The era began on April 24 with an outbreak that took 324 lives across Louisiana and Mississippi. The period ended abruptly in 1936, after more than 200 people died in each of two tornadoes on consecutive days.

1910–1919

After two years, 1910 and 1911, in which no single tornado killed ten people came the worst outbreak of the decade. Ordinarily the tornado season for states as far north and west as Nebraska does not begin until April or May. On March 23, 1913, however, violent tornadoes struck in Omaha and all along the Nebraska-Iowa border. Not until March 13, 1990, did such significant activity reach that far northwest again so early in the season.

In a late-season outbreak (late for the southeastern states), eighteen killer tornadoes hit Arkansas on June 5, 1916. That remains a record for killer tornadoes in one state on one day. The year 1917 tied the record for the most killer tornadoes, with seventy-eight, on a record twenty-nine days. No year has had a killer tornado occur in each of its twelve months. Only two years, 1890 and 1917, have seen a killer tornado in eleven months of the same year. These, like many tornado death records of past years, will likely stand forever, or at least as long as we have watch, warning, and preparedness programs in a civilized society.

In 1916, apparently as part of a Weather Bureau reorganization, tornadoes were again officially documented. Only the most widely visible and most destructive events were reported, however. The annual average was just eighty-nine tornadoes from 1916 to 1919. There was no compelling reason to document all tornadoes, for there were not yet any forecasts to verify. The reign of terror continued as 1912 became the first and only year ever to have killer tornadoes on five consecutive days, April 25–29.

1920–1929

It was in the Roaring Twenties that the tornado death toll reached its peak. The year 1920 saw eleven tornadoes kill twenty or more people. No single year since then has had more than five such tragedies.

In the 1920s communications and tornado awareness had not yet caught up with a growing population. Whether tornadoes were more intense or their distribution was different at this time is impossible to gauge accurately. Housing construction was also very different. It is difficult to judge tornado intensity and compare it to modern tornadoes. The population distribution was also different. There were still many poor rural farmers in the Southeast. The mass migration to the cities and to California would not begin until the Great Depression.

The "tornado of the century" killed, for the first time, more than 200 people in a single city: 234 people, mostly women and children, lost their lives at Murphysboro, Illinois, in the Great Tri-State Tornado of March 18, 1925.

To date California has never had a killer tornado. But on April 8, 1926, a killer vortex did strike California. The powerful man-made vortex was attached to an overhead cloud and was one of thousands of whirlwinds that formed near and over a 900-acre, six-million-barrel oil fire at San Luis Obispo. The vortex originated as a "pillar of flame several thousand feet high" and traveled for more than a mile, destroying a house and killing the owner and his son. Two other people were injured in the open. Debris was carried 3 miles. Other oil fire vortices unroofed homes in the town of Brea.

The Tri-State Tornado property loss record of $16 million stood for only two years. On September 29, 1927, a tornado cut through St. Louis, Missouri, and Granite City, Illinois, taking seventy-nine lives. This was the third major tornado in St. Louis in the memory of many of its citizens; the first of the three was a less damaging event fifty-six years earlier.

By 1929 the beginning of a modern emergency rescue system seemed to be in place. On June 2, 1929, the Hardtner, Kansas, tornado (fig. 12.3) was visible for many miles in all directions. People in Alva, Oklahoma, 17 miles to the south, dispatched ambulances to Hardtner expecting to find the town destroyed. Only a single barn was destroyed, however, as the funnel just missed the town.

On June 10, 1929, French meteorologists received the first radio soundings (*radiosondes*) of temperature and pressure from a high-altitude balloon.

1930–1939

An outbreak across central Alabama on March 21, 1932, produced at least twenty-seven killer tornadoes, almost matching the record of twenty-eight set in 1884. The eight violent (F4–F5) tornadoes in one state, Alabama, on a single day stood as a record until Palm Sunday, April 11, 1965, when Indiana was hit by nine.

The decade 1930–39 was the only one to have two separate tornadoes, each with a death toll of more than 200. In a remarkable coincidence, they hit on consecutive days in 1936. Tupelo, Mississippi (April 5, 216 dead), and Gainesville, Georgia (April 6, 203 dead), both endured great tragedies. It would be six years before another tornado would kill even thirty people. Overall death totals began a noticeable decline that would continue through the rest of the century.

For most Americans, the first view of a tornado came from Hollywood in 1939, when Dorothy and Toto visited the Wizard of Oz. The MGM special effects department created a 35-foot-long, tornado-shaped wind sock out of muslin fabric. It was attached at the closed end and spun around. That model become the most famous tornado image in history; it was probably what most people pictured when tornadoes were discussed.

The origin of weather radar dates to 1939. During World War II a British team, headed by Robert Watson-Watt, made great strides in perfecting higher frequency and shorter wavelength radar that could detect small objects, even raindrops.

Fig. 12.3. In 1929 a tornado at Hardtner, Kansas, posed for one of the most spectacular weather photographs ever taken. The photograph graced textbooks and encyclopedias for the next forty years. Photo from Snowden D. Flora, *Tornadoes of the United States* (Norman: University of Oklahoma, 1953), courtesy U.S. Weather Bureau and Ira B. Blackstock.

In looking back at the period before World War II, we might question whether tornadoes were more intense than they are now. After all, in most years there were two hundred or more tornado-related fatalities, compared with fewer than half that today. No thoroughly reliable method exists to estimate the intensity of tornadoes in the distant past. I suggest, however, that they were not more violent; people were just not prepared for them the way we are today. For perspective, we can look at disasters in general during the period sixty to one hundred twenty years ago. This was a time when wealth and engineering ability allowed us to dig deeper mines and build larger buildings and ships. A growing population was eager for new experiences and steady income. It was also, however, a time before strict building codes and safety procedures were instituted. It was a time when large tornado death tolls occurred alongside similar tolls in other disasters. At the turn of the century, a train accident killing two people was commonplace enough to be ignored in anything but the local newspapers. Today that might be the lead story on national television news.

In the late nineteenth and early twentieth century, all manner of disasters took hundreds, even thousands, of lives annually in the United States. The Johnstown, Pennsylvania, flood took 2,200 lives (1889); and more than 6,000 died in a hurricane at Galveston, Texas (1900). In an era with only minimal building codes, 600 people burned to death in a Chicago theater (1903). An excursion boat fire on the East River in New York City took 1,020 lives (1904). The San Francisco earthquake and fire killed 700 (1906). In 1907, 361 died in a West Virginia coal mine; two weeks later 239 died in a Pennsylvania mine.

Ships were not safe either. About 1,500 drowned after the *Titanic* hit an iceberg (1912); the *Empress of Ireland* took 1,000 people down with her when she sank in the St. Lawrence River (1914); an ammunition ship explosion took 1,500 lives in Nova Scotia (1917). The next year a Minnesota forest fire killed 400. In 1928 more than 2,000 perished in a Florida hurricane and 450 died in the collapse of a California dam. At least 317 people burned to death in an Ohio prison fire (1930); a gas explosion at a Texas school killed more than 300 students and teachers (1937). These were very different times. In retrospect, it is surprising that tornado death tolls were not larger.

The large number of tornado-related fatalities, about 200 per year from 1880 to 1949, may just have been part of this same high-risk period that preceded the safety concerns that are now so much a part of U.S. society.

1940-1949

After a decade of very destructive tornadoes in the southeastern states, the deadliest activity moved westward onto the Great Plains. Of the ten tornadoes that killed thirty or more people, only one was in a southeastern state.

Tornado documentation continued to be rather poor during World War II. A South Dakota outbreak on June 17, 1944, with at least 13 deaths is still officially unlisted to this day, despite being the deadliest outbreak in the state's history (Grazulis 1993). On June 23, 1944, at least 100 people died in a damage swath across West Virginia, a state with no history of violent tornadoes. That tornado was part of an outbreak that also hit supposedly tornado-free parts of Pennsylvania and Maryland. The deadliest tornado of the 1940s, on April 9, 1947, devastated Higgins and Glazier, Texas, then leveled much of Woodward, Oklahoma.

In postwar Japan physics teacher Tetsuya Fujita was working on detailed mapping of typhoons and thunderstorms. He became aware of Horace Byers's Thunderstorm Project after finding the project report in the wastebasket of a U.S. Air Force radar station on Mount Seburiyama. Fujita contacted Byers and sent him a sample of his work on Japanese thunderstorms. Byers was impressed with Fujita's uncanny ability and insight into weather analysis on the local or meso- scale. Byers invited Fujita to the United States and became his mentor at the University of Chicago in the early 1950s.

Over the next forty years, Fujita went on to become the most prolific individual producer and publisher of tornado and severe storm research in the history of meteorology. His work profoundly affected the public's awareness of tornadoes and influenced the course of all research that involved aerial survey of tornado damage, multiple vortices, data collection, high wind risk assessments, downbursts, and even the meteorology of airplane crashes.

Albert Showalter, Joe Fulks, and J. R. Lloyd published tornado forecasting methods in the early 1940s, but history belongs to two air force officers, Ernest Fawbush and Robert Miller. During the war Fawbush served in the

cold climates of the Aleutian Islands and Siberia, while Miller served in the
heat of New Guinea and the Philippines. Fate brought them together at
Tinker Air Force Base near Oklahoma City, and in 1948 Fawbush and Miller
made their historic first successful local tornado forecast (chap. 5). Also in
1948, David Ludlum founded *Weatherwise* magazine, the first devoted to
the study of the weather and written for the general public.

One of the most widely reprinted articles from the early issues of
Weatherwise was the following description of a tornado as viewed from
directly underneath the funnel. On May 3, 1948, Captain Roy Hall, a retired
Army officer and trained observer, made these detailed observations at
McKinney, Texas (see chap. 8 for more details):

> Sixty feet south of our house something had billowed down from above
> and stood fairly motionless, save a slow up-and-down pulsation. It pre-
> sented a curved face, with the concave part toward me, with a bottom rim
> that was almost level, and was not moving either toward or away from the
> house. It was the lower end of the tornado funnel! I was looking at its
> inside, and we were, at the moment, within the tornado itself!
>
> The bottom of the rim was about 20 feet off the ground. The interior of
> the funnel was hollow; the rim itself appearing to be not over 10 feet in
> thickness and, owing possibly to the light within the funnel, appeared
> perfectly opaque. Its inside was so slick and even that it resembled the inte-
> rior of a glazed standpipe. The rim had another motion which was, for a
> moment, too dazzling to grasp. Presently I did. The whole thing was rotat-
> ing, shooting past from right to left with incredible velocity.
>
> I lay back on my left elbow to afford the baby better protection and
> looked up. I was looking far up the interior of a great tornado funnel! It
> extended upward for over a thousand feet, and was swaying gently, and
> bending slowly toward the southeast. Down at the bottom, judging from
> the circle in front of me, the funnel was about 150 yards across. Higher up
> it was larger, and seemed to be partly filled with a bright cloud, which
> shimmered like a fluorescent light. This brilliant cloud was in the middle
> of the funnel, not touching the sides.
>
> As the upper portion of the huge pipe swayed over, another phenome-
> non took place. It looked as if the whole column were composed of rings
> or layers, and when a higher ring moved on toward the southeast, the ring

immediately below slipped over to get back under it. This rippling motion continued on down toward the lower tip.

When the wave-like motion reached the lower tip, the far edge of the funnel was forced downward and jerked toward the southeast. This edge, in passing, touched the roof of my neighbor's house and flicked the building away like a flash of light. Where, an instant before, had stood a recently constructed home, now remained one small room with no roof. The house, as a whole, did not resist the tornado for the fractional part of a second. When the funnel touched it, the buildings dissolved, the various parts shooting off to the left like sparks from an emery wheel.

The very instant the rim of the funnel passed beyond the wreck of the house, long vaporous-appearing streamers, pale blue in color, extended out and upward toward the southeast from each corner of the remaining room. They appeared to be about 20 feet long and six inches wide, and after hanging perfectly stationary for a long moment, were suddenly gone.

1950–1959

The 1950s were full of dramatic advances in research and forecasting, as well as catastrophic events. Weather Bureau forecasters helped to make it the last decade of the century in which a single tornado would kill more than one hundred people. Reporting of tornadoes was improved in an effort to determine the accuracy of forecasts. This boosted the total reported tornadoes from just 200 in 1950 to a high of 856 in 1957.

On June 8, 1951, the first motion pictures of a U.S. tornado were taken at Corn, Oklahoma. This was a pair of tornadoes that seemed to be rotating in opposite directions. Tornado "watch box" forecasting began in 1952, but two of the worst years in history for violent tornadoes lay just ahead. Violent tornadoes would occur on sixteen days in 1953 and seventeen days in 1957, the highest such totals in history.

In 1953 the first book on tornadoes in this century, Flora's *Tornadoes of the United States,* was published. On April 9, 1953, a hook echo was seen and photographed on an Illinois radar screen, and the search for hook echoes became an integral part of warning procedure. Long after the Worcester, Massachusetts, tornado of June 9, 1953, had lifted, it was discovered that the storm's hook echo was identifiable 20 minutes before touchdown. On April

30 a tornado was captured on motion picture film at Warner Robins Air Force Base in Georgia. The film showed buildings disintegrating and shooting skyward in scenes that are unmatched even today (see fig. 6.5). The year 1953 was one of great disasters and the beginning of the modern era of tornado studies.

For the rest of the century, research proceeded at a rapid pace. In 1956 alone there were 107 instrumented aircraft flights into thunderstorms.

The first year in which motion-picture photography played a major role in research was 1957. On April 2 a tornado at Dallas was captured by dozens of photographers, making possible a new era of research in frame-by-frame photogrammetric analysis. Fujita's studies of the Fargo, North Dakota, tornado of June 20, 1957, were a landmark research effort, with an analysis of rotation and storm structure unlike anything done before. The Fargo and Dallas studies improved our understanding of the tornado life cycle as well as the relationship between parent thunderstorms and their tornadoes.

The effort to document all tornadoes, rather than only the damaging ones, gave rise to a new "kind" of outbreak that had been previously documented only in part. It occurred on May 4–5, 1959 and produced forty-nine tornadoes, none of which was a killer and forty-one of which did only F0–F1 damage.

By 1950 experimental military Doppler radar could distinguish airplanes from helicopters by the rotational tendency of propellers. A few people saw the potential usefulness of Doppler radar in tornado research and forecasting. Because it detected motion, the ground clutter from buildings and hills would cease to be a problem. Since a large rotating structure was responsible for spawning tornadoes, Doppler radar seemed like an ideal tool for thunderstorm research and tornado detection. The Doppler radar signal, however, is very complex. Processing requires electronics technology that was not yet available. After the devastating tornadoes of 1953, the idea of trying to refine and put Doppler radar to use was set aside. The focus for the next twenty years was on refining "conventional" radar, which located a storm's position but not the rotation of the mesocyclone.

Tornado-related Doppler radar research began in 1956 when James Brantley of the Cornell Aeronautical Laboratory convinced Vaughn Rockney of the Weather Bureau that Doppler radar had genuine potential for detection of tornadoes. Rockney arranged for the funding of an experimental

Doppler radar to be obtained from the navy and set up for the 1958 tornado season at Wichita Falls, Texas, and Wichita, Kansas. The payoff came on June 10, 1958, when a 206-mph wind speed signature was received at the Wichita station from the El Dorado tornado.

1960–1969

The decade of the Vietnam War and the first moon landing was also the decade in which the supercell concept was born and the United States was hit by its first $100 million tornado. On April 1, 1960, TIROS was launched. The first pictures from space were crude by modern standards, but they launched the era of satellite meteorology. On May 4, 1961, Neil Ward inaugurated the art and science of modern storm chasing (see chap. 3).

In 1962 Keith Browning moved from England to the U.S. Air Force research facility at Sudbury, Massachusetts. He and Ralph Donaldson obtained the radar films of the Geary, Oklahoma, storm of 1961 and studied them in detail. On May 26, 1963, a tornadic thunderstorm was observed overhead by Donaldson at a radar site at Tinker Air Force Base near Oklahoma City. It is with these storms that the "supercell" concept was refined (see chap. 3).

In 1963 the NSSP of SELS and the Weather Radar Laboratory (WRL) at Norman, Oklahoma, merged into the NSSL, with Edwin Kessler as its director. During Kessler's tenure, NSSL would lead the way in the development of a Doppler radar system that could be deployed nationally.

The deadliest outbreak of the decade was on Palm Sunday 1965, when 256 people died across Illinois, Wisconsin, Indiana, Michigan, and Ohio. Ten tornadoes killed 10 or more people, only the second (and last) such outbreak in history (the first was on March 21, 1932). The Palm Sunday outbreak of April 11 produced a record 19 violent tornadoes, nearly twice as many as the previous record of 10 set by the March 21, 1932, outbreak. As extraordinary as this record was, it would stand for only nine years, until April 3, 1974. The death toll on Palm Sunday 1965 was the sixth largest in history and the largest, to that date, since forecasting began twelve years earlier. The Palm Sunday damage patterns spurred Fujita's research into spiral ground markings and the structure of multiple-vortex tornadoes. The high death toll also resulted in a reorganization of the Weather Bureau efforts to enhance public awareness. The reevaluation of warning techniques and a new sense of urgency gave rise to the inauguration of SKYWARN and a 24-hour NOAA weather radio service that continues to this day.

The Topeka tornado of June 6, 1966, set a property-loss record of $100 million. Instead of killing 100 to 200 people, as it might have if it had occurred fifty years earlier, this F5 monster killed only 16. The property loss at Topeka nearly doubled the previous record loss, set at Worcester in 1953. That record would last only four years, however. Joe Eagleman's research on the damage pattern at Topeka introduced scientific methodology to the study of tornado damage and shed light on what might be the safest locations in houses during a tornado. In 1967 the remnants of Hurricane Beulah in central and southern Texas spawned a record-breaking number of tornadoes (115) between September 19 and 23.

The decade ended with some historic research. Ward refined his multiple-vortex tornado model at NSSL, Joseph Golden's waterspout research flights were completed in the Florida Keys, and Ralph Donaldson used Doppler radar to detect a mesocyclone in a supercell. After that latter success in Massachusetts, the development of Doppler radar would be centered at the National Severe Storms Laboratory in Norman.

1970–1979

The decade's storm highlights began with the Lubbock, Texas, tornado on May 11, 1970, and a new damage record of $135 million. The decade ended with the Wichita Falls tornado on April 10, 1979. The Wichita Falls event was the last tornado to kill forty or more people. Its new damage record of $450 million would remain unbroken for twenty years.

The 1970s began a golden age of tornado research. In May 1970 engineers at Texas Tech University used the Lubbock damage to begin comprehensive studies of damage and safety in tornadoes that continues today. Fujita advanced the mapping of tornado paths by relating the deaths at Lubbock to the multiple-vortex structure of the tornado (see fig. 12.4). Doppler radar was installed and in operation at NSSL in 1971. On June 2, 1971, a storm was moving from Kansas into central Oklahoma with a conventional hook echo. A team headed by Rodger Brown detected a 3-mile-wide (low-level) mesocyclone just above cloud base. For the first time

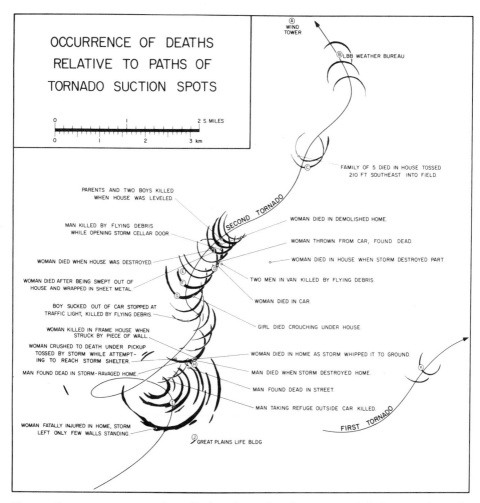

OCCURRENCE OF DEATHS
RELATIVE TO PATHS OF
TORNADO SUCTION SPOTS

Fig. 12.4. Since 1970 many tornado studies have focused on the extreme winds that occur in suction vortices. Fujita's analysis shows that 27 of the 28 deaths in the Lubbock tornado were related to suction vortice damage patterns.

Doppler radar measurements of rotation were directly associated with a conventional radar hook echo.

The first organized storm chase program, a joint effort of the University of Oklahoma and NSSL, was to begin on April 14, 1972. Coincidentally, Neil Ward died, at the age of sixty-two, on April 12, and his funeral was held on the morning of April 14. Conditions failed to develop, and there was no chasing until April 18. On April 19 Brown and his colleagues at NSSL (Brown, Burgess, and Crawford 1973) located twin mesocyclones, each producing tornadoes that moved on parallel paths. The more northern mesocyclone produced a family of tornadoes, a small but violent member of which killed five people in a house near Davis, Oklahoma. The rotation extended to an altitude of 6 miles, about two-thirds the height of the storm. The tornadoes were too far away (about 50 miles) to record a wind-speed measurement. At that distance the beam is too wide, compared to the size of the tornado. Chase teams were in the field on April 19, but not with the armored personnel carrier that was suggested by one engineer, who wanted to use it to penetrate the tornado.

On August 9, 1972, just four years to the day from the first mesocyclone detection, Donaldson had another first at Sudbury, Massachusetts. A meso-cyclone signature was detected, along with a concentrated center in the mesocyclone, just 5 miles away. That concentrated center coincided with a killer tornado at Brookline, Massachusetts. This was the first detection of the position of a tornado by Doppler radar. It was eventually determined that for full-sized Doppler radars, the maximum distance for detecting a half-mile-wide tornado is about 60 miles. A smaller, 50-yard-wide tornado will escape detection at 15 miles.

In 1973 the number of recorded tornadoes topped one thousand for the first time. This was also the year of the first big storm chase success, at Union City, Oklahoma (see chap. 3). At Union City the mesocyclone circulation was detected 40 minutes in advance of a tornado touchdown. An intense shear pattern, producing a tornadic vortex signature (TVS) on Doppler radar, was detected 20 minutes before touchdown and was about half a mile wide. As with the 1972 storm near Davis, the Union City mesocyclone extended to a height of 6 miles. Much of the analysis of radar data and detec-tion of signatures was done well after the storm and not in a real-time, nowcasting situation. Real-time ability would take several years to develop.

At Union City the tornado life cycle was delineated, the tornadic vortex signature was identified, and the dream of a radar-based advanced warn-ing system seemed as if it might become a reality. New research funding was being made available by the Nuclear Regulatory Commission, as part of its comprehensive natural-hazard research program.

With all of these new resources in place, Mother Nature provided the largest-known tornado outbreak in the planet's recorded history. The April 3–4, 1974, "Super Outbreak" began at 2:30 P.M. in an Illinois cornfield, and in the next twenty-two hours 148 tornadoes would touch down and kill 316 (9 in Canada). Government and university scientists converged on the destroyed communities, particularly Xenia, Ohio, where an F5 tornado killed 34 people and damaged or destroyed more than 2,000 houses. The Xenia tornado ripped apart some well-constructed schools, which gave engineers a good look at just what a violent tornado could and could not do. By midafternoon Indiana had been hit by a record-tying nine violent tornadoes. It tied its own record, set in 1965. The record lasted only a few hours. By late evening Kentucky had experienced its eleventh violent tornado of the day.

Using measures such as numbers (probably 148), path length (1,700 path miles), and intensity (30 violent tornadoes), this was an unprecedented outbreak. Massive supercell tornadoes passed directly through town after town, yet the highest death tolls in single cities were 34 at Xenia and 28 at Brandenburg, Kentucky. Fifty years earlier these tornadoes might have killed at least 100 people each. The Super Outbreak of April 3, 1974, brought to the forefront the successes and limitations of tornado forecasts and warnings.

Virtually every tornado occurred in a watch box. Most communities were well warned. It was clear, however, that there might always be events that hit in the wrong place, at the wrong time, and overwhelm the ability to warn everyone, let alone induce them to seek shelter. But there is also a particularly vulnerable segment of the population in any town that may be impossible to reach, at least within the financial capabilities of any government agency (see chap. 14).

At Atlanta on March 24, 1975, there was a unique tornado observation that once again resurrected the old question of a tornado-electricity link. This tornado produced a 12-mile path on the northwest side of Atlanta, doing $56 million in damage, some of it to the governor's mansion. Three people were killed. The maximum damage intensity was F3.

This tornado was unique because of its proximity to sophisticated equipment used to measure the spectrum of radiowave discharges from lightning, called *sferics.* The Electrical Engineering Department of Georgia Tech University had four sferics detectors operating during the tornado's passage, as close as 4 miles from the funnel. The intriguing observation (Greneker et al. 1977) was that the sferics virtually stopped during the time that the tornado was on the ground; the rate dropped to only 10 percent of what it was before touchdown. The sferics returned to the original high rate when the tornado lifted. To the engineers on site, it was evidence that the funnel had created a short circuit between the cloud and the ground. However, just a few year earlier several sferics detectors were in operation during the Union City storm, and there was little or no change in sferics during the life of the tornado. The mystery of tornadoes and electricity continued.

After a jet airliner crashed in 1976 at New York's John F. Kennedy Airport, Fujita began investigating the meteorological conditions that produced the crash. Fujita returned to his photographs of the wind damage taken after the 1974 outbreak. The birth of the downburst and microburst terminology was the result of his 1976 studies (Fujita and Caracena 1977) and of the "starburst" damage pattern photographs from the Super Outbreak.

In the mid-1970s teams of meteorologists at NSSL worked with electrical engineers to create a digital display for Doppler radar. Much of this work is described by David Atlas (1990). The research went hand in hand with the microprocessor revolution in electronics.

A Doppler radar screen, with its pattern of coloring for particles moving away from (red) and toward (green) the radar antenna, is deceptively uncomplicated, belying the nearly one hundred years of continuous research in electronics and electromagnetic wave radiation that preceded its development. It took the pressure of two world wars and several revolutions involving vacuum tubes and then computers, semiconductors, and microprocessors to bring Doppler weather radar into use. It was not invented at a single stroke but slowly developed and refined by the genius and sweat of hundreds of scientists and technicians.

This was a decade of great promise for Doppler radar as a tornado warning tool. Don Burgess of NSSL studied the Doppler radar signatures of thirty-seven mesocyclones that produced twenty-three tornadoes. The average lead time between mesocyclone identification and tornado touchdown was 36 minutes (Burgess 1976). Visual sightings of a funnel cloud usually provide only about 2 minutes of lead time before touchdown. Today the average lead time for all tornado warnings is about 8 minutes. That landmark study by Burgess led to the Joint Doppler Operational Project (JDOP). This collaboration between the National Weather Service, the Air Force Weather Service, and the Federal Aviation Administration led to the go-ahead for development of the current NEXRAD radar system.

In 1975 the Geostationary Operational Environmental Satellite (GOES-1) was launched. Higher resolution cloud images were taken from one position, at an altitude of 22,000 miles. This began the era of satellite photography as we know it today. By 1978 Joseph Klemp and Robert Wilhelmson were making great strides in refining their numerical models of thunderstorms. In 1979 Lemon and Doswell linked tornado formation with the formation of a rear flank downdraft and a divided mesocyclone that was partially within the main updraft.

1980–1989

In the early 1980s Doppler radar refinement had advanced enough to begin the long process of creating and deploying a national Doppler radar network, called NEXRAD. First there had to be construction and evaluation of competing designs of Doppler units from different contractors. NSSL continued work on computer algorithms to aid forecasters in interpreting the Doppler radar information.

In 1988 there began a massive transfer of technology from the research labs to the operational format of the NWS offices. Extensive retraining of the entire NWS staff in the use of the new WSR-88D (1988 Doppler version of Weather Surveillance Radar) facilities was necessary.

The death toll from tornadoes continued to drop despite the increasing U.S. population. This would be the first decade since the Civil War with no more than thirty deaths in any single tornado.

Storm chasing became a widely used and accepted research procedure, and with it our understanding of supercells was expanded. Storm chasers were producing a steady flow of photographs and video footage. The proliferation of home videocameras, beginning about 1985, began to produce detailed closeups of tornadoes taken by people from their backyards. The mapping of outbreaks, once a rarity, was now routine.

On July 21, 1987, a tornado-downburst complex felled 15,000 trees in the Teton Wilderness of Wyoming, at altitudes of up to 10,000 feet. Fujita ranked some of the damage at F4, even though trees are not reliable indications of F4 winds. It was his feeling (pers. comm.) that the winds need to be in that speed range because of the thin atmosphere. At 10,000 feet, the air is only about two-thirds as dense as air at sea level. Throughout the 1980s Fujita refined his model of the microburst, a small (less than 2.5 miles in diameter) downward-moving burst of air from a thunderstorm. The impact of his microburst on tornado documentation was to help determine which events were true tornadoes.

On November 16, 1989, a "tornado" blew down a cafeteria wall of the East Coldenham Elementary School, 6 miles west of Newburgh, New York. At that moment more than 120 first- to third-graders were having lunch in the cafeteria. Nine students were killed. The event remains an official tornado in the NWS tornado database, despite Fujita's personal survey that indicated the damage was clearly caused by a microburst. The governor of New York commissioned Fujita to study the damage path and then rejected his findings as to the nature of its origin (pers. com.). Unfortunately, this nontornado remains (officially) the deadliest weak (F0–F1) tornado in history and the deadliest ever tornado in New York State.

On January 11, 1990, *Newsday* reported that the Falconer Weather Information Service had determined that the event was not a tornado. It also reported that a New York engineering firm had determined that the free-standing center portion of the wall could withstand winds of only 45 mph and that winds of 80 mph probably brought it down. Another independent engineering study found that the wall could have collapsed under pressure from just a 65-mph wind. State safety standards, adopted in 1959, required that walls be able to resist winds of 120 mph. The building construction had begun in 1958 but was renovated in 1984. Only the design, not the construction or the materials, was found to be at fault.

On May 15, 1992, the *Albany Times-Union* reported that the State Supreme Court of New York reversed a lower court ruling that the county was responsible for the deaths. Two year later families of the dead and injured settled out of court for $6,750,000 in a $21 million lawsuit. The trial was set to begin in January 1995, more than five years after the disaster. In the settlement about $6 million was paid by the school's insurer, the remainder by the insurers of the architect and an engineer who worked on the school.

1990–1999

The 1990s saw continued refinement of Doppler radar as both a research and an operational forecasting tool. Local television stations in the more competitive markets installed their own Doppler radar units. Some stations hired chase teams in an effort to get live on-air pictures of a tornado in action. At the beginning of the decade there were the first efforts to deploy the NEXRAD Doppler radar system, usually referred to as WSR-88D. There are now about 160 of these sites, counting those at NWS offices, Federal Aviation Administration airport stations, and military locations.

On March 13, 1990, an outbreak of fifty-nine tornadoes struck primarily in Kansas and Nebraska. Not since March 23, 1913, had any comparable outbreak hit this early in the season so far to the north and west. The tornadoes were widely visible and well forecast. Despite the twenty-six F2–F5 tornadoes, there were only two killers. One took a young boy's life when a chimney toppled into a basement. The other person killed was an elderly woman in a flimsy house that was actually a converted army barracks without a basement. For the first time merging tornadoes were photographed. This outbreak marked the start of a nearly continuous flow of home and chase videos of tornadoes. Since then fifty to one hundred tornadoes have been captured on videotape every year. In some years individual storm chasers have taped fifteen or more.

The forecasting and warning accomplishments displayed so well in March were not repeated on August 28, 1990, when a difficult to see, difficult to forecast, and historically unprecedented violent tornado moved to the southeast across the Chicago suburbs, killing twenty-nine people in and around Plainfield, Illinois. (It is this type of situation that the WSR-88D system should be particularly effective in handling in the future.)

The year 1992 saw its biggest outbreak in the fall rather than in the spring. From November 21 to 23, the southern United States was hit by an outbreak that lasted forty-one continuous hours, one of the longest periods of continuous activity in history. The 1994 tornado season began with another Palm Sunday outbreak. On March 27 a dozen supercells traveled a narrow band across Alabama, Georgia, and the Carolinas. Forty-two people died, 20 of them at a Goshen, Alabama, church (see chap. 4). Of the 18 people who died in Georgia, 15 were in mobile homes.

In spring 1994 and 1995, the largest storm chase project in history took to the road. The Verification of the Origins of Rotation in Tornadoes Experiment (VORTEX) surrounded and probed supercell thunderstorms with twenty cars and vans (mobile mesonets, as they were called) with odd-looking rooftop data-gathering assemblages. Joining the armada were the most sophisticated portable Doppler radars available. These included the Doppler on Wheels and two radar-equipped aircraft. The goal was to understand better the near-surface airflows near mesocyclones that contribute to or trigger tornadoes. The operation was conducted in almost military style and was the first large-scale assault on the mystery of tornado formation. Voluminous data were gathered from storms such as the one at Dimmitt, Texas. It will take years to unravel all the possible clues to tornado formation that lie hidden in the accumulated data.

VORTEX vehicles suffered repeated damage and sometimes needed all their windows replaced. Probe Three even had a bird house (near Comanche, Oklahoma, on April 17, 1995) thrown into the vehicle, only to have it angrily retrieved by the owner after the tornado had passed. Just a few minutes earlier the VORTEX armada was split, as a tornado crossed the road in the middle of the convoy.

Integrated into VORTEX were many innovative ways of studying tornadoes, such as the Tornado Debris Project (Snow et al. 1995). This was an attempt to better understand the internal circulation of a thunderstorm by studying the downwind distribution patterns of debris that was carried long distances by tornadic thunderstorms.

In the 1990s commercial enterprises began to use tornado images. Volvo won an award for its tornado chase commercial that was shown only in Europe and Australia, and *Twister* broke box office records worldwide. Researchers noted, with heavy sighs, that their work could be expanded and funded for decades with just a small fraction of the motion picture profits. Marty Feely, a California-born storm chaser and entrepreneur, established Whirlwind Tours, wich offered vacationers from all over the world the opportunity to search for American tornadoes. More than two million copies of commercially produced home videotapes of tornadoes were sold in the United States alone. In a testament to the abilities of amateur and semiprofessional storm chasers, Charles Edwards built a 70-pound lead-weighted armadillo-shaped camera case he called the Dillocam. In 1997 near Wellington, Kansas, he and a friend, Casey Crosbie, placed the camera in front of a tornado. They and their nervous tourists watched as the funnel passed over the operating camera.

The decade and the century ended with one of the most destructive outbreaks in history. The severity of the May 3, 1999, outbreak in central Oklahoma and Kansas was not apparent to forecasters until just a few hours before the first tornadoes touched down. Despite this, the warning system worked so well that one emergency management expert suggested that people south of Oklahoma City had so much warning that they could have dug a storm shelter in time for the tornado's passage. Key to that ample warning was the television media. The Oklahoma City television stations are equipped with their own Doppler radar. They have been pioneers in radar-based nowcasting. They pride themselves on being able to pinpoint severe storm activity to the street location and get live pictures on the air. As the tornado approached, pictures were broadcast from "towercams," television cameras 1,000 feet high, on top of transmission towers. Their storm chasers are equipped with remote cameras both in cars and in helicopters. Researchers were also chasing with instrumented vehicles. VORTEX chasers measured airflow at ground level, and Bluestein and Wurman probed the funnel with highly refined Doppler radars. In terms of research, destruction, and forecasting, it was the event of the century.

Despite the remarkable nowcasting efforts, there were still forty deaths in central Oklahoma. Most were early in the path, in mobile homes, in frame homes with no basements, or under overpasses. The myth that an overpass is safe shelter was dispelled as people were swept out, dismembered, and thrown to their deaths. The last mutilated body was found a week after the tornado. It was that of a young woman who was thrown from an I-35 underpass, carried to a flooded ditch, and covered with debris. The deaths again revealed the ever-present vulnerable segments of the population. It also showed the power of warnings and awareness. More than five thousand homes were damaged or destroyed, with deaths in just a few of them. Twelve thousand vehicles were damaged or destroyed; eight hundred were wrecked in a single sales lot, with a dozen of them raining down onto a nearby motel. There were no deaths in cars or motels.

Since I first saw the damage caused by the Worcester tornado in 1953, the changes in how we study tornadoes have been revolutionary. Once a distant and rarely photographed apparition, the tornado is now studied at close range by instrumented chase vehicles and captured on home video-tape in almost every month of the year. I view the future with great optimism and excitement, as we continue to pursue tornado knowledge, but with some lingering fears, discussed in the final chapter.

CHAPTER 13

TORNADOES OUTSIDE
THE UNITED STATES

The storm on the McDonald farm one night in August was unusually fierce. With the wind rising to a frightening roar and the house beginning to tremble, Angus, his wife, and his daughter decided they had better wait out the storm in the cellar. The tornado arrived at the isolated farmhouse just as they began to move toward the cellar door. The house was lifted intact and smashed to the ground, throwing the family across the prairie. The daughter probably died instantly. Angus lay unconscious but still alive. Seriously injured, Mrs. McDonald crawled over to her husband and, with her own body and clothing, shielded him the entire night from a torrential downpour of rain and hail. In the morning a passerby heard the cries for help and took the family to town, where Angus died later that day. The town was Wapella, the date was August 28, 1900, and the location was Saskatchewan, Canada. It was one of about one hundred recorded killer tornadoes that have struck that country.

Tornadoes have probably occurred in every country in the world, but they are not extensively studied outside the United States. On most continents tornadoes are extremely rare and not considered a serious threat to life. But there may be much to be learned in these other countries about how tornadoes form and about what conditions cause them to intensify. For instance, one of the best places to study the effects of topography on thunderstorms may be in the Jura Mountains, south of Geneva, along the France–Switzerland border. Swaths of damage in the area date back to 1624 (Dessens and Snow 1993). Another interesting area for research is Bangladesh, which has had horrendous death tolls: as many as one thousand people were killed and tens of thousands injured on a single afternoon of thunderstorms. These incredible nor'westers, as they are called, might well be a combination of downbursts and tornadoes not often witnessed in North America. Any of these unique situations might provide clues to thunderstorm dynamics and tornado formation. The bewildering variety of American tornado situations, with its multitude of variables, make it hard to isolate cause and effect.

My best guess is that about three-fourths of the world's tornadoes occur in the United States. If 1,500 occur in the United States, then perhaps 500 occur in the rest of the world. The majority of the latter are not counted and are probably minor. Most of them occur in about thirty other countries (fig. 13.1). Tornadoes are not minor in Bangladesh, which is about the size of Iowa and has a population four times that of California. The majority of the population is poverty-stricken and lives in fragile housing. There is little wonder that with about nine intense tornadoes a year it has the highest average annual death toll of any nation.

It is not possible to compare accurately the tornado frequency in different countries. The experience in the United States shows that the design of the reporting system can make a 1,000 percent difference in the number of reported tornadoes. There are no international standards in watches, warnings, and verification, so any country-by-country comparisons are highly speculative. England is the only country besides the United States where a serious attempt is made to count tornadoes. There an active private group tries to track down a record of any whirlwind that might fit the broadest definition of a tornado. The average is about thirty per year, a very high concentration given that England is about the size of Iowa, which has a similar annual tornado count.

Although we cannot compare the number of tornadoes, we can compare geography. In Bangladesh and India the positioning of land, sea, and

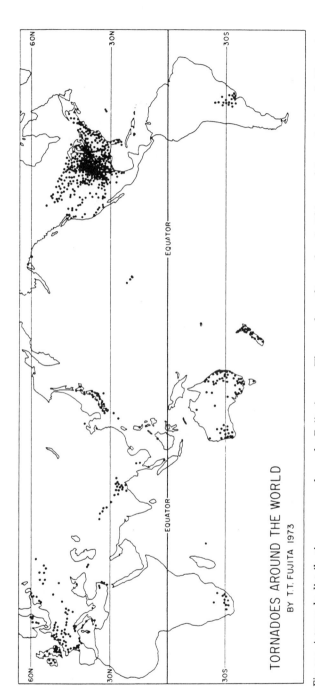

TORNADOES AROUND THE WORLD
BY T.T. FUJITA 1973

Fig. 13.1. A tornado distribution map was drawn by Fujita in 1973. The number of tornadoes in China and Argentina is probably under-estimated.

mountains is somewhat similar to that of the United States. The Bay of Bengal plays the role of the Gulf of Mexico. The Himalayas are in some ways a counterpart to the Rocky Mountains. Parts of Italy have a somewhat similar configuration, with the Mediterranean and Adriatic seas providing moisture to the warm air. The Alps may provide both surface and upper-air tornado formation ingredients. While England does not have the benefit of dry air to enhance severe storms, it has many weather situations that produce thunderstorms and wind shear.

The top ten countries in the world for total tornado deaths in the past one hundred years are probably the United States, Bangladesh, Russia, India, Canada, Italy, South Africa, France, and Argentina, in that order. Until recently, political barriers have prevented the free flow of accurate disaster information for China. In the 1990s there seems to have been about one reported multiple-death tornado a year in China. That could put China ahead of Canada in the above list. These are my subjective judgments based on Richard Peterson's (1982) work and conversations with researchers in the United States and other countries. The definitive study of worldwide tornado distribution has not yet been written. Fujita's (1973) was the last effort at a complete world perspective. The growing interest in the Internet and the World Wide Web may help in the creation of a centralized database for all tornadoes.

Below I list chronologically selected tornadoes or tornado outbreaks in twenty-nine countries. The events are chosen in an effort to put to rest the idea that tornadoes occur only in the United States.

ENGLAND, OCTOBER 17, 1091. According to Terence Meaden (1975), London experienced a tornado more than nine hundred years ago, some details of which were recorded. The funnel plunged four 26-foot-long rafters into the hard surface of a street. They could not be pulled out and, "being an obstacle to passers-by, they were cut off at ground level." Two men were killed when the storm raised the roof at a church. About six hundred houses were damaged.

INDONESIA, APRIL 10, 1815. The eruption of the Indonesian volcano Tamboro blew as much as 100 cubic miles of pulverized rock into the atmosphere. The dust cloud probably cooled the earth and caused "the year without a summer" in the northeastern United States and northern Europe in 1816. The volcano itself killed about 50,000 people. Many others died in a gigantic whirlwind that ripped apart the village of Saugar, 25 miles from the volcano. "Men, houses, cattle, and whatever else came under its influence" were carried into the air.

FRANCE, AUGUST 19, 1845. This is among the worst European tornado disasters and probably the worst outside of Russia. At least 70 people, and perhaps as many as 200, died in the destruction of homes and three large textile and paper mills at or near Monville. One of three mills was a four-story stone building that probably collapsed rather than being swept away. The path was 15 miles long and up to 1,000 feet wide. Large planks were carried for 25 miles, near Dieppe.

AUSTRIA, JUNE 29, 1873. What was probably a tornado was described by Nalivkin (1982) as hitting the International Industrial Exhibition at Vienna. Many people were killed by flying debris, and one of the large balloons at the festival was found later at an unspecified location in Hungary, at least 50 miles to the southeast.

CANADA, AUGUST 6, 1879. Seven people died along a 9-mile-long path near Buctouche, New Brunswick; one hundred buildings were destroyed. This was the farthest east a North American tornado of violent intensity has ever struck.

BANGLADESH, APRIL 7, 1888. The *Times of London* reported that a 500-foot-wide tornado killed 118 and injured 1,200 on the west edge of Dhaka. Soon afterward, another 66 died in the Murchagunja area. There were unsubstantiated rumors that 150 people were killed by hailstones weighing up to 2 pounds each.

MEXICO, MAY 10, 1899. The deadliest known Mexican tornado took place about 100 miles south of Eagle Pass, Texas. At the Hondo coal mine, cars were thrown more than 100 yards and at least 22 people were killed.

RUSSIA, JUNE 29, 1904. At least 30 people died as two tornadoes hit Moscow. The longer track of the two began 20 miles south of Moscow at

Podolsk and passed through villages at the southeast edge of the city. Its path length was about 25 miles. What seems to have been the shorter and weaker path (Nalivkin 1982), hit closer to the center of the city and for a few seconds exposed the bottom of the Moscow River. Stone buildings lost their roofs, wooden homes were destroyed, and lesser buildings "disappeared entirely."

CANADA, JUNE 30, 1912.   A tornado touched down 11 miles southwest of Regina, Saskatchewan, and moved to the northeast. At the south edge of the city it swung to the north and devastated the heart of Regina. Twenty-eight people were killed and two hundred homes and half the businesses in town were destroyed. Losses totaled $4 million in Canada's deadliest tornado disaster to that date.

ENGLAND, OCTOBER 27, 1913.   What may have been England's deadliest tornadic supercell caused damage for five hours and 150 miles. The storm moved almost due north along the border of Wales and the rest of England, from Barry to Chester. The deaths were in the earlier part of the storm, in southern Wales. The *Times of London* reported that buildings were ripped apart in several towns. One death occurred when two men were caught in the open and thrown about 100 feet. Another man was reportedly thrown 1,000 feet to his death at Abereynon, where sixty homes were unroofed. Two children were seriously injured in a chapel at Edwardsville and may have died. England has had only five recorded killer tornadoes in the past two hundred years. This is testimony to the relative weakness of the numerous tornadoes that are recorded there.

ITALY, JULY 24, 1930.   A devastating tornado struck from near Po, passing west of Treviso, near Montebelluna and Mervesa in the Piave River valley, to near Udine. The worst damage was about 20 miles north of Venice, at the north end of the Adriatic Sea. At least 23 people were killed as two hundred homes were torn apart. This area has been hit many times in the past. At Riovigo, southwest of Venice, about 50 people were injured at an amusement park on August 23, 1953. Among the geographic ingredients it has in common with U.S. tornado-prone areas are warm water (the Adriatic Sea) to the south and mountains (the Alps) to the west and northwest.

CUBA, DECEMBER 26, 1940. The *Havana Post* reported that a late season hurricane struck the south shore of the island and caused 80 deaths. Most fatalities occurred in floods. A residential section of Bejucal, 20 miles south of Havana, was struck by a 250-yard-wide hurricane-spawned tornado, which killed 12 people and injured more than 200.

CANADA, JUNE 17, 1946. A tornado touched down just south of Detroit, Michigan, causing $1 million in damage and thirty-five injuries before crossing into Canada. As many as 18 people may have died at Windsor, Sandwich East, and Tecumseh, Ontario.

NEW ZEALAND, AUGUST 25, 1948. The *Wellington Evening Post* reported that 3 people died and 80 were injured in a tornado that hit the towns of Frankton and Hamilton at 11:45 A.M. The Frankton business district had F2 damage to roofs and homes. Two deaths were caused by flying debris, and one person died under a collapsed home. A total of 163 homes and about 50 businesses were damaged.

SINGAPORE, NOVEMBER 2, 1950. The *Malay Tribune* reported that more than one hundred homes were unroofed and seven people injured by flying debris in a tornado that hit Kim Keal Road in the Serangoon section of Singapore. A ten-year-old boy was thrown into a canal and was rescued.

SOUTH AFRICA, NOVEMBER 30 AND DECEMBER 2, 1952. The *Cape Town Times* reported that at least 20 people died and 400 were injured in the village of Albertynesville, 18 miles from Johannesburg. Cars were seen being lifted up to 100 feet in the air. The funnel "appeared to have pinchers, which whipped up everything in its path." Exactly two days later, at 4:30 P.M., Paynesville, 30 miles from away, was hit by a tornado that killed 11 people and "threw cattle high into the air." In the time between the two tornadoes, 15 people were killed by lightning in the area.

BERMUDA, APRIL 5, 1953. The *Hamilton Royal Gazette* reported that on Easter Sunday a girl was killed when hit by a flying door as her home was being unroofed by a tornado at Crawl, Hamilton Parish. As the vortex came ashore as a waterspout, two cars were thrown into the water. Six parishes were hit near the south shore of Devonshire. About fifty homes were damaged, and 9 people were treated at hospitals. Some homes were crushed by falling trees.

PORTUGAL, NOVEMBER 6, 1954. Four people died in a tornado at Castelo Branco. Cars were "thrown into walls" while homes were unroofed and collapsed. Among the 200 people injured were 30 soldiers in a barracks.

POLAND, MAY 15, 1958. The *New York Times* reported that 3 people died and more than 100 were injured at Rawa Mazowiecka, 50 miles south of Warsaw.

INDIA, APRIL 19, 1963. A tornado in northwestern Assam killed 139 people and left 3,760 families homeless in thirty-three villages along a 22-mile path. The funnel moved to the southeast for about 20 miles.

EAST PAKISTAN (PRESENT-DAY BANGLADESH), APRIL 11, 1964. The *Bangladesh Observer* reported that as many as 500 people may have died as a tornado destroyed villages in the Narail and Magura regions of Jessore. Bangladesh newspapers use the words *cyclone, tornado,* and *nor'wester* interchangeably, so it is difficult to determine the exact nature of the storm. The presence of bodies in trees and cooking utensils embedded in trees left little doubt that this was a true tornado.

JAPAN, MAY 24, 1964. A tornado, called a dragon whirl, or *tatsumaki,* in Japanese, damaged 480 homes in the southwestern suburbs of Tokyo. Fujita suggests (pers. com.) that between five and thirty-five tornadoes a year hit Japan.

ITALY, JULY 4, 1965. The *Rome Daily American* reported that one or more tornadoes killed about 25 people and injured 160 in a dozen small towns near Parma. Near Verona, dozens of people were injured by softball-sized hail.

PARAGUAY, OCTOBER 25, 1965. The *New York Times* reported that one hundred homes were destroyed by a tornado that struck the town of Encarnación.

FRANCE, THE NETHERLANDS, AND BELGIUM, JUNE 24–25, 1967.

A two-day outbreak of tornadoes killed 8 people in France on the June 24, 6 at Palluel, with 30 injured, and 2 at Pommereuil, with 50 injured. About two hundred homes were destroyed. On the June 25 Oostmalle, Belgium (10 miles northeast of Antwerp) had many homes destroyed, dozens of cars overturned, and two people killed. Six people died in the Netherlands. At Tricct, west of Arnhem, 4 people died and sixty homes were destroyed. Near Utrecht 18 people were injured as cars were swept from the road. Two people were killed at a camping site near Chaam.

PHILIPPINES, JUNE 13, 1968.

Shortly before midnight a tornado killed 12 people and injured 30 as it swept through two villages south of the site of the former Clark Air Force Base. Forty homes were destroyed. Eight died at Acabebe; 4 died at Masantol.

GERMANY, JULY 10, 1968.

A 17-mile tornado path through the Black Forest damaged more than one thousand homes and killed 3 people.

URUGUAY, OCTOBER 25, 1968.

The *New York Times* reported that a four-year-old boy was killed and 12 others were injured when a tornado touched down in Vichadero.

CYPRUS, DECEMBER 22, 1969.

Six waterspouts hit the southern coastal sections of Cyprus, 10 miles south of Nicosia. Several continued inland as tornadoes with damage paths up to 300 yards wide. Four people were killed, one by a falling tree and three under collapsed buildings.

ITALY, SEPTEMBER 11, 1970.

At the north edge of the Adriatic Sea, near St. Elena Island and the St. Mark's Basin, at Venice, a 25-ton motorized water bus was picked up, spun around, and dropped back into the water, where it sank in 30 seconds. Most of the 60 passengers were sightseers; 22 drowned. The survivors were apparently those who fell off the boat while it was in the air. Two campsites were destroyed at Fusina, where 13 people died and 200 were injured. Ca'savio, near Jesolo (north of Venice), was also hit. The tornadoes moved east from Padua. The death total for the day was more than 40. (Jesolo had been hit by a tornado five years earlier.)

ARGENTINA, JANUARY 10, 1973. The *Buenos Aires Herald* reported that 54 people were killed and 350 were injured as a tornado cut a 300-yard-wide swath through the town of San Justo, 300 miles northwest of Buenos Aires. This early summer (in the Southern Hemisphere) tornado damaged or destroyed five hundred homes. In the last report that I could find, 7 people were said to be "near death." Several homes were said to have "vanished" and huge trees flew like matchsticks. Four people were seen falling to their deaths from a car as it passed by 30 feet in the air.

CANADA, APRIL 3, 1974. A tornado in the Super Outbreak crossed the Canadian border, south of Detroit, and moved northeast across Windsor. Near the end of its path, 8 people died instantly at the Windsor Curling Club ice rink, as one unreinforced concrete block wall and half of the roof fell in. A ninth death occurred in a hospital in January 1975.

AUSTRALIA, NOVEMBER 13, 1976. Three tornadoes touched down in the state of Victoria. The one at Sandon, near Castlemane, killed an elderly couple by throwing their car 100 yards. Theirs was one of several cars parked along the road waiting for the tornado to pass. The funnel was described as "a swirling black mass making a terrible whine like a pig squealing." It was said that "trees fell like grass before a mower." While tornadoes are not especially rare in Australia, killer tornadoes are.

INDIA, MARCH 17 AND APRIL 10, 1978. In the northern suburbs of New Delhi, near the university, 28 people were killed and 700 were injured on March 17. The tornado cut a path 3 miles long and 50 yards wide. On April 10 about 150 people died in a tornado in the Orissa District, mostly in the villages of Purunabandha and Keonjhargarh.

THE NETHERLANDS, OCTOBER 6, 1981. A Fokker F-28 airliner crashed 15 miles south-southeast of Rotterdam after encountering a tornado. Seventeen people were killed as the plane lost a wing and crashed. The flight recorder indicated that the airplane sustained a force six times that of gravity. The tornado was photographed by a policeman, and a few minutes later he photographed what was smoke from the burning plane, both near the town of Moerdijk. Researchers concluded that the airplane flew into "the tornado circulation, in cloud, shortly after the tornado funnel had lifted from the ground" (Roach and Findlater 1983). It was concluded that the increase in altitude noted on the flight recorder was actually a pressure drop associated with the tornado rather than any upward movement of the airplane.

RUSSIA, JUNE 9, 1984. At least 400 people died in and near Ivanova, Gorki, Kalinin, Kostroma, and Yaroslav, 150 to 200 miles northwest, north, and northeast of Moscow. It was probably Russia's deadliest outbreak in history. Most of the deaths were in and near Ivanova, the nearby village of Balino, and a nearby holiday resort.

CANADA, MAY 31, 1985. While a major outbreak of tornadoes was striking Ohio and Pennsylvania a related outbreak had just ended in Ontario, 200 miles to the north. Eight people died and more than one thousand buildings were damaged or destroyed at Barrie, Ontario. A second violent tornado killed two people near Alliston and two more at Grand Valley, Ontario. Sixty-seven people were injured at the Orangetown Shopping Centre. Thirteen tornadoes were counted this day in Ontario.

CANADA, JULY 31, 1987. The most damaging Canadian tornado ever was at Edmonton, Alberta (fig. 13.2). An F4 tornado killed 27 people and injured more than 300 and caused $250 million in damage. The funnel was up to 1 mile wide as it moved almost due north for 22 miles.

BANGLADESH, APRIL 26, 1989. What may have been the world's deadliest tornado took place in the only other part of the world that is prone to strong and violent tornadoes on an annual basis. As many as 1,300 people were initially reported killed and 12,000 injured as a tornado cut a long track, up to a mile wide, about 50 miles northwest and north of Dhaka. The towns of Salturia and Manikganj were leveled, and about 80,000 people were made homeless.

MYANMAR, MAY 15, 1990. A tornado derailed eleven cars of a passenger train between Kawlin and Mandalay. One person was killed and 28 injured.

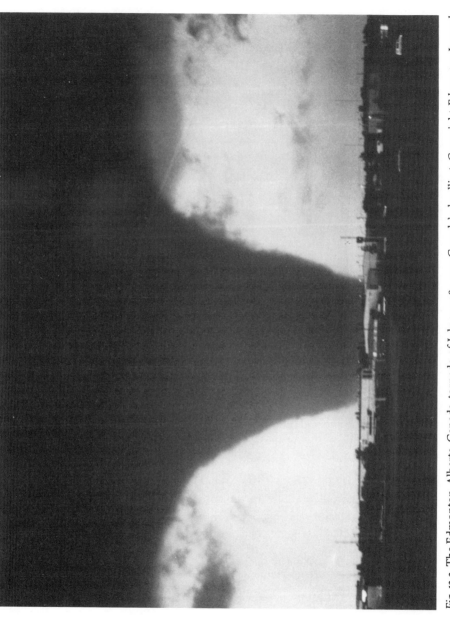

Fig. 13.2. The Edmonton, Alberta, Canada, tornado of July 31, 1987, was Canada's deadliest. Copyright *Edmonton Journal.*

JAPAN, DECEMBER 11, 1990. An unseasonable (wintertime) violent tornado hit Mobara after dark. About one thousand homes were damaged or destroyed and more than 60 people were injured. Ten-ton vehicles were tossed like toys and reinforced steel rods were bent to the ground by an apparent suction vortex. Debris from shattered window panes injured 26 people at a hospital. Another 40 injuries were caused by flying roof tiles and metal sheets.

PANAMA, JULY 6, 1992. What may have been Panama's worst killer tornado hit the southeast edge of Panama City. As electric power lines were severed, people ran into the street from a garment factory. They ran back inside the building when they saw the tornado approaching. The poorly constructed concrete block building collapsed, killing as many as 12 workers and injuring at least 50 others.

CHINA, JUNE 9, 1994. Typhoon Ross went ashore in Guandong Province in southern China, flooding about thirteen hundred villages and drowning more than 200 people while damaging 320,000 homes. The typhoon spawned a tornado that killed 13 people and injured about 100 in the city of Nahhai. It is reasonable to estimate that China has one killer tornado a year.

THE NETHERLANDS, JUNE 8, 1997. About 20 people were injured when a tornado hit a cigarette factory in Bergen. A later tornado hit an airport near Rotterdam and destroyed four planes.

CHAPTER 14

TORNADO RISK

On one evening in 1967, much to the surprise of bartender Dave Williams, the Janesville, Wisconsin, Country Club was "ripped open as if by a can opener." The ballroom roof was strewn across a field. The brick chimney fell into the empty kitchen. Exactly twenty-four hours earlier, one hundred people were in the ballroom and the kitchen was full of workers. It was Tuesday, the only night of the week that dinner was not served. A half hour later, two thousand homes were ripped apart and three people were killed in a St. Louis suburb. Six hours earlier, the roof of the Orrick, Missouri, High School was lifted and dropped. Part of the school roof collapsed, killing two students. It was not the spring tornado season; it was the dead of winter, January 24.

On April 5, 1972, more than 1,500 miles to the west of tornado alley a funnel cloud touched down just north of Portland, Oregon, moved north-northeast across the Columbia River, and smashed into Vancouver, Washington. The tornado struck the unsuspecting and unprepared Ogden Elementary School. There it blasted glass over and into several hundred students, hospitalizing many of them. A woman and two children were crushed in their car by a collapsing wall of a department store. Another woman and her child died under falling walls inside the store. A third woman died in the destruction of the nursery at a bowling alley across the street.

The above examples show just how far and wide tornadoes can reach. Most tornadoes do occur in the states located in what we loosely call tornado alley, and in months that are traditionally called "tornado season." Neither term has any clear meaning. Across the United States there are at least three large "tornado alleys" and many smaller ones. Rather than label the entire Great Plains "tornado alley," I try to quantify its borders later in this chapter.

TORNADO SEASON

We know that North America is the great mixing bowl of tornadic weather patterns. We have the right ingredients, in the right amounts, at the right time, over the right kind of geography, and at the right position on the globe. We are midway between the North Pole and the equator, where tropical heat meets polar cold. Conditions are ideal enough for tornadoes to occur in every month of the year. The United States is probably the only country in the world that can make that claim.

"Tornado season" is generally in the spring. In the winter the United States has plenty of wind shear but little unstable layering with warm humid air below and abnormally cold air aloft, except along the Gulf of Mexico. In the summer there is plenty of warm, humid air and instability but little wind shear. At the transition times of spring and late fall, some areas of the United States have both, and a "tornado season" is the result. Another factor that makes the spring such an active tornado season is that the upper atmosphere warms slower than the lower atmosphere. The air is heated by the ground, which warms under the spring sun. The upper troposphere remains more winterlike. Warm air rising into colder air will tend to keep on rising. In other words, the large temperature difference increases the instability of the atmosphere and makes severe storms more likely. In the spring that colder air often gets rapidly colder with increasing altitude, having what is called a steep "lapse rate." This condition makes the air even more unstable.

Trying to pick the exact day that the tornado season begins and ends requires a definition of the term. One possible definition is the period containing the fewest number of days in which three-fourths of all tornadoes have been counted. Of the 29,515 tornadoes from 1950 to 1991, 75 percent of them have occurred between March 11 and August 12. Some meteorologists may be uncomfortable suggesting that August is still tornado season. Major tornado outbreaks are relatively rare in July and August.

If we redefine "tornado season" as the period containing the fewest number of days when two-thirds of all killer tornadoes occurred, the season would run from March 11 to June 23. On a national level, this is an answer that most people should feel comfortable with. On a state-by-state basis, these dates have little meaning, for every state has its own tornado season.

Figure 14.1 shows a comparison of tornado distribution, by months, of a Canadian border state (Minnesota), a Gulf Coast state (Mississippi), and the entire United States. The monthly distribution is quite obviously different. However, the argument can be made that the tornado season never really ends. Tornadoes occur in every month, and the area where they occur changes each month. Tornadoes have been recorded in the United States on every day of the year. Killer tornadoes have occurred on 352 of the 366 days of the year, including leap year.

TIME OF DAY

The hourly distribution of tornadoes varies a great deal from state to state. Most states, however, have a peak between 4:00 P.M. and 6:00 P.M. (fig. 14.2). That period is several hours after the time of peak solar heating. The hottest part of the day, 1:00 to 3:00 P.M., may be when thunderstorms start growing rapidly, but it takes time for storms to mature to the point where tornadoes start to form. It is not surprising, then, to find that the peak time for tornadoes is a few hours later.

In the western and northern states the distribution is clearly related to afternoon solar heating. In the southeastern states, such as Mississippi, the distribution is not so dependent on solar heating to drive the growth of storms. Large springtime low-pressure systems bring together tornado ingredients—instability, high humidity, and wind shear—at all times of

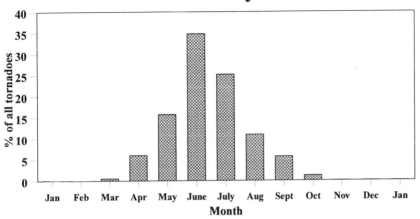

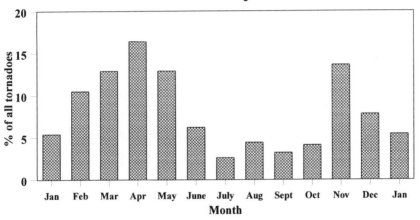

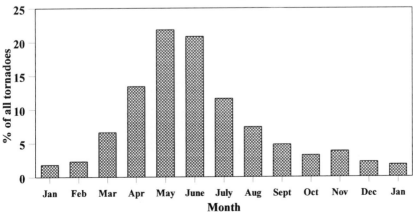

Fig. 14.1. Tornado distribution by month for Minnesota, Mississippi, and the entire United States.

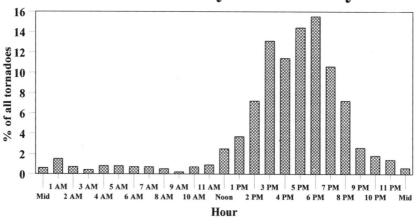

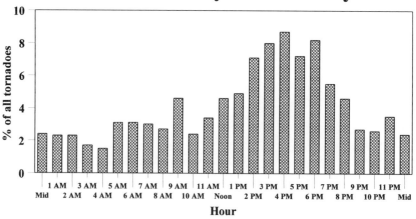

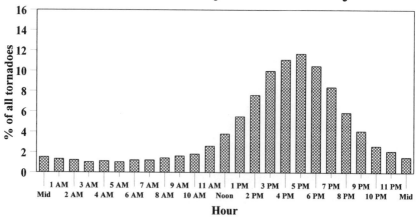

Fig. 14.2. Tornado distribution by hour of day for Minnesota, Mississippi, and the entire United States.

day and night from Louisiana to Georgia. The Gainesville, Georgia, tornado, that killed 203 people in 1936 occurred at 8:30 A.M. The 1994 Palm Sunday disaster at Goshen, Alabama, was part of an outbreak that began midmorning. Of the deadliest tornadoes in U.S. history (see Appendix 1), thirty occurred in the morning.

RISK FROM TORNADOES

There are many types of risk, and different risks to different people. Simple questions such as, Which state has the greatest risk from tornadoes? and In what month is the greatest risk from tornadoes? cannot be answered simply. The questions lack clearly defined terminology. I define three types of tornado risk: (1) the risk of encountering some part of a tornado; (2) the risk to property; and (3) the risk to human life.

The risk of encountering some part of a tornado is relatively easy to calculate as long as we do not try to consider the actual wind speed that is expected. The tornado data that have been gathered for the past forty-five years are probably complete enough so that we can at least get a rough estimate. This first type of risk analysis counts all tornadoes as equal, but they certainly are not equal in destructive potential.

Calculating risk to property requires actual wind speed estimates. This is because some property, such as mobile homes, is damaged by very different wind speeds than other property, such as steel-reinforced concrete schools. The threat that tornadoes pose to a barn (considerable) is very different from the threat that they pose to the containment building at a nuclear power plant (none). For property risk we have to turn to the Fujita Scale (see chap. 7). My focus here will be on the most intense tornadoes, the violent (F4–F5) events that can level a frame house.

The risk posed by tornadoes to human life is a product of the wind speeds that determine property risk and many intangible human factors. It is human behaviors, attitudes, and beliefs that make the risk to life so difficult to define and nearly impossible to quantify. Each "risk" can be analyzed in two ways. We can try to assign an actual numerical value, based on our understanding of the phenomenon. Or we can look at the threat from tornadoes in a relative sense, by comparing one state with another. Here I assign a value on the first two risk types, risk of encounter and risk to property. The risk to life is so complex that I must resort to comparing the death toll in one state to that in another.

RISK OF A TORNADO ENCOUNTER

In this section I create a map from which anyone east of the Rocky Mountains can estimate his or her risk from tornadoes. To show how the map was created, I use the state of Iowa as an example. All of the calculations were done with the SATT2 (Site Assessment of Tornado Threat, version-2) program developed by Frank Tatom at Engineering Analysis in Huntsville, Alabama.

In the period 1950–94 there were 1,140 tornadoes counted in Iowa. On average, those tornadoes had a path length of 6.6 miles and a path width of 192 yards (0.12 mile). Therefore, the average tornado swept an area of 0.79 square mile. The 1,140 tornadoes together swept more than 901 square miles in those 40 years, about 22 square miles a year. Simple division shows that to cover the entire state area of 55,965 square miles at a rate of 22 square miles per year would take about 2,540 years. I call this number the AOI, or average occurrence interval. This is the simplest means of calculating how often a tornado occurs, on average, at any point in the state. Nationally, Iowa stands seventh in AOI (see table 14.1).

As in every other field of study, from advertising to zoology, statistics can be both enlightening and misleading. They can be used to justify lies or provide genuine insight. One might notice in table 14.1 that Vermont ranks slightly ahead of Colorado in this "risk" calculation. This is an absurd premise. Tornado risk is clearly greater in Colorado than in Vermont. Colorado has seen killer tornadoes, long-track supercell tornadoes, and violent tornadoes. Vermont has never had a killer tornado, nor has it been hit by a tornado that produced anything but minimal F2 damage.

Part of the reason for this anomaly is that half of Colorado, the Rocky Mountain region, is almost tornado-free. Another is that a very large percentage of Colorado tornadoes are poorly documented; they leave no clearly defined swath on the open prairie. Many have no listed path length or path width. Others are weak and ignored completely. Vermont tornadoes are a rarity and are eagerly surveyed when they do occur. Vermont tornadoes have wider documented paths because the tracks are well defined by fallen trees.

Table 14.1
STATE-BY-STATE AVERAGE OCCURRENCE INTERVALS, 1950–1995

Rank	State	AOI	Rank	State	AOI
1	Mississippi	2,140	26	Connecticut	11,200
2	Nebraska	2,170	27	Delaware	13,800
3	Kansas	2,220	28	New Jersey	14,500
4	Oklahoma	2,220	29	Florida	16,500
5	Indiana	2,400	30	Maryland	18,100
6	Arkansas	2,510	31	New York	19,300
7	Iowa	2,690	32	North Dakota	21,500
8	Wisconsin	3,220	33	Virginia	22,700
9	Alabama	3,330	34	Vermont	46,700
10	Illinois	3,420	35	Colorado	50,300
11	Georgia	4,030	36	Wyoming	58,100
12	Michigan	4,150	37	New Hampshire	70,900
13	Tennessee	4,740	38	Montana	88,500
14	North Carolina	4,760	39	West Virginia	115,000
15	Ohio	5,350	40	Maine	193,000
16	Louisiana	5,750	41	New Mexico	239,000
17	Pennsylvania	5,850	42	Utah	256,000
18	Missouri	6,140	43	Arizona	394,000
19	Kentucky	6,540	44	Oregon	493,000
20	Texas	6,990	45	California	508,000
21	Massachusetts	7,250	46	Washington	746,000
22	South Dakota	7,350	47	Nevada	1,140,000
23	Minnesota	7,410	48	Idaho	1,300,000
24	South Carolina	7,690	49	Hawaii	16,700,000
25	Rhode Island	8,400	50	Alaska	>100,000,000

These simple calculations ignore many subtle and mathematically complex aspects of risk analysis. For the sake of generating a ballpark answer, however, the method works well enough. These tornado occurrence frequencies are offered as a rough approximation and should not be the basis of any civic planning or decision-making process involving tornado safety procedures or construction.

RISK AT ANY POINT

It is possible to estimate the AOI for any specific spot in the United States. My sample calculation will be for Des Moines, Iowa. In figure 14.3, a circle drawn around downtown Des Moines has a 50-mile radius. That circle has an area of 7,850 square miles. Also in figure 14.3 are the paths of all Iowa tornadoes in the forty-five years from 1950 to 1994. The total area swept by the tornadoes within that circle was about 83.6 square miles. This is an average of 2.7 square miles per year. Dividing 7,850 square miles by 2.7 square miles per year gives a value of about 2,800 years. That is the estimated time for tornado paths to cover the entire area of the circle. Based on this methodology, the AOI for any tornado at Des Moines is roughly once in 2,800 years. The AOI can be estimated for any point in Iowa from figure 14.4 and for any point east of the Rocky Mountains from figure 14.5. The latter figure was plotted using more than 1,000 calculated points.

RISK TO PROPERTY

All types of property are at a different level of risk from tornadoes of different destructive potential. A well-built frame house is at little risk from a tornado with maximum winds of 90 mph but at great risk from a tornado with 200 mph winds. A mobile home is at risk from even the weakest tornado. Therefore, the analysis of risk to property must consider the wind speeds in the storm.

To determine the risk for a specific F-scale class tornado, and thus a specific kind of property damage, the method used to produce figure 14.5 is also used here. If we were concerned only with tornadoes that could destroy a frame house totally, only F4 to F5 tornadoes would be used in the calculation. Figure 14.6 is such a map. The western United States is not shown. The

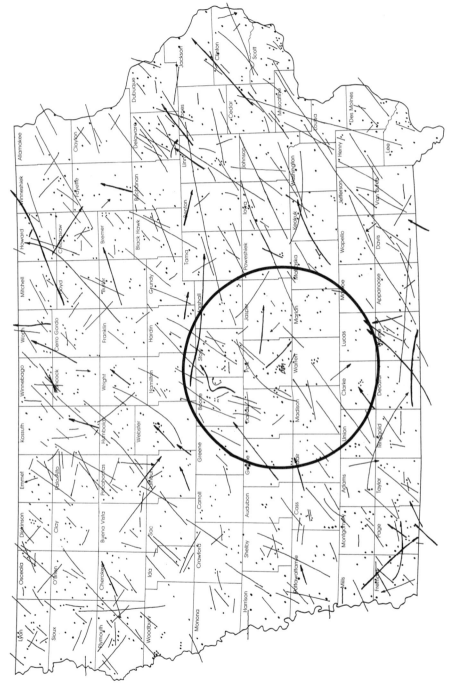

Fig. 14.3. A map of all known Iowa tornadoes, 1950–94, with a 50-mile radius circle drawn around Des Moines.

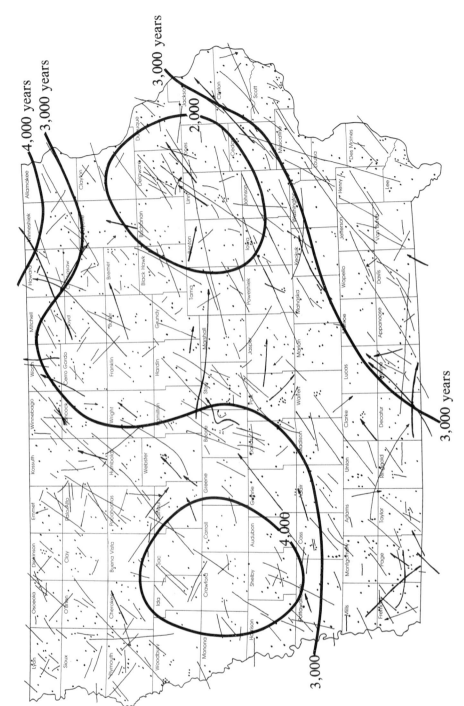

Fig. 14.4. The AOI distribution of risk from all tornadoes in Iowa.

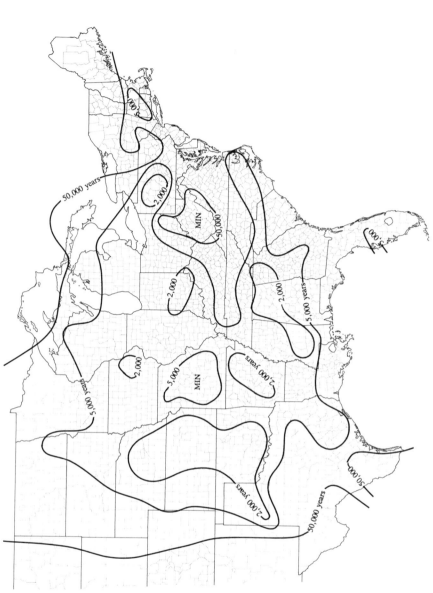

Fig. 14.5. The AOI risk distribution map for the eastern two-thirds of the United States. Each of the areas of maximum occurrence might be called a "tornado alley." The traditional tornado alleys show up better on figure 14.6.

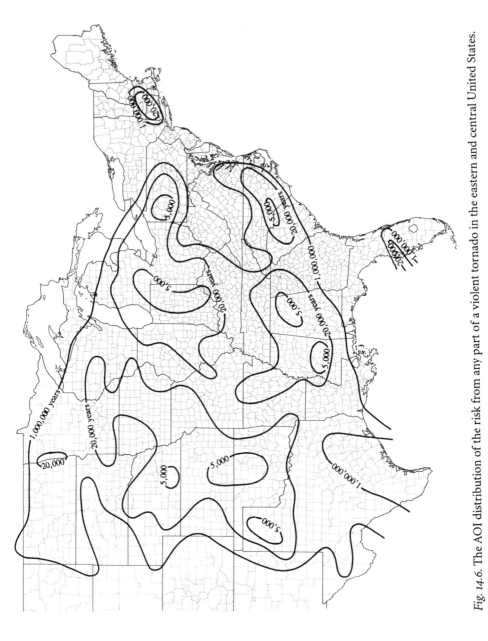

Fig. 14.6. The AOI distribution of the risk from any part of a violent tornado in the eastern and central United States.

distribution is concentrated around some cities. Mapping these small circles locates centers of population, not the actual distribution of tornadoes.

Abbey and Fujita's (1983) study of the Super Outbreak tornadoes of April 3, 1974, has shown that most of the winds in a violent tornado are not violent. On average, less than 2 percent of the swath cut by a violent tornado actually produces F4 or F5 damage. For instance, in figure 14.6 the value at Des Moines for experiencing any part of a violent tornado is once in about 15,000 years. The chance of experiencing winds of 200 mph is probably less than 2 percent, or once in 750,000 years. The likelihood of experiencing F5 winds is probably less than once in 10 million years. Abbey and Fujita note that while the average path width of the F5 tornadoes in the April 3, 1974, outbreak was nearly a half mile, the width of the F5 damage averaged only 32 feet. Their figures can be used to show that only about 0.2 percent (1/500th) of an F5 tornado path actually consisted of F5 damage.

These numbers and methods are used to introduce the general concept of tornado risk analysis. They also offer a few surprises and raise a few questions. I was surprised to see, for instance, the maximum in western Pennsylvania as shown in figure 14.6. The frequency of occurrence values there are comparable to almost anywhere in the Great Plains. Further analysis showed that the entire maximum was caused by a single outbreak in 1985. This Ohio-Pennsylvania outbreak illustrates one of the many problems in judging the long-term risk of relatively rare events such as tornadoes. A single tornado, or a single outbreak, of profound magnitude may greatly skew the statistics. Yet we have no idea how often an event like that occurs. A violent Ohio-Pennsylvania outbreak (like that in 1985) may occur only once in a few hundred or even a few thousand years. A violent Worcester-area tornado (like the one in 1953) may occur only once in a thousand or so years. However, these events are part of our fifty-year database, and we are forced to assume, against our better judgment, that they occur once every fifty years. Although many thousands of tornadoes have been reported, the record is still too sparse to give numbers with confidence. This is particularly true for the rare, F4 and F5 events. To calculate accurate probabilities for violent tornadoes might require one thousand years of data. I think it is safe to say that once we understand tornado formation, computer simulations will give us good risk estimates without having to wait one thousand years for actual occurrences.

Now that we have some maps to work from, we can address the subject of "tornado alleys," the general term for areas of highest tornado risk. There is more than one tornado alley. Any area that seems to experience above-average tornado frequency is eventually labeled a "tornado alley." There are dozens of such regions. The area most commonly referred to as "tornado alley" stretches from Texas to Minnesota (see fig. 14.6). Another stretches to the east from Arkansas and Louisiana to the Carolinas. A third tornado alley is in the Ohio River valley and the southern Great Lakes area from Illinois to western Pennsylvania. There are smaller areas of tornado activity in central Florida and southern New England. Historically, the term "tornado alley" has been used very loosely, and the locations indicated are often based on personal perceptions rather than scientific data. There are no well-defined boundaries, nor will there ever be any.

RISK TO LIFE

The risk to human life depends on much more than the meteorology of the atmosphere. It arises from a complex combination of the destructive potential of tornadoes and many intangible human factors. Unlike the risk of an encounter, or the risk to property, the risk to life is impossible to quantify.

An individual's risk depends on such things as awareness of watches and warnings, the mobility and infirmities of the aged in his or her care, attitudes about preparedness for low-probability risks, attitudes about using a car to escape a tornado, the effectiveness of community warning systems, the distance to safe shelter, and the presence of nearby trees that might block the view of an approaching tornado. Equally important is whether the person is watching a local television station, with posted weather bulletins, or a distant station via satellite dish or cable, with no posted warnings. Risk also involves fear, curiosity, ignorance, obsession, complacency ("ho-hum, there's another tornado watch out today"), denial ("it can't happen here"), greed ("let's take a few short cuts in the construction of the roof of this house"), financial status ("this small trailer is all we could afford"), and love ("I have to get home to my kids despite the rain and sirens"). We must also factor in safety training, the work schedules of two-income parents, the maintenance schedule of sirens, and countless other variables and intangibles.

Tables 14.2 and 14.3 compare the actual loss of life from one state to another. For a few states, the rankings are quite different. By state area, Massachusetts rates very high, largely because of one tornado in 1953 that killed ninety-four people. In table 14.3, based on population, Massachusetts drops to seventeenth place. I consider the rank by population to be more representative of the true risk in this category. Beyond these tables, the simplest way to display the risk to human life may be to plot the location of every killer tornado in U.S. history (fig. 14.7).

The purpose of creating these lists is to generate questions and then to pursue the answers. The data contain interesting curiosities and are a starting point for more serious study about people and what it takes to protect them. The government cannot protect everyone all of the time. Individuals must assess their own risks and their own priorities and take appropriate action. It is likely that the less a person perceives a hazard to be real, the greater the risk from that hazard. Conversely, the more aware one is of the risk, the lower the probability of being killed or injured by it.

Perhaps the perceived risk from tornadoes is enhanced by the fact that thunderstorms, the phenomenon from which tornadoes are spawned, are

Table 14.2
DEATHS PER 10,000 SQUARE MILES, 1953–1998

State	Deaths	Deaths per 10,000 square miles
Massachusetts	104	133
Mississippi	394	84
Alabama	312	62
Indiana	219	61
Ohio	170	41
Michigan	238	40
Arkansas	207	39
Illinois	175	32
Oklahoma	213	31
Kentucky	110	28

Table 14.3

TORNADO DEATHS PER MILLION PEOPLE, 1953–1998

State	Deaths	Deaths per Million People
Mississippi	394	166
Arkansas	207	107
Alabama	312	91
Kansas	195	87
Oklahoma	213	81
Texas	492	44
Indiana	219	42
North Dakota	22	36
Kentucky	110	35
Nebraska	50	34

such a common occurrence. Perhaps it is that tornadoes pose a risk in a different category. Swimming pools and automobiles pose risks that we have consciously chosen to accept and live with. We believe with confidence, rightly or wrongly, that we can control our risks in swimming pools and automobiles. That confidence does not extend to a rain-wrapped tornado on the prowl in the eerie greenish light of an early spring thunderstorm. Tornadoes are uncontrollable and therefore feared by some to a much greater extent, however irrationally. Perhaps some manner of transferred risk is at work here. We worry about remote perils to mask our inability to control the greater threats that are much more real and much less remote.

This discussion of risk is not intended to increase the fear of tornadoes. The risk of encountering any tornado at all is extremely low—just once in one thousand years, even in the very heart of tornado alley. Tornadoes are rare events. Expert chasers drive for days trying to encounter one in the height of the tornado season and have trouble doing it. The risk to life from tornadoes is very low on an overall hazard list. About ten times as many people die each year being hit by falling objects than from being hit by a

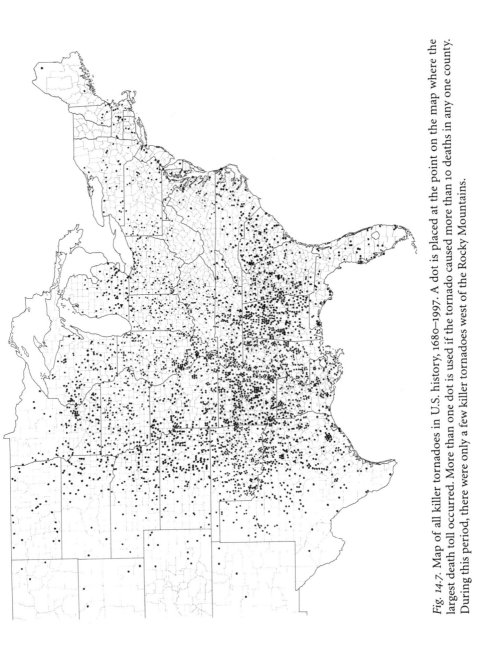

Fig. 14.7. Map of all killer tornadoes in U.S. history, 1680–1997. A dot is placed at the point on the map where the largest death toll occurred. More than one dot is used if the tornado caused more than 10 deaths in any one county. During this period, there were only a few killer tornadoes west of the Rocky Mountains.

tornado. About eight times as many people (more than five hundred each year) die at pedestrian railroad crossings each year, but they rarely make the national news. Yet a single mobile home death can be the lead national story on the nightly news. People have lived their entire lives in tornado alley, eastern Kansas, for instance, without seeing even a distant tornado. Keeping track of weather conditions and paying attention to the wording of severe weather watches will reduce the risk to life to an almost immeasurably small possibility. Just the fact that you are reading this book probably puts you at even lower risk. If you are obsessively worried about tornadoes, you are worried about the wrong thing. Many other hazards deserve far more concern.

CHAPTER 15

FINAL
THOUGHTS

The last tornado that killed one hundred people was at Flint, Michigan, in 1953, the first full year of tornado forecasting. Since that time the combination of watches and warnings and the dissemination of information through schools and the media has seemingly eliminated the massive single-tornado death tolls that once plagued the United States. This has been done despite an increasing population. It seems inevitable, however, that a killer tornado with a death toll of one hundred or more people will strike the United States sometime in the future. I reach this conclusion based on a consideration of certain tornadic events in both the distant and the recent past. I believe that the past is the key to the future.

Figure 15.1 shows that the decline in the annual death toll did not begin in 1953, when the NWS took on a tornado warning role. The roughly bell-shaped curve, formed by the tops of each bar, begins rising in the 1870s and hits a peak in the mid-1920s with the Great Tri-State Tornado. The death tolls then gradually decline throughout most of the rest of the century.

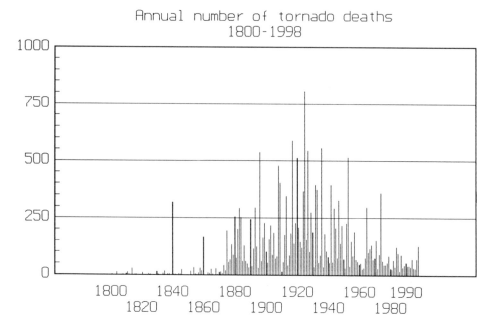

Fig. 15.1. The annual U.S. tornado death toll, 1880–1998.

I attribute the decline to greater awareness, beginning with the spread of information through commercial radio broadcasts, which began in the mid-1920s. To the left side of the curve in figure 15.1, there are two spikes, one in 1840 and another in 1860. Any effort to project this curve into the future should assume that there will be large spikes in the twenty-first century. Tornadoes can and have occurred at exactly the wrong time and in exactly the wrong place. Here are some examples.

In 1840 the tragic coincidence occurred at the Mississippi River port of Natchez, Mississippi. On May 7 boats off Natchez were engulfed by a massive tornado. The river traffic was probably at its peak on a Friday afternoon. The funnel moved northeast precisely at a point where a bend in the river is aligned to the northeast, and the bend was at the bluff on which the city of Natchez was built. Striking at a slightly different angle, and at a less busy time of day, just a mile to the north or south, the event might be only a footnote in weather history, if recorded at all. Instead it is near the top of the all-time U.S. killer tornado list (see the Appendix).

The other anomaly, on June 3, 1860, involved a violent tornado family that coincided with a cluster of vulnerable pioneer communities and a crowded raft on the Mississippi River near Camanche, Iowa. (See chapter 12 for more on the Camanche and Natchez tornadoes.)

There were more close calls in the late 1980s. On December 14, 1987, a tornado touched down 4 miles southwest of West Memphis, Arkansas. In that area the tornado destroyed 270 homes and businesses, leaving 1,500 people homeless and killing 6. One woman died in her mobile home. An elderly bedridden man was crushed by the falling wall of a boardinghouse. A teenager was killed in a parking lot. A one-year-old child was killed in an apartment building. One person died in a car thrown from I-40, and another died in the parking lot of a truck stop. This event hardly seems of historic significance until we look at what was not hit. The tornado missed a dog-racing track, where 7,000 spectators were gathered, by just one quarter of a mile.

On November 15, 1988, there was another example of what might have happened. That was game night for the Southside, Arkansas, high school basketball team. A tornado moved from near Cypress Valley through the town of Southside. A man was killed in Southside when his house was destroyed. The high school gym was totally destroyed, and other school buildings were heavily damaged. Fortunately, by a quirk of scheduling, the basketball team was playing away from home that night.

Many of the most violent tornado outbreaks have occurred in March or early April. This is basketball playoff time, when coaches and administrators may be loath to call off a game because of a mere tornado watch. A "second season" of tornado activity occurs in November, just as teams are anxious to begin their season. I recall from my basketball coaching days the pressure from fans and players to ignore dangerous Vermont snow and ice conditions to travel to important playoff games.

On April 8, 1998, the Birmingham Barons and the Carolina Mudcats minor league baseball teams played through rain, lightning, and tornado warning sirens. Umpires refused to call the game, and fans were left to the safety of the upper concourse while scoreboard lights flickered off and on. Tornado-related deaths that night, several miles west of the ball park, were about 32. Two people died several miles east of the park. More than 20 TVS signatures were noted by Birmingham radar that evening. A few weeks later a tornado passed across the Nashville Oilers football stadium. Fortunately, it was still under construction and thus empty.

On the evening of June 2, 1998, funnel clouds were ripping the roofs from homes within view of Three Rivers Stadium in Pittsburgh, Pennsylvania. Fans left the stands due to the heavy rain, and the Mets-Pirates game was delayed for forty-three minutes. Thunder obliterated the sound of the baseball videos that were playing on the scoreboard, as rotating clouds passed within a half mile of the stadium.

Sporting events and outdoor concerts pose a particular dilemma for forecasters and emergency management staff. With a twenty-minute warning, do they advise the people to stay at the stadium, provide a small target for the tornado, and risk a world-class catastrophe? An announced warning might fill the parking lots and roads with people. The enlarged target might guarantee a major death toll. Yet, should the tornado actually strike the stadium, failure to disperse the crowd might produce the largest death toll in history. No matter what decision is made, fault will certainly be found. The criticism, based on hindsight, may go hand in hand with lawsuits. The capability for a twenty-minute advanced warning brings with it unintended consequences and enormous responsibilities. Legal action, citing inadequate forecasting, is not unknown. In August 1993 two of the people who were injured at Plainfield, Illinois (see chap. 5), along with the survivors of twelve people who were killed, sued the NWS for $74 million. The suit was eventually dismissed.

If the next 100-death killer tornado does not occur at a sporting event, it may occur in a city along the periphery of one of the tornado alleys. The residents of these cities may be much less prepared for tornadoes. The residents and television media in places like central Oklahoma are very aware of tornadoes. Disasters like that shown in figure 15.2 are a possibility in any given year. But most cities have little experience with warnings involving violent tornadoes. Some of these large peripheral cities are Pittsburgh, San Antonio, Austin, Worcester, Springfield, Hartford, Orlando, Atlanta, and Raleigh-Durham. If 22 people can die in a single building at tiny Saragosa, in remote West Texas (May 22, 1987), then the threat of a 100-death tornado is clearly with us. If 27 can die at tiny Jarrell, Texas, many more could perish in a similar situation at Austin, just 35 miles to the south.

Fig. 15.2. The devastation caused at Moore, Oklahoma, by the tornado of May 3, 1999. Photograph by P. Hellstern, *The Daily Oklahoman*, reprinted by permission of SABA.

The uninformed, misinformed, unconcerned, very young, very old, hearing impaired, immobile, inebriated, confused, and foolish will always be with us. Even people who are usually well informed may be engrossed in a satellite TV broadcast that offers no flashing tornado alert on the edge of the screen. Even the most aware people must occasionally rush home from work in the darkness of a spring thunderstorm. Creating a zero-risk situation for tornadoes, or for any hazard, is just not possible. A major tragedy is inevitable. The best we can do is work to keep the toll as low as possible.

In the future someone may try to relate the numbers of tornadoes, or tornado deaths, to human-induced global warming. Any such link of tornado activity with climate change of any kind should be treated with the greatest skepticism. The ingredients that go into the creation of a tornado are so varied and complex that they could never be an accurate indicator of climate change. Higher temperatures may or may not mean more tornadoes. More heat could mean more convection and more thunderstorms, but the latter could also produce heavier rainfall that can smother updrafts in torrential downpours. Higher temperatures may somehow drive the jet stream farther north, away from the Great Plains and the Midwest. This might make drought more likely than tornado outbreaks.

Increased heat and evaporation may increase cloud cover. The resulting reflection of sunlight back into space may trigger a cooling effect. Whatever the climate-changing impact of human activity and increased carbon dioxide turns out to be, it is best measured by temperature, rainfall, and cloud cover, not by tornadoes. Any measure of the annual change in the number of counted tornadoes, especially an increase with all its human components and variables, will be difficult to verify as climatologically valid.

The likelihood of controlling tornadoes any time in the future is extremely low, perhaps nonexistent. The costs and consequences of large-scale tampering with the parent thunderstorms may be far worse than the benefits of such control. Proposed schemes to "control" tornadoes have involved cloud seeding to alter updrafts and precipitation, explosives to disrupt the circulation, and tampering with electrical fields by introducing metal chaff into the thunderstorm. More bizarre proposals, from amateur theoreticians, have included the building of fake mobile home parks on the outskirts of towns. Relying on the tornado's supposed attraction to mobile home parks, the funnel would swing toward the empty mobile homes, thus protecting the towns.

Cloud seeding may produce flash floods that are more costly than the tornado itself. Even if cloud seeding had no effect on the storms, lawsuits would likely follow any natural flood, with claims that the experiment triggered it. Explosives may have to be on the scale of nuclear weapons to alter a tornado. The added heat energy could make the storm stronger rather than weaker. Without a direct link between electricity and the tornado, bits of metal chaff would probably have no impact on tornado formation. And as for the absurd idea of building fake mobile home parks to fool tornadoes, the less said the better.

And what of the 1953 atomic bomb tests in Nevada? Chaos theory (Lorenz 1993) suggests that even small changes in initial conditions, perhaps even the flapping of a butterfly's wings, affect the surrounding air. These movements in turn affect more surrounding air until the effects ripple through the entire atmosphere. All of the world's flappings, exhalings, and movements may eventually create differences in the weather. Just how big the effects are, and how long a time it takes to noticeably alter a national weather pattern, is far beyond the capability of present-day science to say.

It seems possible that aboveground nuclear tests would produce changes in the atmosphere that could eventually influence larger weather patterns. I believe that it is very unlikely that an atomic bomb test had any influence on the 1953 Worcester tornado. However absurd the idea of a link may be, it gnaws at me that the largest aboveground nuclear explosion was detonated just five days before the Worcester tornado. Some day we may be able to model the situation on a supercomputer, but perhaps not in my lifetime. The ripple effects of the Nevada atomic bomb tests may not necessarily have been negative. There is the possibility that man-made influences could weaken tornadoes and make them less numerous rather then strengthen them and make them more numerous, which is often the assumption. Whether the tests altered, caused, raised, lowered, or had no effect on the death tolls will, of course, never be known.

I and thousands of others wait in anticipation for each tornado season. Each season will be unique. The combination of timing, location, size, and intensity of outbreaks will be different from those of any other year. Each new tornado season brings new opportunities for research, new speculations, and perhaps a genuine theory. Remote sensing from satellites may provide hope of filling in the distance and time gaps between weather stations, especially between upper-air observations. Intra- and intercloud lightning, as sensed by satellites, may give us a continuous flow of information about the development of every thunderstorm.

Every year computer simulations run faster and faster, with a finer and finer grid. Someday we will probably have a real-time computer simulation of a severe weather outbreak that runs along with the outbreak itself and continuously updates itself with real-world information. Whether this would mean that we could provide a severe weather warning before any radar indications are present is beyond my ability to speculate.

The future also will bring the nightmare of people running to their basements, knowing that in a few seconds every material thing they have worked for could vanish into thin air. My heart goes out to all those who have had their lives shattered by a tornado. My sincere hope is this book will reduce the severity of the loss for at least a few people.

DEADLIEST
U.S. TORNADOES

About 200 recorded tornadoes have caused 18 or more deaths. The number of deaths in parentheses will often be less than the number in the total deaths column. This is because some deaths occurred outside of town, in small communities, or on rural farms. The death toll might be spread among as many as a dozen small communities, especially in the rural South. Space does not allow a detailed listing of every community with a death. Grazulis 1993, the source for this table, has more extensive descriptions. No effort was made to estimate the Fujita Scale rating before 1870.

Rank	State(s)	Date	Time	Dead	Injuries	F-Scale	Town (deaths), State
1	MO-IL-IN	Mar. 18, 1925	1:01 PM	695	2027	F5	Murphysboro (234), Desoto (69), West Frankfort (127), IL
2	LA-MS	May 7, 1840	1:45 PM	317	109	F?	on Mississippi River (269), Natchez (48), MS
3	MO-IL	May 27, 1896	6:30 PM	255	1000	F4	St. Louis (137), MO; E. St. Louis (118), IL
4	MS	Apr. 5, 1936	8:55 PM	216	700	F5	Tupelo (216), MS
5	GA	Apr. 6, 1936	8:27 AM	203	1600	F4	Gainesville (203), GA
6	TX-OK-KS	Apr. 9, 1947	6:05 PM	181	970	F5	Glazier (17) and Higgins (51), TX; Woodward, OK (107)
7	LA-MS	Apr. 24, 1908	11:45 AM	143	770	F4	Amite (29), Pine (9), LA; Purvis (55), MS
8	WI	June 12, 1899	5:40 PM	117	200	F5	New Richmond, WI (114)
9	MI	June 8, 1953	8:30 PM	115	844	F5	Flint (115), MI
10	TX	May 11, 1953	4:10 PM	114	597	F5	Waco (114), TX
11	TX	May 18, 1902	3:45 PM	114	250	F4	Goliad (114), TX
12	NE-IA	Mar. 23, 1913	5:45 PM	103	350	F4	Ralston (7) and Omaha (94), NE
13	IL	May 26, 1917	12:10 PM	101	638	F4	Mattoon (53) and Charleston (38), IL
14	WV	June 23, 1944	6:30 PM	100	381	F4	Shinnston (30), Simpson (7), Montrose (7), WV
15	MO	Apr. 18, 1880	4:30 PM	99	200	F4	Springfield (7), Marshfield (92), MO
16	AR-MO	May 9, 1927	2:35 PM	98	300	F4	Poplar Bluff (83), MO
17	GA	June 1, 1903	12:45 PM	98	180	F4	Gainesville (98), GA
18	OK	May 10, 1905	6:45 PM	97	150	F5	Snyder (87), OK
19	MA	June 9, 1953	3:25 PM	94	1288	F4	Holden (9), Worcester (60), Shrewsbury (12), MA
20	IA-IL	June 3, 1860	6:20 PM	92	200	F?	in and near Camanche, IA (69); in and near Albany (23), IL

21	LA-MS	Apr. 24, 1908	5:00 AM	400	91	F4	Concordia Parish (30), LA; near Natchez (30), MS
22	MS-AL	Apr. 20, 1920	8:00 AM	700	88	F4	Aberdeen (22), MS; Bexar (9), Waco (19), AL
23	OH	June 28, 1924	4:35 PM	300	85	F4	Sandusky (8), Lorain (72), OH
24	OK-KS	May 25, 1955	10:15 PM	270	80	F5	near Oxford (5), Udall (77), KS
25	MO-IL	Sep. 29, 1927	1:00 PM	550	79	F3	St. Louis (72), MO; Granite City (7), IL
26	KY	Mar. 27, 1890	7:57 PM	200	76	F4	Louisville (76), KY
27	TX	Apr. 12, 1927	7:45 PM	205	74	F5	Rock Springs (72), TX
28	TX	May 15, 1896	4:30 PM	200	73	F5	Sherman (60), TX
29	MN	Apr. 14, 1886	4:20 PM	213	72	F4	St. Cloud (24), Sauk Rapids (37), Rice (11), MN
30	OK	May 2, 1920	8:35 PM	100	71	F4	Peggs (71), OK
31	IA	July 6, 1893	4:35 PM	200	71	F5	Pomeroy (49), IA
32	OK	Apr. 12, 1945	5:40 PM	353	69	F5	Antlers (69), OK
33	IA	June 17, 1882	6:30 PM	300	68	F5	Grinnell (39) and Malcolm (10), IA
34	TN-KY	May 27, 1917	4:00 PM	345	67	F4	Bondurant (21), Hickman (8), Clinton (17), KY
35	MS	Mar. 16, 1942	3:00 PM	500	63	F4	Avalon (5), O'Tuckalofa (19), Tula (4), MS
36	TX-AR	Apr. 15, 1921	2:10 PM	300	59	F4	Avinger (6) TX; Miller and Hempstead Cos. (50), AR
37	MS	Feb. 21, 1971	4:00 PM	700	58	F4	near Cary (14), Pugh City (21), Morgan City (6), MS
38	MS	Mar. 3, 1966	4:00 PM	504	57	F5	Jackson (19), rural Scott County (26), MS
39	MN	June 22, 1919	4:00 PM	200	57	F5	One Mile Lake (4), Lake Alice (2), Fergus Falls (51), MN
40	MS	Apr. 22, 1883	3:00 PM	300	56	F4	Wesson (13) and Beauregard (29), MS
41	AR	Jan. 3, 1949	4:15 PM	435	55	F4	Warren (55), AR
42	AR	Jan. 11, 1898	11:15 PM	113	55	F4	Fort Smith (52), Van Buren (3), AR

Rank	State(s)	Date	Time	Dead	Injuries	F-Scale	Town (deaths), State
43	SC	Apr. 30, 1924	11:00 AM	53	534	F4	rural Sumter County (20), Horrell Hill (12), SC
44	OK	Apr. 27, 1942	3:15 PM	52	350	F4	Pryor (49), OK
45	AR	Mar. 21, 1952	4:50 PM	50	325	F4	Judsonia (30) and Bald Knob (10), AR
46	AL	Mar. 21, 1932	4:30 PM	49	150	F4	rural Perry County (21); Jemison and Union Grove (21), AL
47	AR	Mar. 8, 1909	7:00 PM	49	600	F4	Brinkley (42), AR
48	LA	May 13, 1908	5:30 PM	49	135	F4	Gilliam (34), Bolinger (9), LA
49	MI	May 25, 1896	9:00 PM	47	100	F5	Oakwood (10), Ortonville (22), North Oxford (4), MI
50	LA-MS	Feb. 21, 1971	2:50 PM	46	400	F4	Delhi (10), LA; Delta City (7), Inverness (21), MS
51	IN-KY	Mar. 23, 1917	3:08 PM	46	250	F4	New Albany (46), IN
52	TX-OK	Apr. 10, 1979	5:50 PM	45	1740	F4	Wichita Falls (45), TX
53	IN-MI	Apr. 11, 1965	7:00 PM	44	612	F4	Branch County (19), Hillsdale (11), Manitou Beach (6), MI
54	KS-MO	May 20, 1957	6:15 PM	44	531	F5	Spring Hill (5), KS; south of Kansas City (37), MO
55	AL	Mar. 21, 1932	7:10 PM	41	325	F4	Sylacauga (29) and Bethel Church (7), AL
56	TX	May 6, 1930	3:30 PM	41	200	F4	near Bynum and Mertens (16), Frost (22), TX
57	AR	Mar. 21, 1952	5:00 PM	40	274	F4	England (9) and Cotton Plant (29), AR
58	GA	Apr. 25, 1929	10:00 PM	40	300	F4	rural Bullock County (31), GA
59	TN-KY	Mar. 18, 1925	5:00 PM	39	95	F4	rural Sumner County (27) TN; Beaumont (8), KY
60	LA-MS	Dec. 5, 1953	5:45 PM	38	270	F4	Vicksburg (38), MS
61	TN	Mar. 21, 1952	10:45 PM	38	157	F4	Bolivar (4), Henderson (23), TN

62	AL-TN	Mar. 21, 1932	8:00 PM	38	F4	500	Paint Rock (4), rural Jackson County (32), AL
63	MS	Mar. 31, 1933	10:30 AM	37	F4	170	Sandersville (14), rural Jasper Co.(16), Harmony (6), MS
64	AL	Mar. 21, 1932	4:00 PM	37	F4	200	Northport (37), AL
65	MN	Aug. 21, 1883	5:30 PM	37	F5	200	Rochester (32), MN
66	OK	May 3, 1999	6:00 PM	36	F5	583	Bridge Creek (12) Moore (11), Oklahoma City (12), OK
67	IN	Apr. 11, 1965	7:10 PM	36	F5	320	Dunlap (28), IN
68	KY	May 9, 1933	8:30 PM	36	F4	87	Tompkinsville (18) and Russell Springs (14), TN
69	TX	May 6, 1930	4:45 PM	36	F4	60	rural Karnes and Dewitt Counties (36), TX
70	MS	Apr. 20, 1920	9:55 AM	36	F4	200	Bay Springs (7), Rose Hill (9), Meridian (11), MS
71	SD-MN	Aug. 21, 1918	9:00 PM	36	F4	225	Tyler (36), MN
72	AL	Jan. 22, 1904	12:20 AM	36	F4	150	Moundville (35) and Hull (1), AL
73	AR	May 15, 1968	8:45 PM	35	F4	361	Jonesboro (35), AR
74	AR	June 1, 1947	3:20 PM	35	F4	300	Pine Bluff (16), AR
75	OK	June 12, 1942	8:41 PM	35	F4	100	Oklahoma City (35), OK
76	TN	May 10, 1933	12:15 AM	35	F4	150	Beatty Swamps near Livingston (35), TN
77	AL	Apr. 24, 1908	2:40 PM	35	F4	188	Bergens (12) and Albertville (15), AL
78	OH	Apr. 3, 1974	3:30 PM	34	F5	1150	Xenia (34), OH
79	TX	May 30, 1909	12:15 AM	34	F4	70	Zephyr (34), TX
80	KS	May 8, 1905	11:45 PM	34	F4	50	Marquette (29), KS
81	MO	Apr. 27, 1899	6:10 PM	34	F4	125	Kirksville (34), MO
82	CT	Aug. 9, 1878	6:15 PM	34	F4	70	Wallingford (34), CT
83	IL	Apr. 21, 1967	5:24 PM	33	F4	500	Oaklawn (33), IL

Rank	State(s)	Date	Time	Dead	Injuries	F-Scale	Town (deaths), State
84	IL	Mar. 19, 1948	6:30 AM	33	449	F4	Fosterburg (9), Bunker Hill (19), Gillespie (5), IL
85	AL	Apr. 8, 1998	6:42 PM	32	258	F5	Oak Grove
86	MS	Jan. 23, 1969	5:25 AM	32	241	F4	Hazelhurst (11), near Harrisville (12), White Oak (6), MS
87	KY-IN	Apr. 3, 1974	3:25 PM	31	270	F5	Brandenburg (28), KY
88	AL	Mar. 21, 1932	5:30 PM	31	200	F4	Plantersville (12), Stanton and Lomax (19), AL
89	GA	Feb. 10, 1921	12:30 PM	31	100	F4	Gardner, GA (31)
90	OK	Apr. 25, 1893	6:30 PM	31	100	F4	Moore (30), OK
91	MO	Apr. 18, 1880	4:30 PM	31	100	F4	rural areas south and southwest of Springfield, MO (31)
92	TX	May 22, 1987	7:16 PM	30	121	F4	Saragosa (30), TX
93	MS-AL	Apr. 3, 1974	7:50 PM	30	280	F5	Guin (20), AL
94	WV-PA-MD	June 23, 1944	6:11 PM	30	300	F4	Chartiers (10) Dry tavern (8), PA; Oakland (3), MD
95	MS-TN	Nov. 20, 1900	2:45 PM	30	100	F4	near Lula (15) and Strayhorn (11), MS; Lagrange (2), TN
96	AL-GA	Feb. 19, 1884	2:30 PM	30	100	F4	Piedmont (10) and Goshen (14), AL; Cave Spring, GA (4)
97	VA-MD	Aug. 15, 1818		30		F?	on Potomac River south of Quantico (30), VA
98	IL	Aug. 28, 1990	2:30 PM	29	350	F5	Plainfield (29), IL
99	AR	Oct. 29, 1942	10:30 PM	29	100	F4	Berryville (29), AR
100	MS-TN	Apr. 29, 1909	7:30 PM	29	100	F4	Horn Lake (14) MS; Scotts Hill (9), TN
101	TN	Apr. 29, 1909	11:00 PM	29	70	F4	near Bee Springs (22) and Millville (7), TN
102	TX	May 11, 1970	8:35 PM	28	500	F5	Lubbock (28), TX

103	AL	Apr. 3, 1974	5:50 PM	28	260	F5	near Moulton (14) and near Harvest (9), AL
104	IN	Apr. 11, 1965	7:20 PM	28	123	F4	near Lebanon (11) and near Sheridan (10), IN
105	LA	May 1, 1933	4:00 PM	28	400	F4	southwest of Minden (16) and Minden (12), LA
106	IA-IL	May 18, 1898	4:45 PM	28	150	F4	Preston (5), Riggs (5), Delmar (7), IA; Forreston (4), IL
107	GA-SC	Mar. 20, 1875	12:40 PM	28	70	F4	rural GA (25); rural SC (3)
108	TX	May 27, 1997	2:20 PM	27	12	F5	Jarrell (27)
109	AR	Apr. 16, 1939	2:40 PM	27	62	F4	near Center Point and Tillar, AR (27)
110	SC	Sep. 29, 1938	8:00 AM	27	80	F2	Charleston (27), SC
111	AL	Apr. 20, 1920	12:30 PM	27	100	F4	southeast of Huntsville (27), AL
112	MS	Apr. 20, 1920	8:30 AM	27	60	F4	New Deemer (19), MS
113	GA	Mar. 28, 1920	5:45 PM	27	100	F3	LaGrange (27), GA
114	AL	May 27, 1917	8:45 PM	27	100	F4	Sayre (9) and Bradford (17), AL
115	AL	Mar. 21, 1913	4:30 AM	27	60	F4	Lower Peach Tree (27), AL
116	TN	Nov. 20, 1900	9:30 PM	27	75	F4	near Columbia (27), TN
117	AL	Feb. 12, 1945	5:22 PM	26	293	F3	north edge of Montgomery at Chisholm (26)
118	AL-GA	Mar. 28, 1920	2:45 PM	26	125	F4	near Agricola (17), AL; West Point (9), GA
119	FL	Feb. 22, 1998	12:40 AM	25	150	F3	Kissimmee
120	IN	Apr. 11, 1965	7:25 PM	25	835	F4	Greentown (10), Swayzee (3), south of Marion (5), IN
121	AL	Apr. 15, 1956	3:00 PM	25	200	F4	McDonald's Chapel near Birmingham (25), AL
122	AR-MO-TN	Mar. 21, 1952	8:00 PM	25	150	F4	near Cooter (17), MO; near Owl Hoot (8), TN
123	GA-SC	Apr. 16, 1944	12:30 AM	25	120	F4	Royston (12) and Nuberg (10), GA
124	AR	June 5, 1916	4:00 PM	25	150	F4	Heber Springs (18), AR

Rank	State(s)	Date	Time	Dead	Injuries	F-Scale	Town (deaths), State
125	NE-IA	Mar. 23, 1913	6:15 PM	25	75	F4	Council Bluffs (17), Weston (2), Neola (3), IA
126	KS-NE	May 17, 1896	5:00 PM	25	200	F5	Seneca (6), Oneida (6), Reserve (5), KS; Falls City (4), NE
127	IA	Sep. 21, 1894	8:30 PM	25	60	F4	rural Hancock County, IA (14)
128	KY	Aug. 27, 1854		25	100	F?	Louisville (25), KY
129	IL	Apr. 21, 1967	3:50 PM	24	500	F4	Belvidere (24), IL
130	AR	May 9, 1927	4:20 PM	24	72	F4	Strong (24), AR
131	AR	Mar. 18, 1927	7:30 PM	24	110	F4	Green Forest (24), AR
132	MS	Apr. 20, 1920	7:00 AM	24	180	F4	Ingomar (6), Glen (5), MS
133	TX	Apr. 9, 1919	4:15 AM	24	100	F4	Mineola (3), Spring Hill (6), Blodgett (4), TX
134	MS	Mar. 16, 1919	12:00 PM	24	80	F4	Panther Burn (5), near Isola (16), MS
135	IN	Mar. 11, 1917	2:55 PM	24	110	F4	New Castle (21), Millville (1), Hagerstown (2), IN
136	TN	Oct. 14, 1909	5:30 PM	24	80	F3	Stantonville (15), Pittsburg Landing (6), TN
137	IL	May 27, 1896	6:45 PM	24	125	F4	Birkner (10), near New Baden (13), IL
138	IL	Feb. 19, 1888	4:30 PM	24	80	F4	Mt. Vernon (24), IL
139	IA	June 3, 1860	5:45 PM	24	60	F?	rural areas of Cedar and Clinton County, IA (24)
140	MO-IL	May 21, 1949	6:55 PM	23	130	F4	Cape Girardeau (23), MO
141	GA	Apr. 2, 1936	7:30 AM	23	500	F4	Cordele (23), GA
142	OK	Nov. 19, 1930	9:30 AM	23	125	F4	Bethany (23), OK
143	AR	Apr. 10, 1929	6:00 PM	23	80	F5	near Swifton (23), AR

144	AR	Nov. 25, 1926	5:15 PM	23	90	F4	Heber Springs (17), AR
145	TX	May 14, 1923	4:30 AM	23	250	F5	rural Howard and Mitchell counties (23), TX
146	IN-OH	Mar. 28, 1920	5:15 PM	23	54	F4	near Ossian (9), Townley (4), IN; Brunersburg (6), OH
147	KS	May 25, 1917	2:00 PM	23	70	F5	Andale (12), Sedgwick (8), McLain (2), KS
148	MS	Mar. 2, 1906	6:10 PM	23	60	F4	Meridian (23), MS
149	TX	Apr. 28, 1893	9:30 PM	23	150	F4	Cisco (21), TX
150	NC	Feb. 19, 1884	9:30 PM	23	100	F4	Philadelphia (15), NC
151	SC	June 30, 1814		23	100	F?	Port Royal Sound (23), SC
152	AL	Apr. 4, 1977	3:00 PM	22	130	F5	north of Birmingham (22), AL
153	AL-TN	Apr. 3, 1974	6:25 PM	22	250	F4	near Tanner, Capshaw, and Harvest (16), AL
154	LA	Oct. 3, 1964	6:30 AM	22	165	F4	Larose (22), LA
155	NE-IA	Mar. 23, 1913	5:30 PM	22	50	F4	Yutan (17), NE; Logan (2), IA
156	GA	Feb. 19, 1884	2:00 PM	22	100	F4	Waleska (3), Cagle (8), and Tate (7), GA
157	MS	Apr. 25, 1880	8:30 PM	22	72	F4	Macon 22), MS
158	AL-GA	May 1, 1875	12:00 PM	22	30	F3	Harris County (16), GA
159	WI	June 28, 1865	4:00 PM	22	100	F?	Viroqua (22), WI
160	AL	Nov. 15, 1989	4:30 PM	21	463	F4	Huntsville (21), AL
161	MO-IL	Feb. 10, 1959	1:40 AM	21	345	F4	St. Louis (21), MO
162	TX-LA	Feb. 17, 1938	9:40 PM	21	50	F4	Rodessa (21), LA
163	AL	May 5, 1933	2:30 AM	21	200	F4	Brent (5), Colemont (2), Helena (14), AL
164	AL	Apr. 20, 1920	10:00 AM	21	50	F4	near Arley and Helicon (19), AL
165	IN	Mar. 23, 1913	9:30 PM	21	250	F4	Terre Haute (21), IN

Rank	State(s)	Date	Time	Dead	Injuries	F-Scale	Town (deaths), State
166	IA	May 24, 1896	10:30 PM	21	60	F4	Santiago (3), near Valeria (11), IA
167	KY-IL-KY	Mar. 27, 1890	5:15 PM	21	200	F4	Sheridan (5), Blackford (8), Delaware (5), KY
168	KS-MO	Apr. 21, 1887	5:30 PM	21	250	F4	Prescott (12), KS; Sprague (5), MO
169	OK	May 8, 1882	6:15 PM	21	42	F3	McAlester (21), OK
170	MS	May 7, 1846	2:30 PM	21	62	F?	Grenada (21), MS
171	AR	Apr. 10, 1944	10:35 PM	21	50	F4	Duncan (14), AR
172	WI	June 4, 1958	5:30 PM	20	110	F4	near Menomonie (3), Colfax (15), WI
173	TX	May 15, 1957	9:35 PM	20	80	F4	Silverton (20), TX
174	OK-KS	May 25, 1955	9:26 PM	20	280	F5	Blackwell (20), OK
175	MS	Feb. 1, 1955	2:20 PM	20	141	F3	Commerce Landing (20), MS
176	TN	Mar. 11, 1923	8:00 PM	20	70	F5	Deansburg (2), Pinson (18), TN
177	IL	Mar. 28, 1920	12:15 PM	20	300	F4	Maywood (4), Melrose Park (10), Dunning (6), IL
178	MO	June 5, 1917	8:30 PM	20	68	F4	Overton (4), Rocheport (2), Hinton (3), Centralia (7), MO
179	MN	July 15, 1881	3:30 PM	20	93	F4	Cairo Twp. (6), near West Newton (5) New Ulm (6), MN
180	IN	Apr. 3, 1974	4:50 PM	19	362	F4	Monticello (7), IN
181	IN	Apr. 11, 1965	6:40 PM	19	100	F4	south of Shipshewana (17), IN
182	GA	Apr. 30, 1953	5:10 PM	19	300	F4	Warner Robins (18), GA
183	IN	Mar. 26, 1948	5:10 PM	19	200	F4	Coatsville (14), Hadley (2), Danville (2), IN
184	SC	May 5, 1933	2:30 PM	19	100	F3	Belton (11), SC

185	MS	Feb. 25, 1929	2:30 PM	19	42	F4	Duncan (19), MS
186	TX	May 9, 1927	2:25 AM	19	100	F4	Nevada (16), TX
187	AL	Apr. 8, 1903	1:30 AM	19	100	F4	Hopewell (19), AL
188	IL	May 31, 1858	PM	19	60	F?	Ellison (19), IL
189	OH-PA	May 31, 1985	5:30 PM	18	310	F5	Niles (8), Hermitage (10), PA
190	OH-MI	Apr. 11, 1965	9:35 PM	18	236	F4	Toledo (16), OH; Lost Peninsula (2), MI
191	OH	Apr. 11, 1965	11:05 PM	18	200	F5	Pittsfield (9) and Strongsville (9), OH
192	MI	Apr. 3, 1956	6:30 PM	18	340	F4	Hudsonville (14) and Standale (4), MI
193	AR	Mar. 26, 1949	4:00 PM	18	150	F4	near England (13), AR
194	LA-AR	Dec. 31, 1947	4:00 PM	18	225	F4	Cotton Valley (14), LA
195	GA	Feb. 10, 1940	4:20 AM	18	300	F4	Albany (18), GA
196	AL	Mar. 21, 1932	4:30 PM	18	100	F4	rural Cullman County (18), AL
197	AL	Oct. 25, 1925	2:00 AM	18	60	F4	north of Troy (7), AL
198	WI	Sep. 21, 1924	2:30 PM	18	50	F4	rural Clark County (14), WI
199	TX	Apr. 8, 1919	11:45 PM	18	60	F4	Blue Ridge (8), Ector (3), Ravenna (8), TX
200	MO	May 30, 1917	5:00 PM	18	200	F4	Granite Bend (1), Dongola (7), Zalma (9), MO
201	AR-TN	May 27, 1917	3:00 PM	18	175	F4	near Blytheville (6), AR; Dyersburg (7), Sharon (4), TN
202	NE-IA	Mar. 23, 1913	6:15 PM	18	100	F4	Berlin-Otoe (12), NE; Bartlett (3), Glenwood (2), IA
203	TX	July 5, 1905	3:00 PM	18	40	F4	rural Montague County (18), TX
204	KS-NE	May 30, 1879	4:15 PM	18	60	F4	Irving (9), near Frankfort (5), KS

Suggested Further Reading

No book on tornadoes can be comprehensive, and this book is no exception. If you wish to pursue the subject further, I suggest you explore the other sources of information listed below.

The American Meteorological Society Severe Storm Conference preprints are published every two years by the AMS. They are available in paperback and on CD-ROM. Every other year, severe storm specialists from around the world write papers about their research and present them to the meteorological community. The papers are a good resource for new ideas and references.

Significant Tornadoes, 1680–1991 (Environmental Films, 1993), available through the Tornado Project, includes a description of every known significant tornado (14,000 of them) and contains 400 photographs. An update is also available, covering more recent years.

The Storm Prediction Center's web site has a summary of all severe weather of the previous day and official statistics for the past several years: www.spc.noaa.gov. The web site of the National Climatic Data Center has details on all known tornadoes since 1993 and is updated monthly: www4.ncdc.noaa.gov.

The Thunderstorm in Human Affairs, 2d ed. (Oklahoma, 1988), edited by Edwin Kessler, has an especially good summary of the 1974 superoutbreak.

Tornado Alley (Oxford, 1999) by Howard B. Bluestein, provides perspectives from a long and distinguished career on severe storms and tornadoes, research, and storm chasing.

The Tornado: Its Structure, Dynamics, Prediction and Hazards (American Geophysical Union, 1993), edited by Chris Church, Don Burgess, Charles Doswell, and Robert Davies-Jones, is a remarkable, but unfortunately out-of-print book. It provides an outstanding summary of the previous fifteen years of research, with extensive references.

The Tornado Project (www.tornadoproject.com or The Tornado Project, P.O. Box 302, St. Johnsbury, Vt. 05819) has updated statistics, many hours of tornado video, and World Wide Web links.

Under the Whirlwind (Whirlwind Books, 1998), by Arjen Verkaik, is a well-written, full-color book written from a Canadian perspective.

The Weather Book, 2d ed. (USA Today, 1997), by Jack Williams, is a good place to start for a broad perspective on the weather.

Weatherwise magazine (Heldref Publications) is, to date, the only major weather magazine published in North America.

REFERENCES

Abbey, R. F., Jr., and T.T. Fujita. 1983. "Tornadoes: The Outbreak of 3–4 April 1974." In *The Thunderstorm in Human Affairs*, 2d ed., edited by E. Kessler, 37–66. Norman: University of Oklahoma Press.

Atlas, D. 1990. *Radar in Meteorology.* Boston: American Meteorological Society.

Barnes, S. L. 1968. "On the Source of Thunderstorm Rotation." NSSL Technical Memo ERLTM-NSSL, no. 38.

———. 1970. "Some Aspects of a Severe, Right-moving Thunderstorms Deduced from Mesonetwork Rawinsonde Observations." *Journal of Atmospheric Sciences* 27: 634–48.

Bieringer, P., and P. S. Ray. 1996. "A Comparison of Tornado Warning Lead Times with and without NEXRAD Doppler Radar." *Weather and Forecasting* 11: 47–52.

Bigler, S. G. 1956. "A Note on the Successful Identification and Tracking of a Tornado by Radar." *Weatherwise* 9: 198–201.

Bluestein, H. B. 1983. "Surface Meteorological Observations in Severe Thunderstorms. Part 2: Field Experiments with TOTO." *Journal of Applied Meteorology* 22: 919–30.

———. 1985. *The Formation of a "Landspout" in a Broken-line Squall Line in Oklahoma.* Preprint. 14th Conference on Severe Local Storms, American Meteorological Society. Pp. 267–70.

———. 1999. *Tornado Alley.* New York: Oxford University Press.

Bluestein, H. B., and C. R. Parks. 1983. "A Synoptic and Photographic Climatology of Low-Precipitation Severe Thunderstorms in the Southern Plains." *Monthly Weather Review* 111: 2034–46.

Bluestein, H. B., and J. Unruh. 1993. "On the Use of Portable FM-CW Doppler Radar for Tornado Research. In *The Tornado: Its Structure, Dynamics, Prediction and Hazards,* edited by C. Church, 367–98. Proceedings, Tornado Symposium III. Washington, D.C.: American Geophysical Union.

Booker, C. A. 1954. "On Transmission Towers Destroyed by the Worcester, Massachusetts, Tornado of June 9, 1953." *Bulletin of the American Meteorological Society* 35: 225, 229.

Brooks, E. M. 1949. "The Tornado Cyclone." *Weatherwise* 2: 32–33.

Brooks, H. E., C. A. Doswell III, and R. Davies-Jones. 1993. "Environmental Helicity and the Maintenance and Evolution of Low-Level Mesocyclones." In *The Tornado: Its Structure, Dynamics, Prediction and Hazards,* edited by C. Church, 97–104. Proceedings, Tornado Symposium III. Washington, D.C.: American Geophysical Union.

Brown, R. A., D. W. Burgess, and K. C. Crawford. 1973. "Twin Tornado Cyclones within a Severe Thunderstorm: Single Doppler Radar Observations." *Weatherwise* 26: 63–71.

Browning, K. A. 1962. "Cellular Structure of Convective Storms." *Meteorological Magazine* 91: 341–49.

———. 1964. "Air Flow and Precipitation Trajectories within Severe Local Storms Which Travel to the Right of the Mean Wind." *Journal of Atmospheric Sciences* 21: 634–39.

Browning, K. A., and R. J. Donaldson. 1963. "Airflow and Structure of a Tornadic Storm." *Journal of Atmospheric Sciences* 20: 533–45.

Browning, K. A., and C. R. Landry. 1963. "Air flow within a Tornadic Storm." Preprint. 10th Weather Radar Conference, American Meteorological Society, 116–22.

Browning, K. A., and F. H. Ludlum. 1962. "Airflow in Convective Storms." *Quarterly Journal of the Royal Meteorological Society* 88: 117–35.

Bunting W. F., and B. E. Smith. 1993. "A Guide for Conducting Convective Windstorm Surveys." NOAA Technical Memo, NWS SR-146.

Burgess, D. W. 1976. "Single-Doppler Radar Vortex Recognition: Part I: Mesocyclone Signatures." Preprint. 17th Radar Meteorological Conference, American Meteorological Society, Boston, 189–92.

Burgess, D. W., and R. J. Donaldson, Jr. 1979. "Contrasting Tornadic Storm Types." In *11th Conference on Severe Local Storms,* 189–92. Boston: American Meteorological Society.

Burgess, D. W., and L. R. Lemon. 1990. "Severe Thunderstorm Detection by Radar." In *Radar in Meteorology,* edited by D. Atlas, 619–47. Boston: American Meteorological Society.

Byers, H. R., and R. R. Braham, Jr. 1949. *The Thunderstorm.* Washington, D.C.: U.S. Government Printing Office.

Church, C. R., and J. T. Snow. 1993. "Laboratory Models of Tornadoes." In *The Tornado: Its Structure, Dynamics, Prediction and Hazards,* edited by C. Church, 277–95. Proceedings, Tornado Symposium III. Washington, D.C.: American Geophysical Union.

Church, C. R., J. T. Snow, G. L. Baker, and E. M. Agee. 1979. "Characteristics of Tornado-like Vortices as a Function of Swirl Ratio: A Laboratory Investigation." *Journal of Atmospheric Sciences* 36: 1755–76.

Corcoran, E. 1991. "Calculating Reality." *Scientific American,* (January): 100–9.

Davies-Jones, R. P. 1985. "Tornado Dynamics." In *Thunderstorms: Morphology and Dynamics,* 2d ed., edited by E. Kessler, 197–236. Norman: University of Oklahoma Press.

Davidson, K. 1996. *Twister: The Science of Tornadoes and the Making of an Adventure Movie.* New York: Pocket Books.

Dessens, J. and J. T. Snow. 1989. "Tornadoes in France." *Weather and Forecasting* 4: 110–32.

———. 1993. "Comparative Description of Tornadoes in France and the United States." In *The Tornado: Its Structure, Dynamics, Prediction and Hazards,* ed. C. Church, 427–34. Proceedings, Tornado Symposium III. Washington, D.C.: American Geophysical Union.

Donaldson, R. J. 1970. "Vortex Signature Recognition by Doppler Radar." *Journal of Allied Meteorology* 9: 661–70.

Doswell, C. A., III, and D. W. Burgess. 1988. "Some Issues of United States Tornado Climatology." *Monthly Weather Review* 116: 495–501.

———. 1993. "Tornadoes and Tornadic Storms: A Review of Conceptual Models." In *The Tornado: Its Structure, Dynamics, Prediction and Hazards,* ed. C. Church, 161–72. Proceedings, Tornado Symposium III. Washington, D.C.: American Geophysical Union.

Doswell, C. A., III, S. J. Weiss, and R. H. Johns. 1993. "Tornado Forecasting—A Review." In *The Tornado: Its Structure, Dynamics, Prediction and Hazards,* ed. C. Church, 557–71. Proceedings, Tornado Symposium III. Washington, D.C.: American Geophysical Union.

Eagleman, J. R. 1967. "Tornado Damage Pattern in Topeka, Kansas, June 8, 1966." *Monthly Weather Review* 95: 370–74.

Eagleman, J. R., and V. U. Muirhead. 1971. *Observed Damage from Tornadoes and Safest Location in Houses.* Preprints, 7th Conference on Severe Local Storms, American Meteorological Society, Kansas City. Pp. 171–77.

Eshelman, S. F., and J. L. Stanford. 1977. "Tornadoes, Funnel Clouds and Thunderstorm Damage in Iowa during 1974." *Iowa State Journal of Research* 51: 327–61.

Fawbush, E. J., and R. C. Miller. 1951. "An Empirical Method of Forecasting Tornado Development." *Bulletin of the American Meteorological Society* 32: 1–9.

———. 1953. "The Tornado Situation of March 17, 1951." *Bulletin of the American Meteorological Society* 34: 139–45.

Ferrel, W. 1889. *A Popular Treatise on the Winds.* New York: John Wiley.

Finley, J. P. 1881. "The Tornadoes of May 29 and 30, 1879, in Kansas, Nebraska, Missouri and Iowa." *Prof. Paper No. 4.* U.S. Signal Service.

———. 1884. "Report of the Character of Six Hundred Tornadoes." *Prof. Paper No. 7.* U.S. Signal Service. Available NOAA Library, Silver Spring, Md.

———. 1887. *Tornadoes: What They Are and How to Observe Them.* New York: Insurance Monitor Press.

Flora, S. D. 1953. *Tornadoes of the United States.* Norman: University of Oklahoma Press.

Forbes, G. S. 1976. "Photogrammetric Characteristics of the Parker Tornado of April 3, 1974." *Proc. Symposium on Tornadoes.* Lubbock: Texas Tech University. Pp. 58–77.

Forbes, G. S., and R. M. Wakimoto. 1983. "A Concentrated Outbreak of Tornadoes, Downbursts, and Microbursts, and Implications Regarding Vortex Classification." *Monthly Weather Review* 111: 220–35.

Fujita, T. T. 1958. "Mesoanalysis of the Illinois Tornadoes of April 9, 1953." *Journal of Meteorology* 15: 288–96.

———. 1960. *Detailed Analysis of the Fargo Tornadoes of June 20, 1957.* U.S. Weather Bureau Research Paper No. 42.

———. 1970. "The Lubbock Tornadoes: A Study of Suction Spots." *Weatherwise* 23: 160–73.

———. 1971a. *Proposed Characterization of Tornadoes and Hurricanes by Area and Intensity.* SMRP Research Paper No. 91. University of Chicago.

———. 1971b. *Proposed Mechanism of Suction Spots Accompanied by Tornadoes.* Preprints, 7th Conference on Severe Local Storms, American Meteorological Society, Kansas City. Pp. 208–13.

———. 1973. "Tornadoes around the World." *Weatherwise* 26: 56–62.

———. 1977. "Anticyclonic Tornadoes." *Weatherwise* 30: 51–64.

———. 1981. "Tornadoes and Downbursts on the Context of Generalized Planetary Scales." *Journal of Atmospheric Sciences* 38: 1511–34.

Fujita, T. T., D. L. Bradbury, and C. F. van Thullenar. 1970. "Palm Sunday Tornadoes of April 11, 1965." *Monthly Weather Review* 98: 29–69.

Fujita, T. T., and F. Caracena. 1977. "An Analysis of Three Weather-related Aircraft Accidents." *Bulletin of the American Meteorological Society* 58: 1164–81.

Fujita, T. T., A. and Pearson, 1973. *Experimental Classification of Tornadoes in FPP Scale.* SMRP Research Paper No. 98. University of Chicago.

Fujita, T. T., and R. M. Wakimoto. 1981. "Five Scales of Airflow Associated with a Series of Downbursts on 16 July 1980." *Monthly Weather Review* 109: 1438–56.

Galway, J. G. 1956. "The Lifted Index as a Predictor of Latent Instability." *Bulletin of the American Meteorological Society* 37: 528–29.

———. 1977. "Some Climatological Aspects of Tornado Outbreaks." *Monthly Weather Review* 105: 477–84.

———. 1985. "J. P. Finley: The First Severe Storms Forecaster." *Bulletin of the American Meteorological Society* 66: 1389–95, 1506–10.

———. 1992. "Early Severe Thunderstorm Forecasting and Research by the U. S. Weather Bureau." *Weather and Forecasting* 7: 564–87.

Glass, R. I., R. B. Craven, D. J. Bregman, B. J. Stoll, N. Horowitz, P. Kerndt, and J. Winkle. 1980. "Injuries from the Wichita Falls Tornado." *Science* 207: 734–38.

Golden, J. H. 1974. "On the Life Cycle of Florida Keys' Waterspouts I." *Journal of Applied Meteorology* 13: 676–92.

Golden, J. H., and D. Purcell. 1978. "Life Cycle of the Union City, Oklahoma Tornado and Comparison with Waterspouts." *Monthly Weather Review* 106: 3–11.

Goodman, S. J., and K. R. Knupp. 1993. "Tornadogenesis via Squall Line and Supercell Interaction: The November 15, 1989, Huntsville, Alabama, Tornado." In *Proc. Tornado Symposium III,* edited by C. Church, 183–99. Washington, D.C.: American Geophysical Union.

Grazulis, T. P. 1993. *Significant Tornadoes.* St. Johnsbury, Vt.: Environmental Films.

———. 2000. *Guide to Secrets of the Tornado.* St. Johnsbury, Vt.: Tornado Project.

Greneker, E. F., C. S. Wilson, and J. I. Metcalf. 1977. "The Atlanta Tornado of 1975." *Monthly Weather Review* 104: 1052–57.

Hall, R. S. 1951. "Inside a Texas Tornado." *Weatherwise* 4: 54–57, 65.

Hazen, H. A. 1890. *The Tornado.* New York: N. D. C. Hodges.

Hoecker, W. H., Jr. 1959. "History and Measurement of the Two Major Scottsbluff Tornadoes of 27 June 1955." *Bulletin of the American Meteorological Society* 40: 117–33.

———. 1960. "Wind Speed and Air Flow Patterns in the Dallas Tornado of April 2, 1957." *Monthly Weather Review* 88: 167–80.

Hoecker, W. H., Jr., R. G. Beebe, D. T. Williams, J. T. Lee, S. B. Bigler, and E. P. Segner, Jr. 1960. *The Tornadoes at Dallas, Texas, April 2, 1957.* Weather Bureau Research Paper No. 41.

Ivey, J. 1976. "Patrolman Rode with the Devil." *Weatherwise* 29: 21.

Jakl, V. E. 1920. "Kite Flight in the Center of a Deep Area of Low Pressure." *Monthly Weather Review* 48: 198–200.

Keller, D., and B. Vonnegut. 1976. "Wind Speed Estimation Based on the Penetration of Straws and Splinters into Wood." *Weatherwise* (October): 228–32.

Klemp, J. B. 1987. "Dynamics of Tornadic Thunderstorms." *Annual Review of Fluid Mechanics* 19: 369–402.

Klemp, J. B., and R. B. Wilhelmson. 1978. "The Simulation of Three-Dimensional Convective Storm Dynamics." *Journal of Atmospheric Sciences* 35: 1070–96.

Lee, B. D., and R. B. Wilhelmson. 1996. "The Numerical Simulation of Non-Supercell Tornadoes." 18th Conference on Severe Local

Storms, American Meteorological Society, San Francisco. Pp. 408–11.

Lee, J. T. 1955. "Thunderstorm and Tornadoes of February 1, 1955." *Monthly Weather Review* 83: 45–50.

Lemon, L. R., and C. A. Doswell III. 1979. "Severe Thunderstorm Evolution and Mesocyclone Structure as Related to Tornado Genesis." *Monthly Weather Review* 107: 1184–97.

Lloyd, J. R. 1942. "The Development and Trajectories of Tornadoes." *Monthly Weather Review* 70: 65–75.

Lorenz, E. N. 1993. *The Essence of Chaos.* Seattle: University of Washington Press.

Ludlum, D. M. 1970. *Early American Tornadoes, 1586–1870.* Boston: American Meteorological Society.

Marshall, T. P. 1995. "A Survey of the 1994 Palm Sunday Outbreak." *Storm Track* 18: 1.

Meaden, G. T. 1975. "The Earliest-Known British and Irish Tornadoes." *Journal of Meteorology* 1 (3): 96–99.

Minor, J. E., J. R. McDonald, and K. C. Mehta. 1977. *The Tornado: An Engineering-oriented Perspective.* ERL-NSSL-82, NOAA.

Moller, A. R., C. A. Doswell III, and R. Przybylinski. 1990. *High Precipitation Supercells: A Conceptual Model and Documentation.* Preprints. 16th Conference on Severe Local Storms, American Meteorological Society, Boston. Pp. 52–57.

Murphy, A. H. 1996. "The Finley Affair: A Signal Event in the History of Forecast Verification." *Weather and Forecasting* 11: 3–20.

Olmsted County Historical Society. 1883. *History of Olmsted County.* Chicago: H. H. Hill.

O'Toole, J. M. 1993. *84 Minutes, 94 Lives.* Worcester, Mass.: Data Books.

Nalivkin, D. V. 1982. *Hurricanes, Storms, and Tornadoes.* Washington, D.C./New Delhi: NOAA, National Science Foundation, and Amerid Publishing Co. Translated from Russian.

Peterson, R. E. 1982. *Tornadic Activity in Europe: The Last Half Century.* Preprints. 12th Conference on Severe Local Storms, American Meteorological Society, San Antonio. Pp. 63–66.

Purrett-Carroll, L. 1982. "First Measurements of Size and Velocity of a Violent Tornado." *Weatherwise* 35: 127–30.

Rasmussen, E. N., J. M. Straka, R. Davies-Jones, C. A. Doswell III, F. H. Carr, M. D. Eilts, and D. R. MacGorman. 1994. "Verification of the Origins of Rotation in Tornadoes Experiment." *Bulletin of the American Meteorological Society* 75 (6): 995–1006.

Roach, W. T., and J. Findlater. 1983. "An Aircraft Encounter with a Tornado." *Meteorological Magazine* 112 (February): 1327.

Root, C. J. 1926. "Some Outstanding Tornadoes." *Monthly Weather Review* 54: 58.

Sabones, M. E., E. M. Agee, and M. Akridge. 1996. *The Pulaski County and West Lafayette, Indiana, Tornadoes, 26–27 April 1994: A Case of Supercell (Mesocyclone) and Squall Line Bow-Echo Interaction.* Preprints, 18th Conference on Severe Local Storms, American Meteorological Society. Pp. 746–50.

Schaefer, J. T. 1986. "Severe Thunderstorm Forecasting: A Historical Perspective." *Weather and Forecasting* 1: 164–89.

Schaefer, J. T., D. L. Kelly, and R. F. Abbey, Jr. 1986. "A Minimum Assumption Tornado Hazard Probability Model." *Journal of Climate and Applied Meteorology* 25: 1934–45.

Schlesinger, R. E. 1975. "A Three-Dimensional Numerical Model of an Isolated Deep Convective Cloud: Preliminary Results." *Journal of Atmospheric Sciences* 32: 934–57.

Showalter, A. K., and J. R. Fulks. 1943. *Preliminary Report on Tornadoes.* Washington, D.C.: U. S. Weather Bureau.

Snow, J. T., A. L. Wyatt, A. K. McCarthy, and E. K. Bishop. 1995. "Fallout of Debris from Tornadic Thunderstorm—A Historical Perspective and Two Examples from VORTEX." *Bulletin of the American Meteorological Society* 76 (10): 1777–90.

Stout, G. E., and F. A. Huff. 1953. "Radar Records Illinois Tornado Genesis." *Bulletin of the American Meteorological Society* 34: 281–84.

Straka, J. M., J. Wurman, E. N. Rasmussen. 1996. "Observation of the Low Levels of Tornadic Storms Using a Portable X-Band Doppler Radar." 18th Conference on Severe Local Storms. American Meteorological Society, San Francisco, 11–16.

Tatom, F. B., K. R. Knupp, and S. J. Vinton. 1995. "Tornado Detection Based on Seismic Signal." *Journal of Applied Meteorology* 34: 572–82.

Tice, J. H. 1883. "Electricity and Cyclones." *New York Times,* April 22, 6.

Trapp, R. J., and R. P. Davies-Jones. 1996. *The Dynamic Pipe Effect and its Role in Tornadogenesis.* Preprint. 18th Conference on Severe Local Storms, American Meteorological Society, San Francisco. Pp. 387–90.

Vonnegut, B. 1960. "Electrical Theory of Tornadoes." *Journal of Geophysical Research* 65: 203–12.

———. 1975. "Chicken Plucking as Measure of Tornado Wind Speed." *Weatherwise* 28: 217.

Wakimoto, R. M., and J. W. Wilson. 1989. "Non-Supercell Tornadoes." *Monthly Weather Review* 117: 1113–40.

Ward, N. B. 1972. "The Exploration of Certain Features of Tornado Dynamics Using a Laboratory Model." *Journal of Atmospheric Sciences* 29: 1194–1204.

Wicker, L. J., and R. B. Wilhelmson. 1993. "Numerical Simulation of Tornadogenesis within a Supercell Thunderstorms." In *The Tornado: Its Structure, Dynamics, Prediction and Hazards,* edited by C. Church. Proc. Tornado Symposium III. Washington, D.C.: American Geophysical Union.

Wilson, J. W., and S. A. Changnon, Jr. 1971. *Illinois Tornadoes.* Circular 103. Urbana: Illinois State Water Survey.

Wolf, R., and E. Szoke. 1996. *A Multiscale Analysis of the 21 July 1993 Northeast Colorado Tornado.* Preprints. 18th Conference on Severe Local Storms, American Meteorological Society, San Francisco. Pp. 403–7.

Index